# Developing Monitoring and Evaluation Frameworks

**SAGE** was founded in 1965 by Sara Miller McCune to support the dissemination of usable knowledge by publishing innovative and high-quality research and teaching content. Today, we publish more than 850 journals, including those of more than 300 learned societies, more than 800 new books per year, and a growing range of library products including archives, data, case studies, reports, conference highlights, and video. SAGE remains majority-owned by our founder, and after Sara's lifetime will become owned by a charitable trust that secures our continued independence.

Los Angeles | London | New Delhi | Singapore | Washington DC

# Developing Monitoring and Evaluation Frameworks

**Anne Markiewicz**
*Anne Markiewicz and Associates*

**Ian Patrick**
*Ian Patrick and Associates*

Los Angeles | London | New Delhi
Singapore | Washington DC

Los Angeles | London | New Delhi
Singapore | Washington DC

FOR INFORMATION:

SAGE Publications, Inc.
2455 Teller Road
Thousand Oaks, California 91320
E-mail: order@sagepub.com

SAGE Publications Ltd.
1 Oliver's Yard
55 City Road
London EC1Y 1SP
United Kingdom

SAGE Publications India Pvt. Ltd.
B 1/I 1 Mohan Cooperative Industrial Area
Mathura Road, New Delhi 110 044
India

SAGE Publications Asia-Pacific Pte. Ltd.
3 Church Street
#10-04 Samsung Hub
Singapore 049483

Copyright © 2016 by SAGE Publications, Inc.

All rights reserved. No part of this book may be reproduced or utilized in any form or by any means, electronic or mechanical, including photocopying, recording, or by any information storage and retrieval system, without permission in writing from the publisher.

ISBN 978-1-4833-5833-8

Acquisitions Editor: Helen Salmon
eLearning Editor: Katie Bierach
Editorial Assistant: Anna Villarruel
Production Editor: Bennie Clark Allen
Copy Editor: Michelle Ponce
Typesetter: C&M Digitals (P) Ltd.
Proofreader: Wendy Jo Dymond
Indexer: Wendy Allex
Cover Designer: Michelle Kenny
Marketing Manager: Nicole Elliott

15 16 17 18 19 10 9 8 7 6 5 4 3 2 1

# Brief Contents

| | |
|---|---|
| Preface | xii |
| Acknowledgments | xiv |
| About the Authors | xvi |
| Chapter 1 Introduction to Developing Monitoring and Evaluation Frameworks | 1 |
| Chapter 2 Foundation Concepts | 28 |
| Chapter 3 First Steps: Scoping the Monitoring and Evaluation Framework, Stakeholder Mapping, and Evaluation Capacity Building | 43 |
| Chapter 4 Program Theory and Program Logic as Foundations for the Monitoring and Evaluation Framework | 70 |
| Chapter 5 Evaluation Questions—Determining What We Want to Know | 93 |
| Chapter 6 The Monitoring Plan | 120 |
| Chapter 7 The Evaluation Plan | 148 |
| Chapter 8 Collecting, Managing, Analyzing, and Synthesizing Data to Reach Evaluative Conclusions | 181 |
| Chapter 9 Learning, Reporting and Dissemination Strategies | 218 |
| Chapter 10 Planning for Implementation of the Monitoring and Evaluation Framework | 242 |
| Chapter 11 Conclusion | 254 |
| Appendix | 257 |
| References | 275 |
| Index | 283 |

# Detailed Contents

| | |
|---|---:|
| Preface | xii |
| Acknowledgments | xiv |
| About the Authors | xvi |

**Chapter 1 Introduction to Developing Monitoring and Evaluation Frameworks**     1

    What Is a Monitoring and Evaluation Framework?     1
    Why Invest?     2
    What Functions Does a Monitoring and Evaluation Framework Serve?     4
    What Gap Does This Text Intend to Fill?     6
    Key Features of the Approach     7
    Program-Level Focus     9
    What Are the Differences Between Monitoring and Evaluation?     11
    What Are the Complementarities Between Monitoring and Evaluation?     15
    What Is Included in a Monitoring and Evaluation Framework?     19
    Format and Layout of the Text     20

**Chapter 2 Foundation Concepts**     28

    1. Multiple Purposes for Monitoring and Evaluation     29
    2. Results-Based Management Approach     31
    3. Theory-Based Approach     35
    4. Evaluation-Led Monitoring and Evaluation     38
    5. Participatory Orientation     40

**Chapter 3 First Steps: Scoping the Monitoring and Evaluation Framework, Stakeholder Mapping, and Evaluation Capacity Building**     43

    1. Introduction to Scoping the Framework With Key Stakeholders     44
    2. Key Steps in Scoping the Framework     46
       *Step 1: Identify Requirements*     47
       *Step 2: Determine Participation Arrangements*     50

   *Step 3: Identify Possible and Preferred Approaches*    60
   *Step 4: Review Resource Parameters*    65
   *Step 5: Confirm Purpose and Parameters of*
    *the Framework*    66
  3. From First Steps Onward    68
  SUMMARY CHECKLIST    68
  CHAPTER REVIEW QUESTIONS    69

## Chapter 4 Program Theory and Program Logic as Foundations for the Monitoring and Evaluation Framework    70

  1. Introduction to Developing Program
   Theory and Program Logic    71
   *Program Theory*    72
   *Differences Between Program Theory and Program Logic*    74
   *Program Logic*    74
   *Program Theory and Program Logic for a*
    *Community Education Program*    76
  2. Steps Involved in Developing Program Theory
   and Program Logic    80
   *Step 1: Plan Stakeholder Engagement Strategy*    81
   *Step 2: Develop Program Theory*    83
   *Step 3: Develop Program Logic*    85
   *Step 4: Confirm Program Theory and*
    *Program Logic With Key Stakeholders*    89
  SUMMARY CHECKLIST    91
  CHAPTER REVIEW QUESTIONS    92

## Chapter 5 Evaluation Questions—Determining What We Want to Know    93

  1. Introduction to Developing Evaluation Questions    94
   *Answering Evaluation Questions: A Complementary*
    *Role for Monitoring and Evaluation*    94
   *Developing Agreed, Practical, and Useful*
    *Evaluation Questions*    95
  2. Using Evaluation Domains to Guide Selection of Questions    97
  3. Using Program Theory and Logic to Determine Evaluation
   Questions    107
  4. Steps Involved in Developing Evaluation Questions    110
   *Step 1: Develop Draft Evaluation Questions*    112
   *Step 2: Facilitate Stakeholder Participation*    113

  *Step 3: Scope Number and Range of Questions*
   *Against Data and Resources Available*   115
  *Step 4: Present Questions to Stakeholders for Final*
   *Endorsement*   116
  *Step 5: Finalize Evaluation Questions*   117
 SUMMARY CHECKLIST   118
 CHAPTER REVIEW QUESTIONS   119

**Chapter 6 The Monitoring Plan**   120

 1. Introduction   121
 2. Introduction to Program Monitoring   121
  *Performance Management and Program Monitoring*   123
 3. The Monitoring Plan   125
 4. Steps in Developing the Monitoring Plan   128
  *Step 1: Identify Focus*   129
  *Step 2: Develop Performance Indicators and Targets*   131
  *Step 3: Identify Data Collection Processes and Tools*   142
  *Step 4: Determine Responsibilities and Time Frames*   144
 5. The Future of Program Monitoring   145
 SUMMARY CHECKLIST   146
 CHAPTER REVIEW QUESTIONS   147

**Chapter 7 The Evaluation Plan**   148

 1. Introduction   149
 2. Focusing on Evaluation   150
  *Quality and Value*   151
  *Example of Quality*   152
  *Example of Value*   152
  *Types of Evaluation: Formative and Summative*   153
 3. The Evaluation Plan   155
 4. Steps Involved in Developing the Evaluation Plan   160
  *Step 1: Determine Overall Evaluation Approach*   161
  *Step 2: Identify Evaluation Questions Requiring*
   *Criteria and Standards*   169
  *Step 3: Identify Focus of Evaluation and Methods*
   *for Each Question*   173
  *Step 4: Determine Responsibilities and Time Frame*   176
  *Step 5: Review the Monitoring and Evaluation Plans*   177
 SUMMARY CHECKLIST   179
 CHAPTER REVIEW QUESTIONS   180

**Chapter 8 Collecting, Managing, Analyzing, and Synthesizing Data to Reach Evaluative Conclusions** — 181

   1. Introduction to Data Processes That Support Sound Conclusions — 182
   2. Organizational Context for Data Collection, Management, and Analysis — 184
   3. Data Quality — 187
   4. Steps Involved in Data Collection, Management, Analysis, and Synthesis — 189
      *Step 1: Develop Data Collection Plan* — 190
      *Step 2: Develop Data Management Plan* — 197
      *Step 3: Consider Approach to Data Synthesis* — 203
      *Step 4: Consider Approach to Making Evaluative Judgments and Reaching Evaluative Conclusions* — 210
   SUMMARY CHECKLIST — 216
   CHAPTER REVIEW QUESTIONS — 217

**Chapter 9 Learning, Reporting and Dissemination Strategies** — 218

   1. Introduction — 219
   2. Steps Involved in Learning and Reporting and Dissemination — 220
      *Step 1: Consider Developing or Refining a Learning Strategy That Maximizes Use of Conclusions, Recommendations, and Lessons* — 222
      *Step 2: Consider the Identification of Recommendations and Lessons* — 226
      *Step 3: Provide Guidance on Developing a Reporting and Dissemination Strategy* — 230
   SUMMARY CHECKLIST — 240
   CHAPTER REVIEW QUESTIONS — 241

**Chapter 10 Planning for Implementation of the Monitoring and Evaluation Framework** — 242

   1. Introduction to Planning for Implementation — 243
   2. Key Steps in Implementation of Monitoring and Evaluation Frameworks — 246
      *Step 1: Confirm Program Management Arrangements* — 247
      *Step 2: Work Planning for Implementation* — 248
      *Step 3: Plan for Monitoring and Review of Framework* — 251

| | | |
|---|---|---|
| | Summary Checklist | 253 |
| | Chapter Review Questions | 253 |

## Chapter 11 Conclusion  254

## Appendix  257
## References  275
## Index  283

# Preface

The evaluation literature contains many excellent guides to thinking about the nature of evaluation and provides strong complementary advice on the methods and techniques that are used in practice. An area of less attention, which this text is intended to address, relates to the planning that is required to provide evaluation with an appropriate focus and guide its conduct through a range of stages and steps. While the practice of evaluation is often claimed to be partly an "art" drawing deeply on the insight and experience of the evaluator, it is also a highly organized, sequenced, and methodical undertaking. This text provides guidance to the planning that is required to produce high quality evaluation, incorporating routine monitoring, and offers readers a structured, staged approach to this undertaking.

Many observers have commented on the historically weak relationship that exists between monitoring and evaluation functions. They are often treated like estranged relations, kept apart and treated separately. Monitoring and evaluation may be undertaken by different personnel and different sections within a program or organization, with the results of both streamed separately and not considered together. Such practice represents a weakness and potential loss to the ability to manage programs effectively. In response, this text aims to draw attention to, and integrate the role of monitoring within the broader field of evaluation practice. As demonstrated in the context of the evaluation of programs, both monitoring and evaluation functions have vital and complementary roles to play. Put simply, monitoring relates to the ongoing checking of progress, while evaluation involves deeper, periodic assessment of results. For a program, it makes perfect sense to combine both perspectives to attain the most complete view of its performance. This represents the intent of this text—to provide guidance for the development of an integrated plan for the monitoring and evaluation of a program or related initiative. In practice, such a plan is usually referred to more formally as a Monitoring and Evaluation Framework. The use of the term *Framework* is apt given the range of different sections and tools of which it is typically comprised.

The development of a Monitoring and Evaluation Framework is becoming increasingly recognized as an important initial step in establishing arrangements to determine the performance of a program. The task at hand is far more than a technical undertaking. Determining performance, for example, requires in the first instance, the interpretation of the term and thereafter the necessary background, conceptual grounding, and practical knowhow to do so. Such a balance between theory and practice is reflected in the structure of this text. Beyond this, the text advances and demonstrates several views that are regarded by the authors as positive aspects of evaluation practice. For example, the text encourages a broad interpretation of the notion of *performance*, extending beyond the determination of results of a program. Moreover, arriving at conclusions about program performance requires the incorporation and synthesis of a range of different types of evidence, with the views and perspectives of stakeholders playing an important role. Guidance is therefore provided in this text on the design of a Monitoring and Evaluation Framework, which serves multiple purposes, including establishing results, supporting accountability, and promoting organizational learning and decision making. Similarly, means to engage stakeholders in the development of a Monitoring and Evaluation Framework and its planned implementation are emphasized.

The approach employed to the development of a Monitoring and Evaluation Framework is both theory and evaluation led. This emphasis is reflected in the key concepts introduced early in the text and the important initial stages elaborated to guide its development. These commence with scoping of the Framework, followed by the identification of planned results using program theory and program logic and the development of evaluation questions. Several subsequent chapters focus on the development of a Monitoring Plan and an Evaluation Plan. Importantly, the development of the Monitoring and Evaluation Framework continues with planning for data collection, management, analysis, and synthesis, as well as identifying means to promote learning, reporting, and dissemination. A final chapter focuses on planning for implementation, with reference to the broader program and organizational context in which monitoring and evaluation functions occur. In this manner, the development of a Monitoring and Evaluation Framework is linked to challenges experienced in the management of programs and efforts to promote learning and foster improvements.

In order to demonstrate the application of concepts and steps involved in the development of a Monitoring and Evaluation Framework, the text focuses on one central case example. This case is elaborated through many of the core chapters. A range of associated tables and figures are included that illustrate key concepts covered in the text. To further aid and illustrate application to the field, the text provides readers with a range of practice examples. These have been drawn from the authors' own experiences in both developed and developing country contexts. End-of-chapter review questions have been included, as well as a summary checklist related to each chapter. A summary format providing a template for development of a Monitoring and Evaluation Framework is also included.

This text should thus provide a useful and informative resource for educators, students, commissioners, and practitioners of evaluation, applicable to audiences working with different population groups in both developing and developed country contexts. The text is designed to provide clear practical guidance as to how to plan a Monitoring and Evaluation Framework in a participatory, logical, systematic, and integrated way.

# Acknowledgments

Our practice as evaluators continues to be inspired by the people with whom we work and the associated challenges of developing monitoring and evaluation approaches that are applicable, understandable, and useful. In this pursuit, we are grateful for the support given by fellow evaluators, academics, and staff from the diverse range of organizations with whom we have been privileged to engage. We are fortunate in being able to draw from a wide experience base, covering developing and developed country contexts, including work with Indigenous Australians. Our colleagues and participants in training programs encouraged and motivated us to commit to this writing project.

We would like to thank Helen Salmon, our editor at SAGE, for her stewardship, guidance, and encouragement throughout the project. Thanks also to Anna Villarruel, editorial assistant from SAGE for her support. We would like to acknowledge the reviewers: Linda B. Schrader, Florida State University; Daniela C. Schroeter, Western Michigan University; and Sheldon Gen, San Francisco State University who provided feedback and valuable insights into areas for improvement in the text. Two of our Australian evaluation colleagues, Nea Harrison and Julie Elliot, provided great support in reviewing the draft text. Julie Smith developed the illustrations for this text. Her depiction of the steps involved in preparing a Monitoring and Evaluation Framework is reminiscent of the *Pilgrim's Progress*, albeit with a completed Framework at the end of the journey rather than a celestial city.

Our appreciation goes to the staff and members of the professional associations to which we belong, including the Australasian Evaluation Society and the American Evaluation Association. They have given us a rich and stimulating context for the development of our work as evaluators. The Australasian Evaluation Society has provided an opportunity to develop and roll out a training program on the subject of this text in both Australia and New Zealand.

At the risk of overlooking many people and programs, we would like to highlight a few particularly enriching contexts that have allowed us to develop our model and approach. We would like to acknowledge the International NGO Training and Research Centre (INTRAC) in Oxford, United Kingdom, for supporting the first of our training programs on this subject. Our thanks to Dr. Richard Guy for his encouragement and opportunities to develop and refine our training approach in Papua New Guinea as part of Australia's aid program. The Monitoring and Evaluation Framework developed for the Mongolia Australia Scholarships Program received an Award for Excellence in Evaluation from the Australasian Evaluation Society. We would particularly like to thank Tsetsgee Yundendorj and Anne Lubell in relation to this program. We would also like to acknowledge Bob Eckhardt from the Australian Electoral Commission for his sustained support for our work with the Indigenous Electoral Participation Program.

Finally, our thanks and appreciation must go to our family members who were both understanding and supportive of this undertaking.

# About the Authors

**Anne Markiewicz** is an independent evaluation consultant and the director of Anne Markiewicz and Associates. Commencing her professional career a social worker, Anne held academic positions in social work at two Australian Universities. In 1997, Anne pursued her interest in evaluation and commenced working as an independent consultant. In 2000, she completed a Master of Education in Program Evaluation at the University of Melbourne. Since that time, Anne has completed a significant number of evaluation projects for a range of Australian government departments, nongovernment organizations, and international agencies. She has specialized in evaluating programs with social justice objectives.

Anne's practice as an evaluator has highlighted the need for early evaluation planning to provide a clear and agreed focus, ensure data availability, and support the production of credible evaluations. She has increasingly focused on the development of Monitoring and Evaluation Frameworks for a range of clients. She has designed and delivered an array of related training programs, which encompass areas such as stakeholder engagement, negotiation, and evaluation reporting. This training has been delivered extensively in Australasia, particularly within Australia and Papua New Guinea. Anne has a commitment to evaluation capacity building and has provided mentoring support to a range of government and nongovernment organizations.

Anne is a past board member of the Australasian Evaluation Society, holding positions of secretary and vice president. She has received two awards for excellence in evaluation from the Australasian Evaluation Society. These were the Indigenous Evaluation Award (2008) for an evaluation completed with the Australian Department of Finance and Deregulation and the Outstanding Contribution to Evaluation Award (2013). Anne has published articles on the political context to evaluation, balancing stakeholder interests in evaluation, and the evaluation of programs for Indigenous Australians.

 **Ian Patrick** is an independent evaluation consultant and director of Ian Patrick and Associates. Ian has a number of threads in his career that have supported his move into evaluation. Building on a background in teaching and radio and television production, Ian shifted his focus to international program management. He became aware of the challenges involved in evaluation of complex programs operating in the Asia-Pacific region while working for several Australian universities and managing contractors. Ian completed a PhD in Asian Studies in 1997 and commenced working in academic roles in international development for both the RMIT University and Deakin University, Australia. Ian is currently an honorary senior fellow in Development Studies, School of Social and Political Sciences at the University of Melbourne.

Ian commenced working as an independent consultant in 1998 with roles encompassing evaluation, program design, strategy development, and organizational review. The focus of this work has progressively shifted to concentrate on the evaluation area and has also achieved a balance between Australian and international contexts. He has undertaken evaluation-related assignments for a range of international agencies, Australian government departments, and nongovernment organizations. He has interests in evaluation practice in both public sector and civil society contexts with sectoral experience crossing areas such as law and justice, health, education, rural and urban development, environment, human rights, disaster management, media and the arts, and migration and Indigenous issues.

Ian is a member of the Australasian Evaluation Society and the American Evaluation Association. In 2012, he received the Best Evaluation Policy and Systems Award from the Australasian Evaluation Society for a Monitoring and Evaluation Framework developed for the Mongolia Australia Scholarships Program.

# CHAPTER 1

# Introduction to Developing Monitoring and Evaluation Frameworks

*This introductory section clarifies the purpose and function of a Monitoring and Evaluation Framework and the essential features of the approach used in this text. A close and articulated relationship between monitoring and evaluation functions is identified as fundamental to the approach adopted, with monitoring situated within program evaluation rather than positioned as separate to it. An overview is subsequently presented of the different sections of the Monitoring and Evaluation Framework and of how guidance to its development is structured within the text.*

## WHAT IS A MONITORING AND EVALUATION FRAMEWORK?

A Monitoring and Evaluation Framework is both a planning process and a written product designed to provide guidance to the conduct of monitoring and evaluation functions over the life span of a program or other initiative. The use of Monitoring and Evaluation Frameworks is becoming increasingly important to establish program- and initiative-level progress and results; to subsequently inform management and decision-making processes; to support accountability; and to guide organizational learning for program improvement. Monitoring and evaluation functions are integral to the effective operation of programs and initiatives and increase the overall value derived from them.

A Monitoring and Evaluation Framework represents an overarching plan for undertaking monitoring and evaluation functions for the life of a program and includes a step-by-step guide to its operationalization and application over time. Monitoring and Evaluation Frameworks are ideally developed concurrently with, and inform, a program plan or design. Alternatively, an outline of the Monitoring and Evaluation Framework may be developed during the design stage and elaborated on at an early stage during program implementation.

The Monitoring and Evaluation Framework defines the parameters of routine monitoring and periodic evaluation that will take place over the life of a program or initiative. Typically, these parameters include a focus on evaluation domains, particularly those of appropriateness, effectiveness, efficiency, impact, and sustainability. In some contexts, additional or alternative domains may be used as the focus for investigations through monitoring and evaluation, such as *gender* and other crosscutting issues. The Monitoring and Evaluation Framework shows how data are collected, aggregated, and analyzed on a regular basis in order to answer the agreed evaluation questions. The data generated by the Monitoring and Evaluation Framework should also support formative and summative evaluation processes.

## WHY INVEST?

The need for Monitoring and Evaluation Frameworks is highlighted in the contemporary policy context where the "achievement of results" has become a heightened and primary rationale for program funding and operation. Management strategies such as Results-Based Management (RBM) have strongly influenced the approach adopted by many organizations and placed strong expectations on planning and monitoring and evaluation functions. Under a unifying concern with identification of results, a more integrated relationship between these functions is required. This involves overcoming barriers between planners and those responsible for monitoring and evaluation who traditionally work at different points of the program cycle. The development and implementation of coherent and widely accepted plans are important to the success of programs and initiatives of all types and sizes.

Investing in developing Monitoring and Evaluation Frameworks is an essential step in ensuring that a program is monitored and evaluated over its life span and that informed decisions can be made in order to steer implementation and guide decision making about a program's future. In turn, effective programs have a better chance of delivering outcomes that will potentially improve the circumstances for which the program was developed. These could be located across a range of areas including social, economic, health, psychological, educational, environmental, and cultural areas.

> **Practice Example**
>
> ### Using Monitoring and Evaluation to Inform Program Planning
>
> A program's investment in developing a Monitoring and Evaluation Framework is particularly worthwhile where that program is committed to learning what works for its intended beneficiaries and to adjusting its delivery model based on those learnings. The evaluator worked with a state-based community education program aimed at reducing substance misuse amongst young people living in regional and remote communities. The program was uncertain whether its behavior-change strategies were effective in achieving the intended outcomes for this particularly hard-to-reach target group. The program invested in the development of a Monitoring and Evaluation Framework. After 12 months of implementation of the Framework, including structured data collection and analysis, the program was able to determine that the awareness-raising strategies it had been using up until that time were not as effective as anticipated. The monitoring and evaluation activities undertaken within the parameters of the Monitoring and Evaluation Framework identified positive alternative delivery approaches that were likely to be more effective, such as working in collaboration with other youth-focused organizations that had established relationships with the target group. As a result, the program redesigned its delivery model and specific strategies used including adopting an enhanced focus on partnership building. The program developed new staff position descriptions, undertook training of its personnel, and put these into operation in a new program phase. The Monitoring and Evaluation Framework was also subsequently updated in line with the new program model and approach. This example illustrates the benefits of investing in monitoring and evaluation for achieving the most appropriate program design and also the manner in which planning and monitoring and evaluation functions can operate in a constructive, mutually supportive manner.

## WHAT FUNCTIONS DOES A MONITORING AND EVALUATION FRAMEWORK SERVE?

With a sharpened focus and concern with results, Monitoring and Evaluation Frameworks have evolved to make assessments that extend beyond tracking implementation, and a traditional concern with activities and outputs, to focus on outcomes. Similarly, as the nature of programs and other delivery mechanisms become more sophisticated, designs for Monitoring and Evaluation Frameworks have emphasized versatility and ability to adapt to different program circumstances.

Other expectations placed on monitoring and evaluation are to encompass and competently assess a range of areas of program performance such the appropriateness of the design and efficiency of delivery. While increasing sophistication is required, approaches to monitoring and evaluation are also expected to be readily comprehensible and promote the active participation of a broad range of stakeholders. Further, for the results and products of monitoring and evaluation to be of value, they need to be effectively disseminated and actively used. Such expectations and needs place considerable onus on Monitoring and Evaluation Frameworks to effectively encompass and guide a comprehensive monitoring and evaluation process.

In summary, Monitoring and Evaluation Frameworks can address a range of different purposes, including the following:

- **Results.** Using approaches and tools that anticipate and provide a basis for identifying and assessing results, both expected and unexpected
- **Management.** Providing a guide to tracking progress in program implementation against program plans, performance indicators and targets, and a basis for correcting the relationship between program inputs, activities, and outputs where needed
- **Accountability.** Accounting and reporting on the use of resources allocated and results achieved to a range of stakeholders such as government, funders, organizational governance and management personnel, members of the public, and program beneficiaries
- **Learning.** Generating and disseminating knowledge about good practice, learning from experience as to what works and what does not, and why a program was successful or not, in its particular context
- **Program Improvement.** Improving the design and performance of a program during its implementation and making overall judgments as to the quality, value, effectiveness, and importance of a program

- **Decision Making.** Using the results generated by monitoring and evaluation to inform decisions such as on program design, resource allocation, program direction, and program continuation

> **Practice Example**
>
> ### Multiple Purposes for Monitoring and Evaluation Frameworks
>
> A Monitoring and Evaluation Framework was developed for a large regional family violence prevention program that was funded to operate for 10 years. The Framework which was developed in the program's first year of operation was designed to support a range of purposes. Different purposes were more critical at different stages of the program's life cycle. In the shorter term, the emphasis of the Framework and its respective monitoring and evaluation functions was placed on the learning aspect. This entailed providing data to identify whether the program design and its strategies were in fact appropriate to its context and effective in maintaining and developing the support of allied partners and services. Also in the short term, an emphasis was placed on establishing how well the program was being implemented. This involved placing a priority on the delivery of timely performance information to management. In the medium term, the Framework emphasized generating sufficient data for accountability and program improvement purposes. The program was required to report against different accountability-related milestones at various intervals, the first of these being 3 years after its commencement. Program improvement was to be informed through identifying results, determining the degree to which they were effective, and deriving associated learning. For the final years of the program, the Monitoring and Evaluation Framework emphasized identification of longer term results that the program had contributed to, both expected and unanticipated. Results areas included reduction in levels of family violence, improved gender relations, and increased capacity of local government and community-based organizations to sustain the initiative. Such results were expected to inform decision making about the future direction of the program.

## WHAT GAP DOES THIS TEXT INTEND TO FILL?

The development of Monitoring and Evaluation Frameworks is a core skill area in evaluation practice, but it is not always well addressed in evaluation education and professional training. Specific knowledge and skills are required in order to design the framework, including using participatory processes to engage stakeholders and then moving to implementation. These skills include the ability to foreshadow outcomes and subsequently identify and measure results achieved. The use of program theory and logic is advanced in this text as a key means to this end.

To equip the reader for these tasks, the text provides an appropriate grounding in key concepts used, and for this purpose, draws on evaluation theory and the broader literature. This literature relates to monitoring and evaluation practice in both developed and developing country contexts. While there are some differences between the two settings, the similarities are sufficient to provide generalizable principles for application to both settings.

The intent of the text is ultimately to support practice, and considerable focus is given to providing a clear structure and guidance for the development of a Monitoring and Evaluation Framework. Practical stages and steps in this process are identified, with accompanying information on developing the different sections of the Monitoring and Evaluation Framework. A range of plans and other tools are introduced, and completed examples are incorporated to aid the application of new material.

The approach of the text is to illustrate and promote the critical role of monitoring and evaluation for both a program and the broader organizational context in which it may operate. All too frequently, monitoring and evaluation appear as an add-on or as a discretionary activity for programs, while organizations fail to use what monitoring and evaluation have to offer to support learning and improve decision making and practice. This text, therefore, advocates for the early planning for the monitoring and evaluation of a program. Experience suggests that the earlier this is undertaken, and a Monitoring and Evaluation Framework is prepared and implemented, the more readily results will be known, adjustments can be made, and learnings derived.

This text should provide a useful and informative resource for educators and students, program managers, and commissioners and practitioners of evaluation. It aims to equip those responsible for, or involved with, monitoring and evaluation functions with the knowledge and skills to develop and implement a Monitoring and Evaluation Framework. The text should be applicable to those working in a range of settings, in both developing and developed country contexts. It provides practical guidance as to how to plan for monitoring and evaluation processes in a participatory, logical, systematic, and integrated way.

## KEY FEATURES OF THE APPROACH

The text draws on and is consistent with a contemporary, purposeful planning approach known as *Results-Based Management*. This approach links together planning, monitoring, and evaluation processes with an emphasis on integration and interdependence between these functions. The type of Monitoring and Evaluation Framework advanced is intended to actively counter a tendency to split off evaluation as a separate activity, with little relationship to monitoring. In contrast, the approach of this text may be regarded as evaluation-led in that a critical role is accorded to evaluation questions to focus the investigations undertaken. The approach taken in this text should achieve an improved balance between monitoring and evaluation functions with both contributing to more effective management, accountability, learning, and program improvement.

The following key principles of the evaluation-led approach are adopted in this text:

- Evaluation is seen as the overall discipline and endeavor that provides the point of reference for a Monitoring and Evaluation Framework. Monitoring is regarded as a subset of evaluation and guided by its theoretical and practice conventions. This orientation averts monitoring being accorded greater prominence due to a perceived more immediate link to management and accountability functions. In an evaluation-led approach, learning and program improvement are placed in a central position.
- The Monitoring and Evaluation Framework incorporates a range of areas of inquiry. Identifying and measuring outcomes is emphasized similar to many other approaches to monitoring and evaluation. Assessment of the change arising from a program, or impact, is only one of five evaluation domains, however, and complemented through investigation of a program's appropriateness, effectiveness, efficiency, and sustainability. These include forming judgments about program quality, value, importance, fidelity of implementation, and on issues of attribution. In the approach adopted here, the use of program theory and logic provides clarity and definition to assessment of impact and also suggests linkages to investigations related to the other domains.

- One set of evaluation questions provides a common and unifying focus for both monitoring and evaluation functions and the respective plans that are generated to guide these areas. Integration of monitoring and evaluation is therefore promoted.
- A range of performance measures are used to assess performance. The Monitoring and Evaluation Framework does not "institutionalize" performance indicators, baselines, and targets as the sole measures employed but rather uses them judiciously alongside other measures. More balanced assessments are thereby produced, drawing on results produced by both monitoring and evaluation.

Key steps involved in the approach include development of the building blocks of program theory, program logic, and evaluation questions. This is followed by generation of integrated monitoring and evaluation plans and strategies for data collection, management, and analysis. A strategy for learning, reporting, and communication is identified, followed by planning for implementation. All steps emphasize stakeholder participation and capacity development in the manner that they are undertaken. The overall approach reflected in the Monitoring and Evaluation Framework is consistent with and follows three central steps inherent to Program Theory-Driven Evaluation. These are developing a program theory, formulating and prioritizing the evaluation questions against that theory, and answering the evaluation questions using the evaluation method considered most fit for purpose (Donaldson, 2007).

This approach to developing Monitoring and Evaluation Frameworks has been shown to be suitable and effective in application with a variety of programs operating in both the government and nongovernment sectors, in a range of country contexts. Particular strengths of the approach identified are as follows:

- It is simple, easy to comprehend, and follow.
- It provides practitioners with a method they can apply to a range of different program contexts and to programs of different size and structure.
- Its utility lies in its structured, systematic approach, progressing from identifying desired results through to generating evaluation questions and using these questions to guide linked monitoring and evaluation processes.
- It meets the range of different end purposes (management, accountability, learning, program improvement, decision making).

# Chapter 1 Introduction to Developing Monitoring and Evaluation Frameworks

- It achieves a balance between monitoring and evaluation functions by showing how the two processes are interrelated in practice, not just in theory.

## PROGRAM-LEVEL FOCUS

This text concerns an aspect of *program evaluation*, which is a well-recognized term that identifies and demarcates evaluation practice that is focused on programs. This text is not, for example, concerned with evaluation of personnel within an organization, which represents a separate practice area. Developing Monitoring and Evaluation Frameworks for programs means that the focus is broadly placed on social interventions. This represents the most common focus of programs, across an array of areas such as education, health, justice, and human rights. A program can be defined as a set of planned, systematic activities and services directed to the achievement of goals and objectives through working toward results.

From a more operational perspective, our focus on Monitoring and Evaluation Frameworks for programs involves a demarcation from several broader social constructs. These include the sector (e.g., health sector) and systems level (e.g. government agencies operating in particular setting). Specific types of designs are used for Monitoring and Evaluation Frameworks for organizations, sectors, and systems for which this text does not provide particular guidance. Further specification of the nature of a program is obtained in its distinction from a project. The terms are often used in a synonymous manner, but as Bamberger, Rugh, and Mabry (2012) observe, "a program is usually understood to include a number of different projects and is intended to produce broader and possibly longer term outcomes and impacts" (p. 619). Despite these differences, the principles and broad parameters of Monitoring and Evaluation Frameworks as outlined in this text are likely to be transferable to other strata such as systems and policies.

Monitoring and Evaluation Frameworks operating at different levels may be developed so that they collect related information and so that the results of one may usefully inform the other. For example, a program-level Monitoring and Evaluation Framework may share related questions and outcome areas with subsidiary project-level Monitoring and Evaluation Frameworks. This arrangement where frameworks at different levels (system, program, project, etc.) inform others is known as *cascading*. Cascading Monitoring and Evaluation Frameworks may be vertically integrated across levels, as well as horizontally integrated across related projects or programs. This is depicted in Figure 1.1.

**Figure 1.1** Cascading Monitoring and Evaluation Frameworks

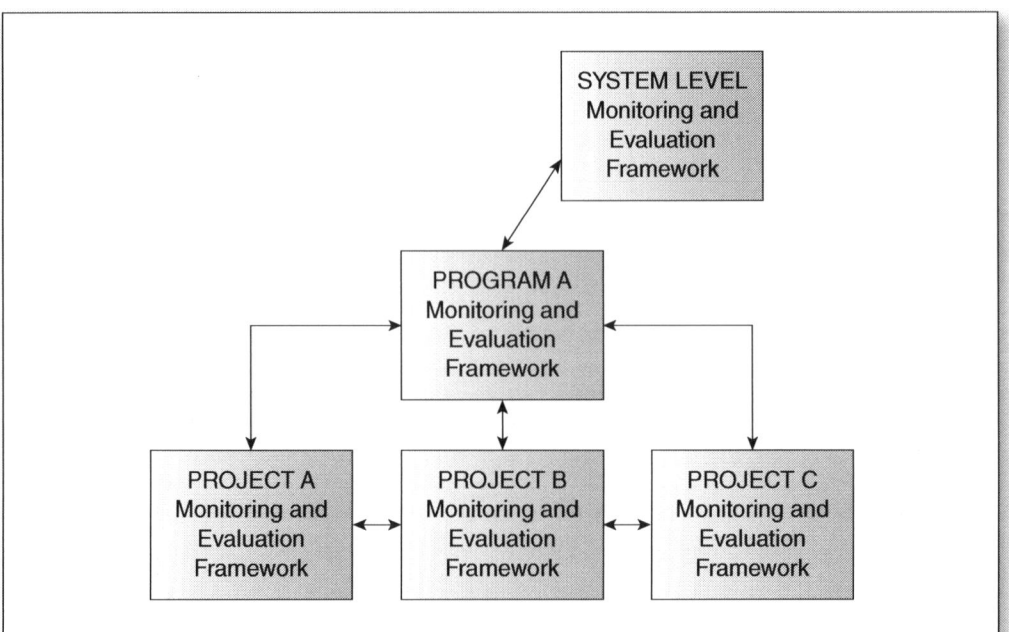

### Practice Example

## Cascading Monitoring and Evaluation Frameworks

A Monitoring and Evaluation Framework was developed for a state-based program aimed at reducing the rate of homelessness across a range of targeted communities. Consideration was given to related requirements for assessment of performance at the national and local levels. The state-based program was cofunded through a national homelessness strategy and had funded a large number of discrete local-level projects across the state. The development of the Monitoring and Evaluation Framework needed to consider how to identify outcomes that could be reported at both the state and national levels against respective performance benchmarks. The source of much of this information was the results of local-level projects. The evaluators examined a Monitoring and Evaluation Framework already developed for the national strategy and identified a range of outcome areas and indicators used. They then used these to inform the development of a Monitoring and Evaluation Framework for the state-based program, and on a simplified basis, for application to the individual projects funded within the state. In doing so, they checked on the availability of, and ability to collect, data at the state and local levels. Three Cascading Monitoring and Evaluation Frameworks were therefore in operation, including a preexisting framework for the national level and two related Frameworks developed with the assistance of the evaluator for the state and local levels, respectively.

Although the two Frameworks developed were considered useful, once implemented, some issues were experienced. Unexpected constraints arose as to the availability of data at the state level, and it appeared that some partner organizations had exaggerated their ability to collect and analyze it. State-level personnel, together with the evaluators, therefore discussed these matters with national-level personnel and negotiated some changes in the number and scope of performance indicators to be used. This outcome was seen as particularly productive at the state level with personnel feeling more empowered to enter into constructive dialogue with national-level staff. Previously, performance indicators were perceived as imposed from outside, often creating unrealistic data burdens for funded projects. Data gathered were also viewed as not always relevant or useful. The net result was a set of cascading and agreed Monitoring and Evaluation Frameworks that linked the national-level strategy, the state-level program, and the range of funded state projects.

## WHAT ARE THE DIFFERENCES BETWEEN MONITORING AND EVALUATION?

Program evaluation represents an area of professional practice concerned with the evaluation of programs. As a broad practice area, and as reflected in the approach taken in this text, it encompasses the two specific functions of monitoring and evaluation. These functions, both individually and in a mutually reinforcing manner, contribute to the effectiveness of program evaluation. Monitoring and evaluation functions are unified in both employing social research methods to undertake systematic investigations and, as advanced in this text, serving to answer a common set of evaluation questions. Despite this commonality, the role and functions of monitoring and evaluation are distinct, and careful differentiation is required to maintain clarity and efficacy within a monitoring and evaluation system guided by a Monitoring and Evaluation Framework. The predominant focus of monitoring is on tracking program implementation and progress, including program activities and processes, outputs produced, and initial outcomes achieved. Monitoring focuses on both what is being done in a program and how it is being done, serving as a means to identify any corrective action that is necessary. Predetermined performance indicators and targets are often used as an important point of reference for monitoring. Monitoring is primarily used to support management and accountability purposes.

Evaluation, by contrast, moves beyond the tracking focus of monitoring. Its predominant orientation is on forming judgments about program performance. Evaluation functions are undertaken periodically and sometimes more episodically. The analysis conducted as part of evaluation is usually based on the synthesis of a range of data, including that gained through monitoring. Evaluation is concerned with identifying a deeper and nuanced understanding of change and issues associated with a program and developing explanations for what is identified. Based on these assessments, evaluation commonly involves making judgments in relation to the program and also formulating conclusions and recommendations for the future. Evaluation aims to inform policy and program development based on reflection and learning. Monitoring and evaluation functions take many different forms in practice and are adapted for application to a range of different contexts.

For the purpose of this text *monitoring* is defined as

> the planned, continuous and systematic collection and analysis of program information able to provide management and key stakeholders with an indication of the extent of progress in implementation, and in relation to program performance against stated objectives and expectations.

Definitions of evaluation abound in the literature and continue to evolve. To avoid redefining the term evaluation, the text has drawn from the foundation work of Scriven (1991), drawing from his classic definition of evaluation. In this text, *evaluation* is defined as

> the planned, periodic and systematic determination of the quality and value of a program, with summative judgment as to the achievement of a program's goals and objectives.

The process of evaluation builds on monitoring information to identify the degree to which outcomes and longer term impacts have resulted and objectives have been achieved. Evaluation identifies approaches that worked well and those that did not, reasons for success or failure, and learning from both. Evaluation undertakes broad inquiry into the processes of implementation, determining its level of success and any associated issues. The evaluation process also provides a level of judgment in relation to the program overall.

Evaluations can take place formatively or summatively or both. An evaluation is considered formative when it adopts a focus on program processes and implementation with the aim of improving program design and future performance. In contrast, summative evaluations are particularly concerned with making judgments about a program's overall performance and are thus more focused on the identification of program results, usually at the end of a program's life. However, evaluations may also be constructed to be more or less formative or summative and carried out at different stages of a program's life cycle, depending on the context and need for specific types of information. In this text, both formative and summative evaluations are regarded as aspects of the broader construct of program evaluation.

The key differences between monitoring and evaluation are summarized in Table 1.1.

**Table 1.1** Monitoring and Evaluation Functions

|  | *Monitoring* | *Evaluation* |
|---|---|---|
| Main Agents | • Managers and program staff | • Evaluators working with key stakeholders including program staff |
| Main Interests | • Support management decision making<br>• Internal and external accountability | • Learning for policy and program improvement, including for more strategic decision making |
| Timing | • Continuous, timely | • Periodic, less timely, and less regular |
| Scope | • Implementation, including day-to-day activities, what the program produces (outputs), and immediate outcomes<br>• Whether the program is implemented to plan (fidelity)<br>• Use of funds and other program resources, including staff | • Achievement of objectives<br>• Changes at outcome and impact levels and levels of attribution to program<br>• How well program resources were used<br>• Program fit to context, stakeholder needs, and policy environment |

*(Continued)*

**Table 1.1** (Continued)

|  | *Monitoring* | *Evaluation* |
|---|---|---|
|  | <ul><li>Level of engagement and immediate responses of stakeholders to program</li><li>Immediate developments in program policy context and environment</li><li>Performance against indicators and targets</li></ul> | <ul><li>Stakeholder engagement and reactions</li><li>Overall quality and value of program</li><li>Likelihood of continuation of benefits from the program</li></ul> |
| Resourcing | <ul><li>Embedded as part of management processes</li></ul> | <ul><li>Usually requires dedicated resources as part of overall program budget</li></ul> |
| Measures | <ul><li>Indicators and targets</li><li>Often uses only one method to measure each variable</li></ul> | <ul><li>Criteria and standards</li><li>Generally multimethod in approach within a more rigorous methodological design</li></ul> |
| Reasons for Progress or Change | <ul><li>Not able to explain why or why not performance areas were achieved</li></ul> | <ul><li>Attempts to explain reasons for achievement or nonachievement of performance areas (including those covered by indicators and targets)</li></ul> |
| Attribution | <ul><li>Does not deal with issues of attribution</li></ul> | <ul><li>Attempts to identify contribution</li></ul> |
| Conclusions | <ul><li>Program progress and performance issues</li></ul> | <ul><li>Lessons learned, what has worked and what has not, with recommendations for program improvement</li></ul> |
| Reporting | <ul><li>Regular reporting (e.g., quarterly, annually)—often based on funder requirements</li><li>Simpler reporting formats used such as tables and charts</li></ul> | <ul><li>Reporting at agreed intervals including midterm and end term</li><li>Detailed evaluation reports</li></ul> |

### Practice Example

#### Designing a Monitoring and Evaluation Framework to Guide Routine Monitoring and Periodic Evaluation

A Monitoring and Evaluation Framework was designed for a national community health program delivering services to Indigenous communities. In this program, a range of monitoring data was routinely collected. Such

# Chapter 1   Introduction to Developing Monitoring and Evaluation Frameworks

> data included demographic patterns and trends in the Indigenous communities, administrative data related to service delivery and utilization, and accountability data related to delivery of program outputs. However, the comprehensiveness, analysis, and use of the monitoring data were limited. The development of a Monitoring and Evaluation Framework involved determining program theory and program logic, which then informed identification of the evaluation questions. The existing monitoring data were aligned against the evaluation questions. This provided clarity for the program in highlighting how existing monitoring data could be used, while also identifying gaps in both existing data and associated knowledge about program performance. Significant data gaps identified included limited available information on service user characteristics and satisfaction with service delivery. These gaps would be filled by monitoring and complementary evaluation activities. Greater focus would be placed on the collection of monitoring data related to service user characteristics. Evaluation would particularly add value in providing explanations and deeper understanding about the issues experienced by service users and their satisfaction with services used. The Monitoring and Evaluation Framework that was developed provided focus for this complex community health program and enabled it to better track implementation, assess results, and use learning to adjust program design.

## WHAT ARE THE COMPLEMENTARITIES BETWEEN MONITORING AND EVALUATION?

Promoting a fit between monitoring and evaluation makes perfect sense. Organizations that manage and implement programs benefit from the information that monitoring provides about progress in implementation of a program and initial outcomes produced. Monitoring results can be compiled into progress reports for senior managers, funders, and other stakeholders. The complementary role of evaluation is to inform program development and support learning. Deeper investigations and assessments made against agreed criteria, which are intrinsic to evaluation, will show how the program model can be improved and highlight the reasons for success or otherwise in a range of performance areas.

Despite the compelling rationale for complementarity, historically there has often been an uncomfortable fit between monitoring and evaluation functions. Organizations striving to produce an integrated approach to monitoring and evaluation have been challenged by practice barriers where the personnel who undertake monitoring and evaluation may derive from different disciplinary backgrounds and often work separately. The historical separation of monitoring and evaluation into two camps can appear to be reinforced by the different epistemologies and end purposes of these practices, often depicted as the difference between trying to prove or to improve. While the results of monitoring have immediate application in the context of program implementation, evaluation "has a deeper heuristic and penetrating nature" (Nielsen & Ejler, 2008, p. 176). Evaluation has the bolder, but necessary, role of questioning the context, the manner in which implementation is undertaken, and the value of results achieved.

Given the earlier, it is unsurprising that some discontent and critique punctuate the relationship between monitoring and evaluation. Monitoring is a process that often disappoints evaluators. Good monitoring requires sustained organizational capacity for the production and use of performance information. Where this is absent, underdeveloped monitoring systems compromise the validity and reliability of the information collected. A compounding problem occurs in the case of overengineered monitoring systems with overambitious or too numerous indicators that overextend the organization's capacity and resources to collect the requisite data. This may reflect a top-down orientation in the development of monitoring systems that are out of sync with timelines and those involved with providing, collecting, or ultimately using the desired information (Chen, 2005; Nielsen & Hunter, 2013). Such trends reinforce a need to not only improve the quality of monitoring undertaken but, for evaluators, to also question data quality in performance management, to test data validity, and to provide a complementary understanding of program benefits (Nielsen & Hunter, 2013).

Evaluations, by contrast, can disappoint managers as they are not always able to provide timely, readily available, and usable information to guide operational decision making. Evaluation reports and findings are not necessarily produced in an accessible format. Evaluations are often conducted retrospectively and not well synchronized with significant program milestones, budget cycles, or other decision points (Nielsen & Ejler, 2008). Evaluations are therefore often considered to provide "too much information, too late to inform and improve management programming decisions" (Nielsen & Ejler, 2008, p. 180). Furthermore, undertaking evaluations can pose a cost burden for smaller scale programs that are not able to develop discrete budgets for evaluation. Managers may thus prioritize monitoring over evaluation functions.

Efforts to address constraints in the use of evaluation have focused on refining its practice so that it is more compatible with management practices and information needs. Related initiatives include focusing evaluation to address emerging organizational strategic needs (Dudding & Nielsen, 2013); promoting an organizational culture where monitoring and evaluation results are shared amongst managers; and development of accessible, reliable databases which are a common reference point for both monitoring and evaluation functions (Boll & Høeberg, 2013).

Overall, the literature identifies a need to explore the different ways that monitoring and evaluation functions can effectively complement each other, and on this basis, look for means to enhance their interaction. Analyses of complementarity between performance measurement and evaluation have covered the public, not-for-profit, and international development sectors including a focus on organizational and policy dimensions (Boll & Høeberg, 2013; Dudding & Nielsen, 2013; Nielsen & Ejler, 2008; Nielsen & Hunter, 2013; Rist, 2006). Across these analyses, five different types of complementarity have been identified, as summarized in Table 1.2.

**Table 1.2** Complementarity Between Performance Measurement and Evaluation

| *Types of Complementarity* | |
|---|---|
| Sequential | • Monitoring generates questions to be answered in evaluation, and evaluation studies identify areas that require future monitoring. |
| Informational | • Monitoring and evaluation draw on the same data sources but ask different questions and frame different analyses. |
| Organizational | • Monitoring and evaluation data operate in collaboration with both sources of information used, often channeled through the same administrative unit. |
| Methodological | • Monitoring and evaluation share similar processes and tools for structuring and planning, obtaining data, analyzing, and making judgments. |
| Hierarchical | • Performance data are used at various levels of the delivery chain, at times for monitoring and at times for evaluation. |
| Integrative | • Monitoring and evaluation functions are integrated through a focus on answering a common set of framing evaluation questions. Information from both monitoring and evaluation is combined to answer the evaluation questions. This unity of focus avoids the development of parallel, unrelated systems.<br>• Monitoring and evaluation approaches are designed at one time and unified within a shared Monitoring and Evaluation Framework.<br>• Monitoring and evaluation draw from a pool of common methods, tools, and analytical skills, with choices made according to need, timing, expertise, resources, and feasibility. |

As identified earlier, the forms of complementarity between monitoring (performance measurement) and evaluation are diverse. Some are functional and others contextual in orientation, with some particularly applicable to larger organizational and geographic units. Drawing on the preceding, this text supports the need to identify a form of complementarity that more closely aligns to the development of an overarching Monitoring and Evaluation Framework that includes both monitoring and evaluation functions, integrated by their reference to a common set of evaluation questions and the use of common data collection methods, tools, and skills. The resultant form of complementarity is distinguished by its integrated and synergistic characteristics.

This integrative approach, as advanced in this text, is consistent with calls for mutual reinforcement between the two practices. As Nielsen and Hunter (2013, p. 121) note, "complementarity is a two-way street; monitoring practices may inform evaluation studies and *vice versa*." For assessment of a program, monitoring provides an inadequate source of information on its own. However, when appropriately robust, and correctly aligned, monitoring provides the necessary basis for evaluation. Nielsen and Ejler reflect this intent:

> Indeed, monitoring and evaluation studies should be seen as closely interlinked and complementary; monitoring providing data for evaluation and thus constituting one of several data sources, and evaluation being the necessary add-on to monitoring in order to focus on causality and deeper explanations conducted from time to time to qualify monitoring data. (2008, p. 181)

The alignment of both practices is strengthened by a common focus on answering evaluation questions. By adopting this integrated approach, functions of accountability and learning may coexist more comfortably. This approach averts the rift in practice between accountability through monitoring alone and program development based on evaluation learnings occurring as an afterthought or add-on to monitoring.

An integrated approach to the use of monitoring and evaluation functions represents a significant bonus to the development of a broader performance management system. This is evidenced in more direct and efficient harnessing of different kinds of performance information and improving synergy with other performance management functions, such as program planning. These relationships are highlighted in Figure 1.2.

**Figure 1.2** Performance Management

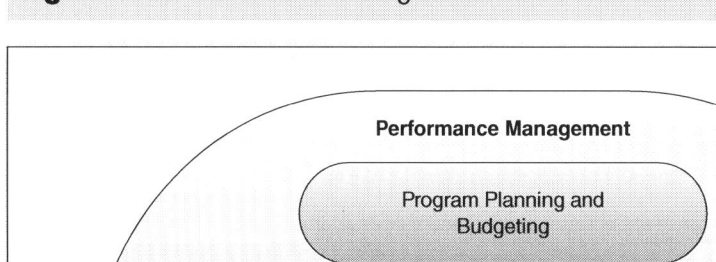

## WHAT IS INCLUDED IN A MONITORING AND EVALUATION FRAMEWORK?

The following reflect the major content areas of a Monitoring and Evaluation Framework and also represent the basis for a Table of Contents to guide its development:

1. *Introduction to the Framework* sets out the context and background to the program, providing a profile of the program and its aims and objectives. The Introduction should identify the parameters and functions of the Monitoring and Evaluation Framework and the approach adopted to promote participation of stakeholders.

2. *Program Theory and Program Logic* indicates the intended causal connections and relationships between a program's efforts and the intended

results. In practice, some variations in approach and terminology are found in this area, which may have implications for the degree and manner in which a Monitoring and Evaluation Framework is expected to foreshadow the results of a program.

3. *Evaluation Questions* outline the areas of investigation that will structure the monitoring and evaluation functions, usually classified under domains, typically those of appropriateness, effectiveness, efficiency, impact, and sustainability.

4. *The Monitoring Plan* outlines what is to be monitored, and how, against the agreed evaluation questions.

5. *The Evaluation Plan* outlines what is to be evaluated, and how, in reference to the evaluation questions. It should articulate with and refer to the Monitoring Plan.

6. *Data Collection, Management, and Analysis* comprises a data collection plan, data management plan, and guidance for data analysis and synthesis.

7. *Reporting and Communication Strategy* details the approach to producing and disseminating monitoring and evaluation reports for accountability and learning in order to guide program implementation and inform decision making.

8. *Implementation* identifies how the framework will be put into practice through development of a work plan.

9. *Data Collection and Reporting Formats* includes the tools and proformas that have been developed for data collection and reporting, usually included as appendices to the main document.

## FORMAT AND LAYOUT OF THE TEXT

The six main stages involved in developing a Monitoring and Evaluation Framework each involve associated steps, as shown in Figure 1.3. Together these provide a structure for the text as detailed in Table 1.3. One or two chapters are devoted to each stage. Additionally, two initial chapters provide an introduction and outline foundation concepts.

**Figure 1.3** Stages in Development of a Monitoring and Evaluation Framework

| Stage 1 | Stage 2 | Stage 3 | Stage 4 | Stage 5 | Stage 6 |
|---|---|---|---|---|---|
| **Scoping the Framework** | **Program Theory Program Logic Evaluation Questions** | **Develop Monitoring and Evaluation Plans** | **Data Collection, Management, Analysis, and Synthesis** | **Learning, Reporting and Dissemination** | **Planning for Implementation** |
| • Identify requirements<br>• Determine participation arrangements<br>• Identify possible and preferred approaches<br>• Review resource parameters<br>• Confirm purpose and parameters of the Framework<br>• Document and distribute agreements reached | • Plan stakeholder engagement<br>• Develop/review program theory and program logic<br>• Confirm program theory and program logic with key stakeholders<br>• Develop draft evaluation questions<br>• Facilitate stakeholder participation<br>• Scope number and range of questions against data and resources available<br>• Present questions to stakeholders for final endorsement<br>• Finalize evaluation questions | • Identify focus of monitoring<br>• Develop performance indicators and targets (where appropriate)<br>• Identify data collection processes and tools<br>• Determine responsibilities and time frames for monitoring<br>• Determine overall evaluation approach<br>• Identify evaluation questions requiring criteria and standards<br>• Identify focus and evaluation methods for each question<br>• Determine responsibilities and time frames for evaluation<br>• Review monitoring and evaluation plans | • Develop data collection plan<br>• Develop data management plan<br>• Consider approach to data analysis and synthesis<br>• Consider approach to making evaluative judgments and reaching evaluative conclusions | • Consider developing a program and organizational learning strategy that maximizes utilization of evaluative conclusions and recommendations<br>• Consider processes for the identification of recommendations and lessons<br>• Provide guidance on developing a reporting and dissemination strategy | • Confirm program management arrangements<br>• Develop a work plan for implementation<br>• Plan for monitoring and review of Framework |

**MONITORING AND EVALUATION FRAMEWORK**

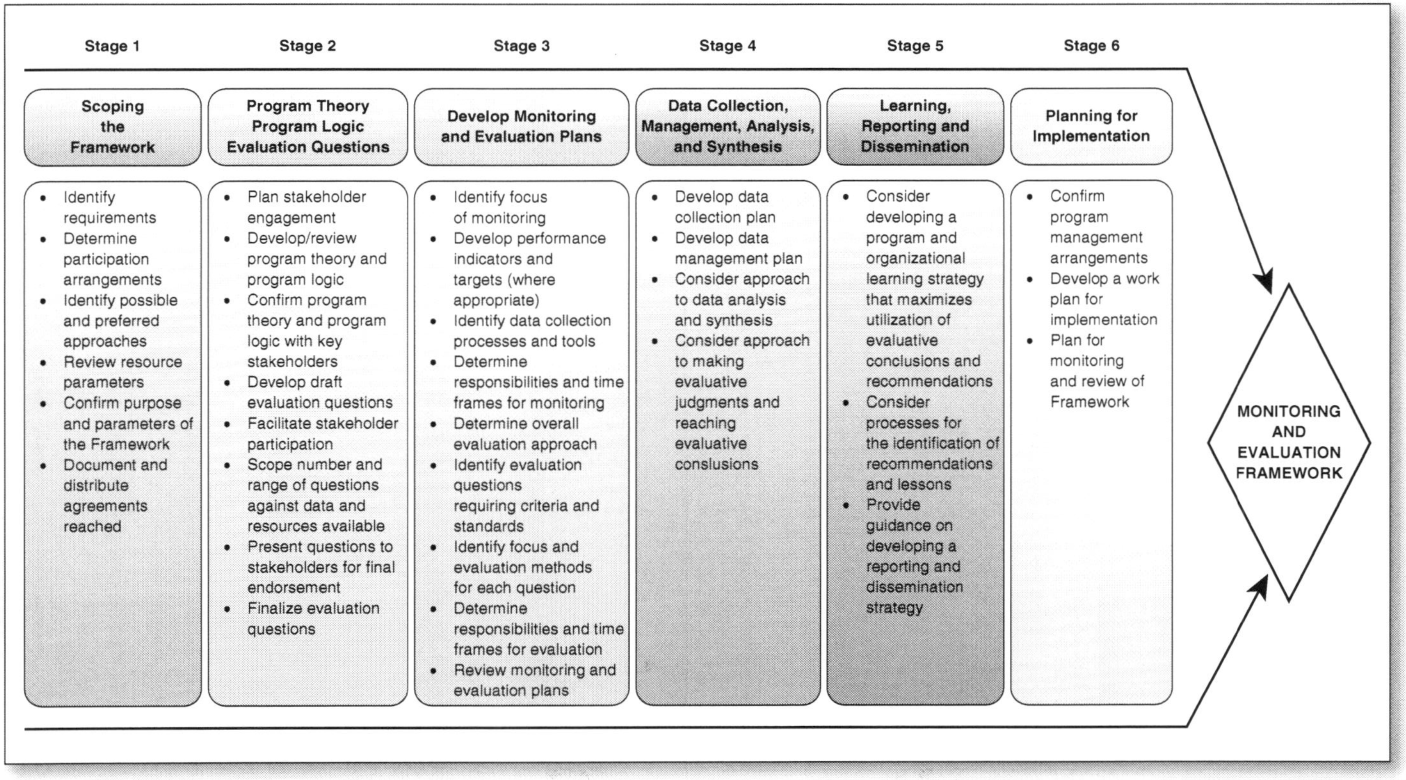

**Table 1.3** Text Structure

| *Introduction and Foundation Concepts* | | Chapters 1 & 2 |
|---|---|---|
| Introduction | | Chapter 1 |
| Foundation Concepts | | Chapter 2 |
| *Stage 1: Scoping the Monitoring and Evaluation Framework* | | Chapter 3 |
| Steps | | |
| 1 | Identify requirements | • Examine documentation that provides context and background to the Monitoring and Evaluation Framework.<br>• Clarify with the core program team their expectations, needs, and priorities.<br>• Elicit views as to the purpose of the Framework and its focus.<br>• Clarify audiences and information needs of key stakeholders.<br>• Clarify time frames for development and implementation of the Framework, including for main deliverables such as reports. |
| 2 | Determine participation arrangements | • Identify stakeholders who should be involved in the development and implementation of the Framework or involved as audiences for its results.<br>• Determine roles for key stakeholders.<br>• Plan for participation and how it is to occur.<br>• Brief key stakeholders on context and background to the Monitoring and Evaluation Framework.<br>• Elicit stakeholder requirements and expectations.<br>• Identify and address stakeholder needs for evaluation capacity development. |
| 3 | Identify possible and preferred approaches | • Elicit the preferred (and often differing) evaluation approaches of all involved parties, including the paradigms, values, and methods they would ideally like to see reflected in the Framework.<br>• Consider the merits and limitations of possible approaches and methods canvassed.<br>• Reach consensus as to the preferred approaches, paradigms, methods, and values to be considered and agreed upon following the development of the agreed evaluation questions. |
| 4 | Review resource parameters | • Assess system capabilities for generating and managing both routine monitoring and periodic evaluation data.<br>• Scope budget and other available resources.<br>• Reconcile scope of the Monitoring and Evaluation Framework to budget and available resources and data. |
| 5 | Confirm purpose and parameters of the Framework | • Confirm the purpose, focus, and scope of the Monitoring and Evaluation Framework.<br>• Document and distribute agreements reached. |

# Chapter 1  Introduction to Developing Monitoring and Evaluation Frameworks

| *Stage 2: Foundations for the Monitoring and Evaluation Framework* | | | *Chapters 4 & 5* |
|---|---|---|---|
| *Develop Program Theory and Program Logic* | | | *Chapter 4* |
| Steps | | | |
| 1 | Plan stakeholder engagement strategy | • Establish a process for engaging key stakeholders in development of the program theory and the program logic, such as convening a stakeholder workshop, forum, or other arrangement. | |
| 2 | Develop program theory | • Convene appropriate participatory arrangements with key stakeholders.<br>• Identify sources of information to be used in developing the program theory, such as literature, research, studies, practice experience, and other evidence.<br>• Identify key assumptions to be tested during the evaluation.<br>• Develop draft program theory in conjunction with key stakeholders. | |
| 3 | Develop program logic | • Convene appropriate participatory arrangements with key stakeholders.<br>• Identify the key assumptions and outcome areas to be tested during the evaluation.<br>• Develop program logic with key stakeholders and with reference to the program theory. | |
| 4 | Confirm program theory and logic with key stakeholders | • Present the program theory to key stakeholders to determine its<br>    ○ plausibility and consistency with the evidence base, and<br>    ○ coherence, logical flow, and the clarity of its communication.<br>• Confirm the program theory and the program logic as key reference points for developing the evaluation questions for the Monitoring and Evaluation Framework. | |
| *Develop Evaluation Questions* | | | *Chapter 5* |
| Steps | | | |
| 1 | Develop draft evaluation questions | • Draw on prior clarification as to the purpose of the Monitoring and Evaluation Framework.<br>• Review documentation that provides context and background to the Monitoring and Evaluation Framework.<br>• Develop an initial set of evaluation questions using the five evaluation domains to prompt areas of investigation and categorize questions generated. | |

*(Continued)*

**Table 1.3** (Continued)

| | | |
|---|---|---|
| | | • Consider the relative significance of each domain given the purpose of the Framework.<br>• Use the program theory and the program logic and other available materials to assist in identification of the evaluation questions including those that focus on achievement of critical results areas. |
| 2 | Facilitate stakeholder participation | • Facilitate broad stakeholder engagement in selecting and agreeing on evaluation questions. This ideally will involve a Monitoring and Evaluation Planning Workshop held at an early opportunity. |
| 3 | Scope number and range of questions against data and resources available | • Scope data availability to respond to proposed evaluation questions.<br>• Scope the number and range of questions proposed against the resources available, including budget, staff availability, and capacity for monitoring and evaluation. |
| 4 | Present questions to stakeholders for final endorsement | • Re-present evaluation questions to the key stakeholders involved in Step 2 for final endorsement. |
| 5 | Finalize evaluation questions | • Develop a final agreed set of evaluation questions for inclusion in the Monitoring and Evaluation Framework. |
| *Stage 3: Develop Monitoring and Evaluation Plans* | | *Chapters 6&7* |
| *Develop the Monitoring Plan* | | *Chapter 6* |
| Steps | | |
| 1 | Identify focus | • Identify focus of monitoring in order to provide answers for evaluation questions. |
| 2 | Develop performance indicators and targets | • Develop performance indicators and targets where these are appropriate to the questions.<br>• Identify relevant baselines, as appropriate for conditions to which indicators refer. |
| 3 | Identify data collection processes and tools | • Identify data collection processes and tools that will require development. |
| 4 | Determine responsibilities and time frames | • Determine responsibilities and time frames for the implementation of monitoring activities. |

| *Develop the Evaluation Plan* | | | *Chapter 7* |
|---|---|---|---|
| *Steps* | | | |
| 1 | Determine overall evaluation approach | <ul><li>Select the most suitable approach and methods to be adopted from the range of options available.</li><li>Consider evaluation principles and standards for guidance.</li><li>Identify ethical issues that may emerge during the implementation of the Monitoring and Evaluation Framework.</li></ul> | |
| 2 | Identify evaluation questions requiring criteria and standards | <ul><li>Identify evaluation questions that require criteria and standards.</li><li>Identify the headline evaluation questions that relate to determining a program's quality and value.</li><li>Develop criteria for determining quality and value.</li><li>Develop standards against the criteria.</li><li>Develop an evaluation rubric that includes the criteria and standards.</li></ul> | |
| 3 | Identify focus of evaluation and methods for each question | <ul><li>Consider types of evaluative processes that will augment monitoring conducted in order to answer the evaluation question.</li><li>With reference to each evaluation question, identify the focus of evaluation and the types of evaluation methods to be used.</li><li>Identify the parameters of selected methods, specifying the breadth and depth of the inquiry to be conducted.</li></ul> | |
| 4 | Determine responsibilities and time frame | <ul><li>Determine responsibilities for undertaking evaluation activities and whether they will be internally or externally conducted.</li><li>Identify agreed intervals and time frames for implementation of the Evaluation Plan.</li></ul> | |
| 5 | Review the Monitoring and Evaluation Plans | <ul><li>Reassess capacity for data collection across the Framework in its entirety, including routine monitoring and periodic evaluation.</li></ul> | |
| *Stage 4: Data Collection, Management, Analysis, and Synthesis* | | | *Chapter 8* |
| *Steps* | | | |
| 1 | Develop data collection plan | <ul><li>Confirm data needs for implementation of the Monitoring Plan and the Evaluation Plan.</li><li>Determine which data are already collected by the program.</li><li>Identify additional types of data collection methods to be used.</li><li>Identify the focus of each method, sampling approaches, implementation requirements, and any potential ethical issues.</li><li>Determine specifications for the development of data collection tools.</li></ul> | |

*(Continued)*

**Table 1.3** (Continued)

| 2 | Develop data management plan | • Identify the range of data to be managed.<br>• Identify requirements for database systems.<br>• Determine how data analysis will be undertaken.<br>• Consider required data reports and their contents.<br>• Consider and plan for the development of staff capacity for data management.<br>• Plan for regular reviews of the data system. |
|---|---|---|
| 3 | Consider approach to data synthesis | • Consider how monitoring and evaluation data will be integrated and who will be responsible for undertaking data synthesis.<br>• Consider how synthesized data will be used to assess performance against indicators and targets, and against criteria and standards, and determine who will be responsible for undertaking such synthesis. |
| 4 | Consider approach to making evaluative judgments and reaching evaluative conclusions | • Consider how synthesized data can be used to form evaluative judgments and who will be responsible for undertaking this.<br>• Consider how evaluative judgments made translate to the identification of evaluative conclusions.<br>• Ensure that the range of evaluative conclusions developed can lead to an overall conclusion in relation to the program. |

| *Stage 5: Learning, Reporting, and Dissemination* | *Chapter 9* |
|---|---|

*Steps*

| 1 | Consider developing or refining a learning strategy for the program that maximizes use of conclusions, recommendations, and lessons | • Consider developing or refining a learning strategy for the program that guides the learning process, identifying when and how learning is expected to occur.<br>• Ensure that the Monitoring and Evaluation Framework identifies and promotes opportunities for reflection and learning. This includes attention to<br>    o linking learning to program improvement and to redesign where required,<br>    o identification of transferable recommendations and lessons for the benefit of other programs and contexts, and<br>    o increasing opportunities for the use and influence of conclusions, recommendations, and lessons. |
|---|---|---|
| 2 | Consider processes for the identification of recommendations and lessons | • Consider how to translate conclusions into recommendations and lessons that will be useful and used.<br>• Scope the need for recommendations, their nature, and number.<br>• Consider how to best engage stakeholders in identification of recommendations and lessons without compromising independence or objectivity. |

# Chapter 1  Introduction to Developing Monitoring and Evaluation Frameworks

| 3 | Provide guidance on developing a reporting and dissemination strategy | • Develop a reporting and dissemination strategy that best supports potential use of evaluative conclusions, implementable recommendations, and useful lessons.<br>• Provide guidance for the production of reports and effective reporting processes.<br>• Give consideration to different types of reports and their audiences.<br>• Consider best methods for communicating messages to different audiences. |
|---|---|---|

| *Stage 6: Planning For Implementation of the Monitoring and Evaluation Framework* | | *Chapter 10* |
|---|---|---|
| *Steps* | | |
| 1 | Confirm program management arrangements | • Provide guidance regarding program and organizational elements required for effective operation of monitoring and evaluation functions, as identified in the Monitoring and Evaluation Framework. These include the areas of management of key stakeholder relationships, personnel management, financial management, information technology, and administrative systems.<br>• Identify any specific areas of program or organizational capacity development required to implement the Framework.<br>• Provide guidance regarding any necessary adjustment or development of program guidelines and procedures to support implementation of the Monitoring and Evaluation Framework. |
| 2 | Develop a work plan for implementation | • Develop a work plan for implementation of the Monitoring and Evaluation Framework. This should identify required activities, when they are to be undertaken, and who is responsible for them. Use a Gantt chart or similar planning tool for this purpose. |
| 3 | Plan for monitoring and review of the Framework | • Determine how the implementation of the Monitoring and Evaluation Framework will be monitored and reviewed. Include arrangements that will examine the relevance of the content and organization of the Framework as well as the effectiveness and efficiency of its implementation.<br>• Build arrangements for ongoing monitoring and periodic review of the Monitoring and Evaluation Framework into the work plan. Include arrangements for periodic updating of the Framework and continued focus on developing program and organizational capacity for monitoring and evaluation as required. |

# CHAPTER 2

# Foundation Concepts

*This chapter introduces and discusses the concepts that are central to the approach adopted in this text. Subsequent chapters elaborate on the groundwork established here. The five foundation concepts which collectively represent and support the approach to the design of a Monitoring and Evaluation Framework are depicted in Figure 2.1 and summarized in the text that follows.*

The following key concepts inform the design of a Monitoring and Evaluation Framework:

1. **Multiple purposes for monitoring and evaluation:** The purposes served by monitoring and evaluation are likely to include tracking the progress of program implementation, identifying results, providing a basis for accountability to funders and stakeholders, facilitating learning, guiding program improvement, and informing decision-making processes.

2. **Informed by Results-Based Management (RBM):** The approach is informed by and incorporates RBM principles. These promote a dynamic and interlinked relationship between planning and monitoring and evaluation.

**Figure 2.1** Foundation Concepts

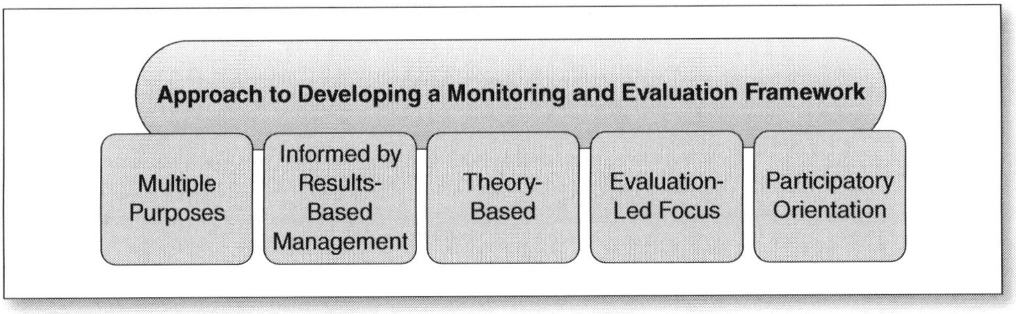

Approach to Developing a Monitoring and Evaluation Framework

- Multiple Purposes
- Informed by Results-Based Management
- Theory-Based
- Evaluation-Led Focus
- Participatory Orientation

3. **Evaluation-led focus for monitoring and evaluation**: Evaluation represents the broader, overarching form of inquiry being undertaken and therefore provides a leading focus for the approach. Monitoring represents a subset of evaluation. Evaluation questions guide both monitoring and evaluation activities, and their organization within evaluation domains provides a focus for areas of investigation.

4. **Theory-based:** A theory-based approach clearly establishes anticipated causal relationships, identifies anticipated results from a program, and uses these theories to organize and guide the evaluation process.

5. **Participatory orientation:** The approach promotes the input and influence of stakeholders in the process of design of the Monitoring and Evaluation Framework and in the monitoring and evaluation activities that it contains.

Each of these concepts is discussed in turn in the following sections.

## 1. MULTIPLE PURPOSES FOR MONITORING AND EVALUATION

The value of a Monitoring and Evaluation Framework lies not just in its development but in the use of the information that it generates to track the progress of implementation, to identify results and account for funding provided, to improve program performance and enhance service delivery, to support learning and program development, and to inform policy development and decision making. The purpose of this text is to provide guidance on developing a Monitoring and Evaluation Framework that incorporates and supports this full range of functions.

In practice, those developing a Monitoring and Evaluation Framework will need to consider the generic functions identified above as guidance but also consider the specific needs and expectations arising from the particular context. The political context in which evaluation operates is a reality, and its influence and effect on practice has been widely discussed (Datta, 2011; Weiss, 1983). The evaluator's role includes identification and mediation of a range of expectations that can arise from different stakeholders (Markiewicz, 2005). These stakeholders can be both external and internal to the program and its host organization. Issues of timing, feasibility, and resource availability will also influence the scope and focus of a Monitoring and Evaluation Framework.

Most commonly, a Monitoring and Evaluation Framework developed for a program will aim to encompass a full range of functions. This reflects factors intrinsic to programs that are typically designed to address complex needs and problems and operate in sophisticated organizational contexts. Program design is a highly skilled area and also subject to increasing levels of demand and scrutiny. This is typically reflected in program guidelines provided by funders and regulatory and governing organizations. In what Kettner, Moroney, and Martin (2013, p. 4) refer to as the "Era of Accountability," high expectations are directed to programs to measure and report on results while also justifying their cost effectiveness. These expectations clearly have an impact on arrangements made for monitoring and evaluation.

Maintaining an appropriate balance between functions in a Monitoring and Evaluation Framework requires knowledge of evaluation issues and practice and also discussion and negotiation skills in order to explore and accommodate different needs and focus areas. A clear understanding of what is entailed by the different functions of evaluation is a starting point. For example, while accountability is essentially concerned with being answerable to those with power over a particular context, this is not necessarily confined to providing information and explanations to funding bodies or internal management. This is typically characterized as *upward accountability*. Accountability requirements also need to be considered toward stakeholders such as constituents and members of organizations, toward beneficiaries and other stakeholders in civil society, and toward peers and similar organizations (Guijt, 2010).

Accountability pressures, particularly in an upward direction, are one of several factors that can skew the design of a Monitoring and Evaluation Framework, placing an inordinate degree of emphasis on the identification of results. Other related pressures can derive from factors such as organizational promotion and even competition with rival organizations in relation to their results profile. While results are a critical area of organizational performance, it is important that other dimensions are not obscured or minimized. For example, monitoring and evaluation may pay limited attention to program quality. Instead, their perspective may be limited to examining "what differences the social program has made in the lives of its participants and not the experience of being in it" (Greene, 1999, p. 163). An appreciation of program quality yields insight into how the identified outcomes were reached, or in other words, the nature of the means that were used to achieve the ends. Furthermore, assessments of program quality need to consider and incorporate the diversity of different participant experiences and not be reduced to just one answer (Greene, 1999).

Learning is another dimension to which program monitoring and evaluation, and its guiding Monitoring and Evaluation Framework, can make a critical contribution. This includes deriving and using lessons on what does and does not work and what is applicable to similar programs. More methodological and process-orientated aspects of learning are also important and have intrinsic value. These include learning new ways of engaging with stakeholders, undertaking ethical and effective evaluation practices, and developing capacities for reflection, research, analysis, and dialogue (Preskill, 2008). Tensions are often identified in relation to a program's ability to incorporate learning due to pressures of upward accountability. In this context, monitoring and evaluation systems may become too focused on measurement and grading performance, data systems are overtaxed, and limited time, capacity, and resources remain for a learning focus (Ebrahim, 2005). Attempts to resolve these tensions seek to reposition and reaffirm learning as intrinsic to accountability. Learning is viewed as necessary to ascertain whether a program had delivered as anticipated and is supported through practical steps such as timing learning events to feed into required reports (Guijt, 2010).

Similarly, the status of learning and its critical role within monitoring and evaluation processes is reinforced where organizational leadership promotes a culture. Such support from leadership needs to extend across the field of monitoring and evaluation. Where monitoring and evaluation are viewed as mechanisms for program improvement and betterment of service delivery, it is more likely to embrace all the functions and purposes indicated earlier. Effective leadership, ownership of monitoring and evaluation purposes and processes, evaluation capacity building, and adequate resourcing of the monitoring and evaluation system are highlighted in this text as important elements of successful evaluation practice.

Overall, it is critical that a Monitoring and Evaluation Framework is not constructed simply to support compliance with accountability requirements. Despite a range of challenges involved, the Monitoring and Evaluation Framework needs to reflect a range of purposes, many of which are generic, but which are also refined and given particular definition according to the specific context. Such an approach is highlighted in this text.

## 2. RESULTS-BASED MANAGEMENT APPROACH

Results-Based Management (RBM) is a management approach that has achieved wide currency in the public sector. It has drawn on management practices in the private and not-for-profit sectors, in addition to asserting its own level of influence in these contexts. In essence, RBM aims to gear organizational and program efforts to improving performance and the achievement of results. This emphasis and accompanying concerns with accountability have heightened expectations of what monitoring and evaluation should deliver. RBM is identified as part of a broad movement of public sector reform orientated toward outcomes and efficiency that had its inception in the 1980s. It has made an impact on many governments worldwide but with local differences and levels of acceptance (Chouinard, 2013; De Vries & Nemec, 2013; McDavid, Huse, & Hawthorn, 2013).

RBM has been defined as a management strategy by which all actors "ensure their processes, products, and services contribute to the achievement of desired results (outputs, outcomes and higher level goals or impact)" (United Nations Development Group, 2011). The actors are expected to use the information and evidence generated to improve decision making, accountability, and reporting. RBM is strongly associated with a need to increase the use of reliable evidence as a basis for decisions made, as opposed to the conventions of "usual practice" or simply drawing the perceptions of a limited range of stakeholders. In this context, the RBM approach identifies a critical role for monitoring and evaluation to establish the evidence that is required. To promote the use of such evidence, it further advocates for breaking down traditional divides between planners and managers and those assessing organizational and program performance. In this manner, monitoring and evaluation are functionally integrated not only within a broader program or organizational setting but also within a shared commitment to achieving results.

A range of management approaches share a similar orientation to RBM. These include an early originator, Management by Objectives (Drucker, 1954) and the later Managing for Results (Drucker, 1964; Moynihan, 2006). Management for Development Results (MfDR) is prominent in international development contexts (Asian Development Bank, 2011; Organisation for Economic Co-operation and Development [OECD] Development Assistance Committee [DAC]). All expound a cyclical management process involving result setting, identifying and assessing performance information using monitoring and evaluation processes, and returning findings on results to management to make further adjustments to organizational direction and commitment of resources. The interconnectedness that is inherent to this approach has been used as a guiding principle for this text.

The RBM approach (United Nations Development Programme [UNDP], 2011) is represented in Figure 2.2. This management approach with its cyclical, iterative, and integrated orientation also typifies what is known as *performance management*. The term is used with this sense in this text in contrast to more general usage where it often appears as a descriptor for a range of efforts to focus the performance of an organization.

While few proponents of monitoring and evaluation practice question the value of an integrated approach between planning, monitoring, and evaluation functions, the RBM approach has been subject to considerable critique. The approach and its accompanying mind-set have been critiqued for displaying an "obsessive measurement disorder" (Natsios, 2010). Such a perspective is based on concern that the approach relies too strongly on quantification, affirming

**Figure 2.2** Results-Based Management Life Cycle Approach

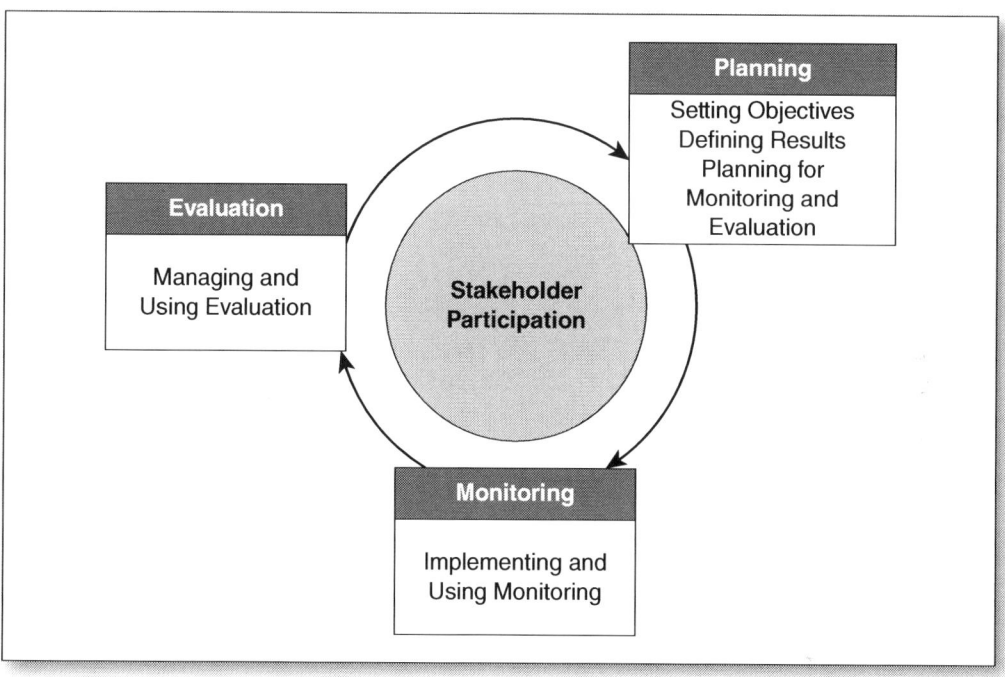

that which can be easily measured and discounting that which cannot (Eyben, 2013). An accompanying risk is to similarly discount the value of transformational initiatives that may be relatively less amenable to measurement. RBM has also been critiqued for reinforcing top-down perspectives where what is valued and measured is not in accord with the needs of implementing partners, operational personnel, and beneficiaries.

Exponents of social theories including complexity theory and systems theory have identified what they consider to be flaws in the linear, cause-and-effect type thinking that characterizes RBM (Hummelbrunner, 2010; Ramalingam, Jones, Toussant, & Young, 2008). A major evaluation of the implementation of RBM in the United Nations system identified that the approach had failed to identify how outcomes may be influenced by multiple actors and external risk factors. Its perceived formalistic perspective was seen to stifle the innovation and flexibility required to achieve those results (United Nations, 2008). Further concerns have identified RBM as adding to an administrative burden in contemporary organizations with a range of procedural requirements and incompatible systems, rules, and regulations. Measurement systems have frequently been described as overengineered with too many indicators employed. Systems developed in this manner have commonly experienced many constraints in implementation, especially in developing country contexts with limited capacity for data collection.

Despite the critiques of RBM and its limitations, this text has proposed that the approach and its broader governing principles have merit. The key feature of the approach is to promote a culture of results and integration between the functions of planning, monitoring, and evaluation. This is in contrast to any prescriptive dictates about any particular methods selected to establish change and measures employed. In practice, there are a variety of different interpretations of what constitutes RBM. As Hatton and Schroeder (2007) state, "it is not easy to find two people who will describe RBM in the same way" (p. 428). In practice, RBM approaches can use a variety of different methods to establish change including quantitative indicators, theory-based evaluations, or impact evaluations, and complexity theory can also be used to understand complex change (Vahamaki, Schmidt, & Molander, 2011).

Although not without its challenges, many perceived issues with RBM are likely to derive from the competing paradigms that play out in its application rather than in its broader intent. Positivistic perspectives and strong concerns with accountability reinforce calls for use of particular methods. These include more scientific and precise measurement involving more singular use of quantitative data due to their perceived greater validity and reliability. Such perspectives are opposed by a constructivist or interpretive approach, which is concerned with learning in complex nonlinear environments by eliciting stakeholder voices using participatory methods (Armytage, 2011). Armytage (2011) observes that the dominance of a more positivistic paradigm "may explain the current trend toward performance-based models, which markedly emphasize monitoring at the expense of evaluation" (p. 274).

To avoid adoption of uniform approaches to RBM, this text suggests that it should not be regarded as a prescriptive or restrictive model but rather as a management approach or perspective that it is nuanced in its application. Key to the approach is the interlinked and balanced relationship between planning, monitoring, and evaluation; the incorporation of monitoring with its focus on tracking progress and more learning-focused evaluation; and a broad base of inquiry driven by evaluation questions. Such inquiry includes a key focus on identifying outputs, outcomes, and impacts that are what are typically formally identified as the results of an initiative. A range of other performance areas such as the appropriateness and efficiency of an initiative are also assessed to provide a broader view of performance.

Risks of adopting an RBM approach characterized by reductionist, linear, or positivist thinking are reduced where a range of methods and measures are used to establish change, including but not confined to use of indicators and targets. Both qualitative and quantitative perspectives are encouraged. The approach advocated of developing plans for monitoring and evaluation simultaneously promotes the adoption of evaluative thinking. This approach is outlined in greater detail in Chapter 6, "The Monitoring Plan."

## 3. THEORY-BASED APPROACH

This text adopts a theory-based approach and incorporates this into the formulation of a Monitoring and Evaluation Framework. The approach is fundamental and widely applied in evaluation practice and is an important distinguishing feature. A theory-based approach can be broadly understood as developing models of how a program works, and through the practice of evaluation, examining the viability of the model, including its level of appropriateness and accuracy. Such an approach includes the process of theory making, theory testing, and any required readjustment of the theory as a result. As part of this process, the evaluator is required to identify and understand the assumptions that underlie anticipated changes brought about by the program. Different stakeholders may perceive how the program works and its assumptions differently, and the role of the evaluator is likely to involve mediating such differences and arriving at a consensus position (Chen, 2015).

One notion of theory-based evaluation that reflects the above schema, and resonates with the intent of this text, is that developed by Donaldson (2007) who identified three steps involved in undertaking his approach termed "program theory-driven evaluation science" (p. 10). These are

1. developing program impact theory,

2. formulating and prioritizing evaluation questions, and

3. answering evaluation questions.

Donaldson (2007) details how this involves a process of working with stakeholders and drawing on research to develop a common understanding of how a program addresses an issue, identifying questions, and then answering these questions using the most rigorous methods available given the context. While Donaldson's approach has received considerable support, the evaluation field reflects wide variation in how theory-based evaluation is understood. As Coryn, Noakes, Westine, and Schroter note,

> even though a common vocabulary, definition, and shared conceptual and operational understanding has largely been elusive, theory-driven forms of evaluation have, nonetheless, increasingly been espoused by numerous evaluation scholars and theorists, practitioners and other entities as the preferred method for evaluation practice. (2011, p. 200)

While sharing a common basis in theory-led evaluation, this text uses two different concepts to delineate between more conceptual and more operational models of how the program operates. *Program theory* aims to make explicit the reasoning as to how and why a program's actions will produce the intended results. A *program logic* identifies and maps the intentional and sequential progression from a program's actions to its intended results over time. A program logic also categorizes a program's results according to a range of factors including timing. Both program theory and program logic, as discussed in Chapter 4, are used to generate evaluation questions and serve as reference points against which the actual program, as implemented, is compared.

Despite strong support for theory-based approaches to evaluation, there are also those who express reservations. Scriven (1991) has argued that if evaluators undertake development of program theory, this can deflect their focus away from the conduct of the evaluation itself. Scriven's view is that the task of developing a program theory should be completed by social scientists or program theory specialists, not evaluators. Furthermore, Scriven has argued that it is the role of evaluators to determine only whether programs work, not how they work (Coryn et al., 2011). In support of Scriven's position, some evaluators support "goal free" evaluation that focuses on what a program actually does rather than what it intends to do (Youker, 2013). In this case, they are likely to deliberately avoid identifying and learning about the stated objectives and anticipated outcomes of a program.

Stufflebeam and Shinkfield (2007) express related reservations stemming from the perceived complexity of program theory and the frequently inadequate time available for its proper development. The authors observe that "in claiming to conduct a theory-based evaluation, evaluators often seem to promise much more than they can deliver" (Stufflebeam & Shinkfield, 2007, p. 186). They express further concern that through developing program theory, evaluators may potentially usurp a program's responsibility for program design, that evaluators face a conflict of interest in evaluating a program theory that they themselves have developed, and that evaluators tend to present an unvalidated and untested program theory as fact. Coryn et al. (2011) refer to a range of publications of Coryn where he identified some misplacement of priorities with theory-driven evaluation being more focused on evaluating the underlying program theory rather than the program itself. Furthermore, he expressed concerns that evaluation questions are generally not well connected to the program theory and that the approach is overly abstract with little guidance provided as to how to use it in practice.

Others have observed that despite claims to the opposite, program theory is frequently undertaken in a partial or simplistic manner. Rogers (2007) observes, for example, an evaluation using a program logic model may only investigate whether a particular result occurred and provide little or no associated explanation. Additionally, only some aspects of the logic may be investigated without explanation of the focus adopted. Such observations are consistent with that of Coryn et al. (2011), who made assessments of a wide range of practice examples of theory-based evaluation against identified principles of this approach. They found, for example, that program theories postulated were often narrowly formulated on the basis of existing scientific theory and did not incorporate stakeholder views to develop a comprehensive theory. Similarly, questions formulated on the basis of the program theory were often descriptive in nature, rather than evaluative questions that prompted investigation of the program's quality and value.

The approach used in this text, notes both a generally high value accorded to the theory-led evaluation approach, as well as cautions expressed regarding limitations in the manner in which it is implemented. A theory-based approach to evaluation offers considerable explanatory value in providing a model of how a program causes intended or observed outcomes and also at least partially focuses the investigations undertaken through the evaluation (Rogers, Petrosino, Huebner, & Hacsi, 2000). The position of this text is to strike a balance between a pragmatic approach to development of program theory and logic, while retaining adequate methodological integrity to meet their purposes. Care is taken that the approach is not overly complex and that development is not too time-consuming. Such a balance is further influenced by the need for user-friendly constructs that will be applied when engaging with stakeholders involved in contributing to the development of program theory and logic. While possibly open to critique for oversimplification, accessibility and participation are promoted amongst stakeholders and professionals charged with their use.

A further strength of the approach adopted in this text is the use of program theory and program logic to inform development of evaluation questions that otherwise may have been developed through a more random, free-form brainstorming process. The interconnection between these three constructs is further demonstrated in the manner in which the evaluation questions lead logically to the development of a monitoring plan and an evaluation plan, which then inform methodology development, data collection, and analysis processes. This integrated approach is consistent with the notion of program theory-driven evaluation science as proposed by Donaldson (2007). It also aims to address limitations identified in the literature through providing clarity in how a theory-based approach can be planned and implemented as directed by a Monitoring and Evaluation Framework.

## 4. EVALUATION-LED MONITORING AND EVALUATION

Monitoring and evaluation are intrinsically linked and important functions, although they have evolved from different historical roots and theoretical foundations. In this text, an evaluative approach is used to establish the theory and principles that are used to guide both monitoring and evaluation processes. Such an orientation stands in contrast to many other traditional approaches to developing Monitoring and Evaluation Frameworks, where the central focus is placed on monitoring inputs, activities, and outputs in order to track program implementation. In such traditional approaches, evaluation, if included, is positioned as an add-on to complement the centrality of monitoring activities. In many practice areas, and particularly in international development, what is termed *evaluation* is often more characteristic of monitoring. As a consequence, the emphasis on monitoring can overshadow the more "vexing challenges of evaluation" (Armytage, 2011, p. 262).

The central positioning of monitoring within a Monitoring and Evaluation Framework has occurred in part because monitoring has provided funders and managers with more tangible, immediate, and regular information than evaluation has been able to with its focus on producing in-depth, periodic studies. In view of this paradox, the question of whether evaluators should "engage in cross-fertilizing performance-management and monitoring efforts with evaluation thinking and techniques" has been raised and responded to by suggesting that evaluators "must elevate evaluative thinking and processes at the core of organizational operations" (Nielsen & Hunter, 2013, p. 121). In concert with this intent, this text has consciously adopted an approach where evaluation theory and principles are used to guide the nature of inquiry that takes place through program monitoring.

The issue of emphasizing monitoring at the expense of evaluation may also be attributable to an inherent tension that exists between the functions of accountability and learning (Armytage, 2011). In the earlier discussion, the many different purposes of a Monitoring and Evaluation Framework were described as inherent rather than a set of options from which a few are chosen. In adopting this perspective, the artificial divide which overly equates monitoring with accountability and evaluation with learning will hopefully be reduced.

In order to adopt an evaluation-led approach, this text draws on a range of evaluation concepts. The following are critical to the text:

- Commitment to use of a participatory approach
- Use of theory-based approaches
- Development of evaluation questions to guide inquiry
- Framing areas of inquiry against the domains of appropriateness, effectiveness, efficiency, impact, and sustainability
- Use of mixed methods or pluralist approaches to guide methodology development and data collection
- Support for implementation-focused, formative as well as summative, evaluation processes
- Development of agreed criteria and standards for assessing program quality and value
- Assessment of fidelity of program implementation
- Identification of results with consideration to issues of attribution
- Development of useful and useable reporting processes with wide dissemination of findings
- Commitment to organizational learning and evidence-informed decision making
- Commitment to organizational evaluation capacity building

Underpinning the concepts, are fundamental evaluation values as identified and expounded by various professional evaluation associations. These include values such as ethical conduct, public interest, inclusiveness and diversity, cultural responsiveness, quality and competence, confidentiality and respect, integrity and truthfulness, accountability, and reflective evaluation practice (American Evaluation Association [AEA], 2004; Australasian Evaluation Society [AES], 2013). An evaluation-led approach is also reinforced through the use of evaluation questions to guide both monitoring and evaluation processes and the use of a wide range of measures beyond indicators and targets. The approach is also characterized by drawing on a common pool of methods, tools, and analytical skills that are then used within monitoring and evaluation functions according to need, timing, expertise, available resources, and feasibility. This approach avoids the development of parallel, unrelated systems.

Overall, this text affirms critical principles and theories that are derived from the field of evaluation. These apply to both monitoring and evaluation and define their interrelationship. Sound monitoring is critical and has important inherent functions. It also provides information, drawn from regular data gathering exercises, that forms a basis for many evaluation processes. In this manner, the two functions complement each other and support the drawing of balanced and integrated assessments.

## 5. PARTICIPATORY ORIENTATION

Stakeholder participation is an important feature in both the process of developing a Monitoring and Evaluation Framework and in determining its contents. The latter will involve choices made regarding the approach and methods adopted. The evaluation field is characterized by wide debate regarding what level and type of participation is optimal in practice. Recognizing the complexity of this area, and how levels of participation are partly determined by context, this text does not make dictates about this area. Instead, the approach taken is to advance the principle of encouraging as much participation as is possible and feasible and to reflect this in the development of the Monitoring and Evaluation Framework.

The definition of what participation means in monitoring and evaluation, and in social programs more generally, is open to many interpretations (Cullen & Coryn, 2011). It can be viewed, for example, as promoting the representation and voice of different stakeholders in concert with democratic principles (MacDonald, 1976). Stakeholder involvement enables the range of diverse, varied, and often competing perspectives and interests to be canvassed and represented. This reflects a democratic process where the diversity of values and interests in society are represented (Greene, 2006). It can also be viewed from a social justice perspective, which seeks to redress power imbalances, build capacity, and promote the levels of control of stakeholders who may be otherwise marginalized (House & Howe, 2000). In addition to the quest for democratic representation and social justice, the involvement of stakeholders is also undertaken with the aim of increasing the utilization of evaluation findings and placing value on participation as part of an empowerment approach to evaluation. Examples of approaches primarily based upon principles of utilization include Patton's (2008) utilization-focused evaluation where he proposes substantial consumer involvement in the evaluation process in order to increase the utility of evaluation findings. Fetterman and Wandersman (2005) put forward an approach where evaluation supports stakeholders and program beneficiaries, through evaluation capacity-building efforts, to evaluate their own programs in order for them to achieve self-determination and empowerment.

As demonstrated by the preceding examples, different social values and political perspectives underpin different approaches to participatory evaluation practice. A schema frequently used to characterize participatory practice uses a continuum that commences with no participation, moving through to provision of information, consultation, partnership with stakeholders, to control by stakeholders (Pretty, 1995). King (2005) emphasizes that while most evaluations involve some degree of participation, this does not necessarily make them participatory. A distinction can thus be made between the notion of "participation in evaluation" and what may be termed as "participatory evaluation." King (2005) notes that the importance of interacting with stakeholders to gain their perspectives and input has been widely recognized as important to good evaluation practice. However, her argument is that consultation does not in itself define participatory practice, with the latter requiring stakeholders to be actively engaged throughout the evaluation process in making decisions across a broad range of areas such as evaluation design, data collection, and dissemination.

Critical views, such as that of King (2005) observe that forms of participation in evaluation from lower levels of the continuum are misidentified and more token in orientation. Other perspectives, such as that of Cullen, Coryn, and Rugh (2011), use a more pragmatic and less absolutist schema to categorize participatory evaluation. They identify three major variables, these being (a) who maintains control of the evaluation process, (b) stakeholder selection for participation in different stages of the evaluation process (design, data collection, data analysis, etc.), and (c) depth of participation within different evaluation stages. Incorporating this schema within a survey of levels of participation in evaluation in an international development context, they identify wide degrees of variation, while also identifying that evaluators mostly retain control over the evaluation process. The authors also cite another survey undertaken in the United States/Canada context (Cousins, Donohue, & Bloom, 1996) that highlights comparable results.

A contributing cause to variations in levels of participation in evaluation is likely to be a tendency toward tokenism in incorporating participation in practice. This in turn reflects the status of *participation* as a buzzword (Cornwall & Brock, 2005), readily claimed as a defining characteristic of evaluation but often with little substance. Beyond this, there are many constraints and challenges in application, including levels of required knowledge and skill among evaluators, time and expense involved in implementing participatory practice, lack of familiarity or comfort with participatory methods among stakeholders, potential domination of participatory processes by some individuals over others, and resistance that may be experienced from certain stakeholder groups including funders, governing bodies, and powerful elites.

Despite such challenges, there are compelling reasons to promote the concept of participation in both the development of a Monitoring and Evaluation Framework and the specific arrangements determined for monitoring and evaluation functions. The justification derives from political and values perspectives, in support of evaluative principles. Drawing on the work of Mayoux (2005), reasons for supporting participation may be summarized as follows:

**Rights**: Participation, particularly of marginalized people, is a human right and advances their empowerment.

**Relevance**: Participation of a wide range of stakeholders increases the relevance of evaluation questions and their alignment with the realities of peoples' lives and the policy context.

**Accuracy**: Participatory methods overcome the limitations of reliance on fragmentary individual views and thereby increase the reliability of the information collected and promote the generation of realistic recommendations.

**Effectiveness**: Involvement of the main stakeholders in the development of a Monitoring and Evaluation Framework and evaluation planning builds awareness and ownership, increasing the likelihood of effective implementation and the use of findings and recommendations.

**Process**: Adopting participatory evaluation processes builds skills, capacities, and networks and thereby makes a contribution to social conditions, civil society, and empowerment.

Opportunities to promote participatory practice in both the development of the Monitoring and Evaluation Framework and in specific arrangements for monitoring and evaluation are likely to vary according to different contexts and the orientation of involved stakeholders. Furthermore, participation levels may vary at different stages of the process, allowing for different possibilities for participation at different times (Plottu & Plottu, 2010). While it is therefore difficult to be prescriptive, participatory practice is likely to involve strong cooperation or even partnership between the evaluator and stakeholders. There is likely to be a shift in power dynamics so that stakeholders are involved in influencing or making decisions in relation to both approach and process (Cousins & Whitmore, 1998). As highlighted above, there are many advantages in promoting such ends.

Chapter 3, building on the concept of stakeholder participation, outlines how this takes place in practice through the development of a Monitoring and Evaluation Framework. Chapter 3 discusses concepts of stakeholder selection and mapping, the management of stakeholder relationships, and approaches to evaluation capacity building.

# CHAPTER 3

# First Steps: Scoping the Monitoring and Evaluation Framework, Stakeholder Mapping, and Evaluation Capacity Building

*This chapter discusses the process of scoping the Monitoring and Evaluation Framework. This involves identifying what is known about the context and purpose of anticipated monitoring and evaluation activities, specific issues to be addressed, and the level of resources available and required for this purpose. Together, these represent important understandings about the Monitoring and Evaluation Framework and provide the basis for its development.*

*Planning is required in order to identify and engage stakeholders in the process of developing the Monitoring and Evaluation Framework and for any necessary capacity building to support their participation. Stakeholders are regarded as those people with a stake in a program, its monitoring and its evaluation, or its results. Stakeholders are usually drawn from three main groups, which are policy makers, program funders, and senior managers; program managers, program deliverers, and program partners; and program beneficiaries or their representatives.*

## 1. INTRODUCTION TO SCOPING THE FRAMEWORK WITH KEY STAKEHOLDERS

A range of choices and associated decisions apply to the development of a Monitoring and Evaluation Framework. These include reaching agreement as to the purpose the Framework is to serve, its priorities, and parameters. Particular attention needs to be given to determining the appropriate breadth and depth of the Monitoring and Evaluation Framework, in accord with the size and scale of the program and the available budget for monitoring and evaluation. Overly ambitious Monitoring and Evaluation Frameworks are too frequently developed, resulting in poor implementation or implementation failure. Decisions on the nature of the Monitoring and Evaluation Framework will be influenced by the intersection of the knowledge, experience, approach, values, and interests of the evaluation team with that of program personnel and key stakeholders. Ostensibly, the evaluation team will have been selected on the basis of their expertise and experience. Team members will therefore bring with them perspectives and approaches that will have significant influence, while at the same time working collaboratively to elicit and incorporate those of key stakeholders.

Initial tasks involved in developing the Monitoring and Evaluation Framework include clarifying expectations and requirements of the core program team, establishing how stakeholder participation will occur, considering possible and preferred approaches, reviewing resource parameters against expectations, and confirming the Framework's purpose and parameters. Evaluation

# Chapter 3  First Steps: Scoping the Monitoring and Evaluation Framework

team members, program personnel, and key stakeholders are likely to hold either explicit or implicit preferences and expectations regarding the development of the Framework that need to be openly identified and debated, with consensus then achieved. For example, parties involved in the process are likely to draw from differing social science and evaluation paradigms and approaches based on their foundation education, their subsequent education and training, their career paths, and their personal experiences. These preferred evaluation approaches, or heuristics, will then affect the way that evaluation questions are selected (Fitzpatrick, Sanders, & Worthen, 2011). Furthermore, some involved parties will face different contextual and political influences that will impact on their expectations and requirements. The expectations, requirements, and preferences held by the parties involved should thus be well scoped and negotiated by the evaluation team during the early stages of developing the Monitoring and Evaluation Framework.

Program and stakeholder perspectives are critical to ensure that a range of views are incorporated and that maximum levels of support for the Framework are achieved. For those developing a Monitoring and Evaluation Framework, debates can take place as to the desired level of representation of stakeholders, who should be involved and who should not, and which voices will be heard. Stakeholders, once involved, can provide input and debate many aspects of the design and implementation of a Monitoring and Evaluation Framework. These include the manner in which the program theory and the program logic are developed, the range and type of evaluation questions used, key performance indicators and targets selected, the type of approach and methods employed, the nature of findings generated, and processes used for reporting and dissemination of results. All of these considerations can be subject to discussion and negotiation. A range of views is likely to arise as to what constitutes a credible approach to monitoring and evaluation that is acceptable and capable of meeting the information requirements and diverse needs of the different stakeholder interests represented.

In facilitating discussion of purpose and scope, priorities, and parameters, there is a need for a heightened awareness of the diversity of political interests and agendas likely to emerge in the process of developing a Monitoring and Evaluation Framework. The political nature of evaluation is evident through the range of competing stakeholder interests and multiple perspectives represented (Weiss, 1983). Stakeholder perspectives are often informed by their organizational mandate. Government agencies and not-for-profit organizations often have defined ways of operating and possibly a track record in undertaking monitoring and evaluation activities in a particular manner. Even when successful in capturing the nature of the prevailing expectations and interests, policy shifts and turnover of key personnel frequently result in subsequent changes to these expectations. Reflecting on the political nature of the process, Kusek and Rist (2004) comment that "constructing a results-based M&E system is an inherently political act entailing both political risks and benefits" (p. 45). The capacity of monitoring and evaluation activities, as guided by the Monitoring and Evaluation Framework, to produce findings that are critical or identify performance failures places them firmly in a political context.

In the most challenging of circumstances, program and external stakeholders may enter the process with a vested interest that the program continue and be altered in certain directions or ways or that it should cease to operate altogether. It is possible that stakeholders will anticipate that planning for monitoring and evaluation, as reflected in the Monitoring and Evaluation Framework, will work to support their interests in this regard. Pressure can be placed on those undertaking monitoring and evaluation to identify certain findings and make specific recommendations (positive or negative depending on the circumstance) that are consistent with prevailing political agendas.

The preceding are examples of the inevitable contextual, political, and stakeholder realities and challenges that need to be identified and well managed during the course of developing a credible and defensible Monitoring and Evaluation Framework. Some of the more extreme and unhelpful risks of stakeholder involvement can be ameliorated by undertaking evaluation capacity-building activities that emphasize the value of adopting a transparent, open, and learning-oriented approach to the process. Through developing a team-based approach that values and supports the integrity of the Framework, a positive culture can be instigated and supported that also acts to moderate the influence of any extreme views or interests.

## 2. KEY STEPS IN SCOPING THE FRAMEWORK

Table 3.1 outlines the recommended steps involved in scoping the Monitoring and Evaluation Framework.

**Table 3.1** Steps Involved in Scoping the Monitoring and Evaluation Framework

| *Stage 1: Scoping the Monitoring and Evaluation Framework* | | |
|---|---|---|
| *Steps* | | |
| 1 | Identify requirements | • Examine documentation that provides context and background to the Monitoring and Evaluation Framework. |

# Chapter 3  First Steps: Scoping the Monitoring and Evaluation Framework

| | | |
|---|---|---|
| | | • Clarify with the core program team their expectations, needs, and priorities.<br>• Elicit views as to the purpose of the Framework and its focus.<br>• Clarify audiences and information needs of key stakeholders.<br>• Clarify time frames for development and implementation of the Framework, including for main deliverables, such as reports. |
| 2 | Determine participation arrangements | • Identify stakeholders who should be involved in the development and implementation of the Framework or involved as audiences for its results.<br>• Determine roles for key stakeholders.<br>• Plan for participation and how it is to occur.<br>• Brief key stakeholders on the context and background of the Monitoring and Evaluation Framework.<br>• Elicit stakeholder requirements and expectations.<br>• Identify and address stakeholder needs for evaluation capacity development. |
| 3 | Identify possible and preferred approaches | • Elicit the preferred (and often differing) evaluation approaches of all involved parties, including the paradigms, values, and methods they would ideally like to see reflected in the Framework.<br>• Consider the merits and limitations of possible approaches and methods canvassed.<br>• Reach consensus as to the preferred approaches, paradigms, methods, and values to be considered and agreed upon following the development of the agreed evaluation questions. |
| 4 | Review resource parameters | • Assess system capabilities for generating and managing both routine monitoring and periodic evaluation data.<br>• Scope budget and other resources available.<br>• Reconcile scope of the Monitoring and Evaluation Framework to budget, available resources, and data. |
| 5 | Confirm purpose and parameters of the Framework | • Confirm the purpose, focus, and scope of the Monitoring and Evaluation Framework.<br>• Document and distribute agreements reached. |

## *Step 1: Identify Requirements*

Requirements for the design of the Monitoring and Evaluation Framework can often be identified through a review of documentation that provides relevant program context and background. The review should assemble available plans and related documentation that details the program intent and design. Program funding agreements or guidelines should be located for reference. Where program theory or program logic has already been developed, this provides a good starting point for the review of program intent. The program for which the Monitoring and Evaluation Framework is being developed may be part of a larger organizational initiative or a coordinated sectoral or national strategy. In that case, Monitoring and Evaluation Frameworks may already be in place to assess performance at these broader levels. Where available, such Frameworks are likely to provide important points of reference, such as with higher level evaluation questions and indicators and targets. In some contexts, expectations may be in place for alignment between monitoring and evaluation approaches used within particular organizations or contexts. This may apply, for example, in use of common indicators so that results may be more readily aggregated. Other source documents of value can also include relevant research and evaluation findings drawn from available literature.

Early steps in the process of developing a Monitoring and Evaluation Framework involve clarifying its purpose and focus. Clarification of the purpose of a Monitoring and Evaluation Framework involves identification of the exact functions it is to serve, while clarifying its focus entails identification of the priority of the issues requiring attention. Establishing the parameters of the Monitoring and Evaluation Framework involves scoping the resources available against expectations and data availability against data requirements. Time frames for the completion of the Framework and its main deliverables, such as reports, also require early identification. These processes are best undertaken through inception meeting discussions held with funders, the program team, and other relevant primary key stakeholders.

During the preparatory stage of developing a Monitoring and Evaluation Framework, it can be useful to undertake a readiness assessment in a similar manner to undertaking an evaluability assessment for an evaluation. Kusek and Rist (2004) suggest that in undertaking a readiness assessment it is important to determine the motivations, demands, and incentives for the system. This is particularly important when considering that the development of the Monitoring and Evaluation Framework may be compliance driven in response to demands by the funder, with a low level of commitment by the program to its use or application for program development. These factors will then undermine the utility of the Framework as it may end up as a document that is completed and then filed away. It is therefore important to explore the drivers for the development of the Framework in order to better contextualize its purpose and functions. Kusek and Rist also suggest that the readiness assessment should identify the champions for the Framework and clarify the roles and capacity building requirements of involved stakeholders. Stakeholder mapping and engagement processes are thus important for the development of the Monitoring and Evaluation Framework. These factors are discussed further in the following section.

> **Practice Example**
>
> ### Reaching Agreement on the Purpose and Focus of a Monitoring and Evaluation Framework
>
> The development of a Monitoring and Evaluation Framework for a newly funded crime prevention program highlighted different perspectives on its purpose and focus. The program was managed by a nongovernment organization and funded by a state-level Department of Justice. Both parties were involved in meetings with the evaluator regarding the development of the Framework. Personnel from the Department of Justice were concerned that the Framework would particularly focus on the identification of changing levels of criminal activity in target communities. Their expectation was that the program would lead to a strong reduction in this activity. In contrast, personnel from the nongovernment organization were more concerned with identification of the degree to which the program had improved the well-being of service users and the capacity of their communities to support them. Furthermore, while the Department of Justice personnel were interested to use the findings from monitoring and evaluation to justify the continuation of their funding for the program, program personnel were concerned with using findings to promote the service delivery model and its achievements. For the nongovernment organization, the value of the program to its partners and their level of support for the program were critical success factors. These different perspectives were discussed and debated over several meetings facilitated by the evaluator. Consensus was achieved when it was agreed that the Framework would focus on tracking changes in the level of criminal activity in target communities, while also focusing on the identification of service user and community outcomes and examining the quality and value of the service model involved.

## Step 2: Determine Participation Arrangements

As discussed in Chapter 2, facilitating stakeholder participation is integral to developing a Monitoring and Evaluation Framework. This section discusses approaches to stakeholder mapping and engagement. The process of identification and selection of stakeholders, and determining the roles they will adopt in the development and implementation of the Monitoring and Evaluation Framework, is known as *stakeholder mapping*. This process also involves identifying which stakeholders have an interest in the results and reports generated by the monitoring and evaluation process. The latter group are likely to include stakeholders additional to those involved in the design and implementation of the Framework.

### Stakeholder Mapping and Selection

Considerable interest is apparent in the evaluation literature in relation to approaches to stakeholder mapping and engagement (e.g., Bryson & Patton, 2010; Fitzpatrick et al., 2011). Related discussion is found in the international development, community development, and business literature in terms of approaches to project management, governance, social engagement, and empowerment (e.g., Mayers, 2005; Newcombe, 2003; Schmeer, 1999). Stakeholder mapping provides a necessary foundation for effective participation, complemented by strategies to build the capacity of these stakeholders as required. The intent here is to strengthen stakeholder input into the development of the Monitoring and Evaluation Framework, while at the same time increasing levels of ownership and use of its potential results. Building stakeholder skills in areas such as data collection and analysis can also be of independent value, including supporting the empowerment of marginalized groups.

The selection of which voices will be included during the development of a Monitoring and Evaluation Framework is a critical one that will vary according to its purpose and use. To promote use of the products of the Framework, it advisable to involve those stakeholders with knowledge of the program and its context and those who are in operational roles. Where there is an intention to influence policy, this will require representation from policy makers and senior managers. The involvement of program beneficiaries or their representatives can work to provide a "reality check" on the evaluation process, promoting a focus based on the needs and perceptions of those that the program is intended to assist. Involvement of a broad range of stakeholders is also likely to assist in determining whether particular kinds of data are available and feasible to collect.

# Chapter 3  First Steps: Scoping the Monitoring and Evaluation Framework

Another decision involved in selecting stakeholders is to consider the optimal number of core stakeholders that can be feasibly involved in the development of a Monitoring and Evaluation Framework. Time and budget constraints will inevitably create pressures that act to limit the range of stakeholders able to be involved. Some prioritization is therefore likely to be required in relation to inclusion of certain groups and individual key stakeholders in a participatory design process (Bamberger et al., 2012).

Stakeholders can be divided into categories according to how closely connected or removed they are from an interest in the design and implementation of the Monitoring and Evaluation Framework. A broader group of interested and concerned stakeholders can be identified from which a smaller group who would be more strongly involved are pinpointed. From the smaller key stakeholder group, an even more select group of people can be identified who may be regarded as specific stakeholders who will work to help with focus, make design and methodological decisions, interpret results, and promote usefulness and credibility (Patton, 2012). Referring to program evaluation, Patton (2012) suggests that between 6 to 10, and no more than 15, core stakeholders are desirable for inclusion. This number of stakeholders would be sufficient to achieve both diversity of perspectives and manageability in designing an evaluation, negotiating and setting priorities, and undertaking interpretation of findings. This principle would be equally applicable to the design of a Monitoring and Evaluation Framework.

An initial step in mapping different stakeholder groups is to identify primary stakeholders and their interests and potential roles in developing, implementing, or being an audience for the results of the Monitoring and Evaluation Framework. Stakeholders can be expected to have a variety of interests and show varying levels of availability and capacity to contribute to monitoring and evaluation related functions. While individual differences will be evident, certain stakeholder groups can be expected to have particular interests. For example, program funders who are often external to the program may be particularly concerned with program outcomes and return on investment, policy makers with effectiveness and equity, program managers with operational efficiency, program delivery personnel and partners with quality and reach of service delivery, and program beneficiaries or their representatives with service delivery outcomes. Each group is thus likely to enter the process with different interests and expectations of what monitoring and evaluation and an associated Framework will provide. They will potentially adopt different roles, with capacity, availability, and the context and purpose of monitoring and evaluation also influencing role take up.

The types of roles that different groups may play are detailed in Table 3.2.

A variety of different checklists and matrices have been developed in the evaluation literature that aim to map relevant stakeholders and foreshadow the roles they will play and their stake or interests in the process. Some of these extend to identification of levels of power and influence in a particular context. Other approaches follow the ladder of participation approach in

**Table 3.2** Types of Stakeholders and Their Potential Roles

| *Stakeholder Representation* | *Potential Stakeholder Roles* |
|---|---|
| A<br>• Program funders<br>• Policy makers<br>• Program designers<br>• Senior managers | • Input into the *focus and scope* of the Monitoring and Evaluation Framework<br>• Involvement in the development and confirmation of the **key constructs** upon which the Framework will be based, such as program theory, program logic, evaluation questions, and evaluation rubrics<br>• **Endorsement** of the final Framework to ensure its alignment with broader policy and program objectives and imperatives<br>• Interest in the **products** arising from the Monitoring and Evaluation Framework, such as findings generated, evaluative conclusions, recommendations, and reports produced |
| B<br>• Program managers<br>• Program developers<br>• Program implementers<br>• Service delivery partners | • Input into the *focus and scope* of the Monitoring and Evaluation Framework<br>• Involvement in the development and confirmation of **key constructs** upon which the Framework will be based<br>• Consultation regarding the contents of **Monitoring and Evaluation Plans**<br>• **Endorsement** of the final Framework to ensure it is feasible and achievable given resource parameters and time constraints.<br>• **Implementation** of the Framework<br>• Interest in **products** arising from the Monitoring and Evaluation Framework |
| C<br>• Program beneficiaries<br>• Beneficiary representatives | • Involvement in the development and confirmation of **key constructs** upon which the Framework will be based<br>• **Implementation** of the Framework (depending on context)<br>• Interest in **products** arising from the Monitoring and Evaluation Framework, such as findings generated, evaluative conclusions, recommendations, and reports produced |

## Chapter 3  First Steps: Scoping the Monitoring and Evaluation Framework

identifying levels of stakeholder participation in the process along a continuum from information only, to consultation, partnership, empowerment, and full control. This text uses a simple stakeholder mapping matrix, as appears in Table 3.3. The left hand column of the matrix uses a classification system comprising three broad groupings of stakeholders (as appears in Table 3.2), while the column adjacent to this allows individual stakeholder types to be specified.

**Table 3.3**  Stakeholder Mapping Matrix

| Stakeholder Mapping Matrix | | | | | | | |
|---|---|---|---|---|---|---|---|
| Category | Group | Consult, Re-focus, and Scope | Develop Key Constructs | Develop Overall Framework | Endorse Final Framework | Implement Framework | Audience for M&E Products |
| **A** <br> Program funders <br> Policy makers <br> Senior managers | | | | | | | |
| **B** <br> Program managers <br> Program delivery personnel <br> Program partners | | | | | | | |
| **C** <br> Program beneficiaries <br> Beneficiary representatives | | | | | | | |

> **Practice Example**
>
> ### Mapping and Selecting Stakeholders for Developing a Monitoring and Evaluation Framework
>
> A state-based program responsible for providing family support services was interested in engaging with a large group of stakeholders in order to achieve buy-in and support for the development of a Monitoring and Evaluation Framework. Initially, program personnel suggested the formation of a large working group of 30 or more interested stakeholders. After discussion with the evaluator, it was agreed that stakeholders would be grouped according to their interest and potential roles in developing the Framework. An inner circle would include six to eight key stakeholders who would be directly involved in the construction of the Framework. The inner circle formed included representatives from the funding body and the family support agencies. A middle circle comprised of six to eight key stakeholders who would be engaged at various junctures throughout the process. The middle circle of stakeholders included representatives from partner organizations operating closely affiliated programs, a peak organization, and beneficiary representatives. Several workshops were to be held combining the inner and middle circle groups, comprising around 12 to 16 people. These stakeholders would become involved in many of the conceptual tasks such as developing program theory, program logic, and evaluation questions.
>
> An outer circle of another 12 to 16 people was identified as having a stake in the program and would be actively consulted throughout the process. They would not necessarily be available or interested in working on the actual development of the Framework and would not be involved in workshops and working groups. The outer group of stakeholders included personnel from government departments and programs with an interest in the program area. The process of forming three concentric circles of different stakeholder groups enabled a more tailored approach to participation to be adopted. Different groups had roles to play according to their interest and capacity. The approach worked well for the program, providing a streamlined and efficient approach to stakeholder engagement.

Subsequent chapters discuss in more detail how key stakeholders become actively involved in the development of the building blocks of program theory, program logic, and evaluation questions.

**Chapter 3** First Steps: Scoping the Monitoring and Evaluation Framework 55

The stages where stakeholder participation should be actively supported in the development of a Monitoring and Evaluation Framework are summarized in Figure 3.1. These include involvement in constructing program theory and program logic, developing evaluation questions and evaluation rubrics, involvement in the formulation of the Monitoring Plan and the Evaluation Plan, and as an audience for findings and reports.

**Figure 3.1** Points of Stakeholder Participation

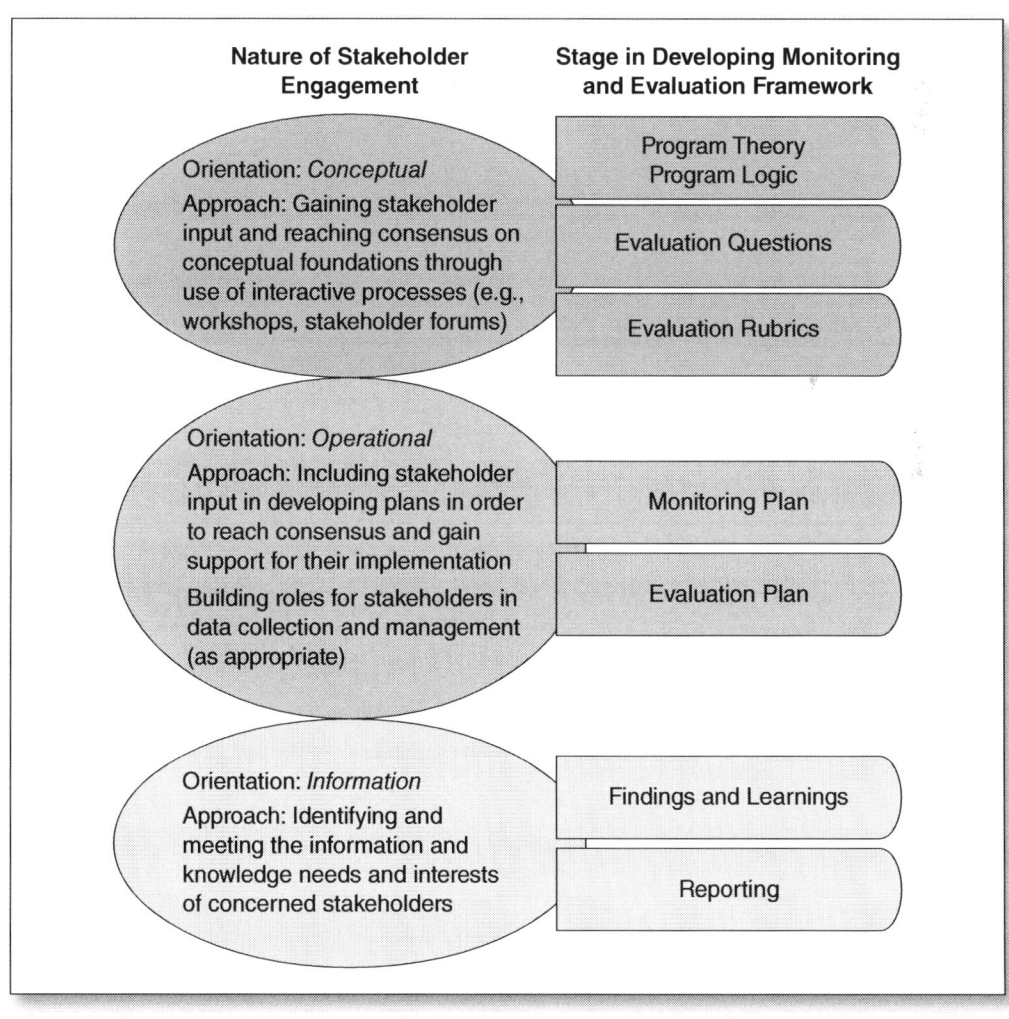

### Stakeholder Management

Once key stakeholders have been identified, selected, and engaged, a process of ongoing relationship building is required to facilitate positive interactions and promote constructive working relationships so that the Monitoring and Evaluation Framework is appropriately designed and implemented. The section above has broadly categorized key stakeholders within the three distinct groups of funders, policy makers, and senior managers; the program personnel and practitioners who operationalize the program; and the program beneficiaries. Each of these distinct groups will require different approaches to facilitate and sustain their active involvement in the process, as well as to build their capacity to be positive contributors as required. Some stakeholder groups, and subgroups and individuals within them, will hold different levels of power and influence. For example, some program personnel and program beneficiaries may have relatively low levels of power and influence. Cultural and gender differentials may also characterize some groups and require consideration in the development of an engagement strategy (Mertens & Wilson, 2012).

Stakeholders require information as to the context and background of the Monitoring and Evaluation Framework. Their requirements and expectations of monitoring and evaluation, and by extension of the Framework, need to be elicited. This process can be challenging when stakeholders have little experience of this area or have unrealistic expectations. In this situation, strategies for evaluation capacity building may be required, which are discussed in the next section.

> **Practice Example**
>
> **Planning for Stakeholder Engagement in the Development of a Monitoring and Evaluation Framework**
>
> A series of workshops was planned as part of the development of a Monitoring and Evaluation Framework for a program supporting the settlement of newly arrived migrants and refugees. The purpose of the workshops was to involve stakeholders in development of program theory and program logic and then for them to agree on a set of evaluation questions. An evaluator was engaged to lead the development of the Framework and to facilitate the series of workshops. Ahead of the planned workshops, the evaluator learned that many of the stakeholders who would be participating held differing views as to the purpose and direction of the program.

> Program personnel indicated that they were concerned that the workshops would become tense and conflictual. The evaluator therefore decided to emphasize strong preparation for the workshops and a methodology that would provide significant opportunities for stakeholders to contribute their differing views. In advance of the workshops, draft program theory and program logic diagrams were distributed for consideration, together with a set of draft evaluation questions. The sessions had clearly stated outcomes. Through active facilitation, a range of different perspectives were elicited and debated in a constructive manner. Consequently, anticipated issues and conflict did not eventuate. Following the workshops, few changes were made to the circulated draft diagrams and questions, as stakeholders believed that their perspectives and contributions had been well acknowledged and included. Circulating draft materials ahead of the workshops, adherence to a planned and structured process, strong facilitation skills, and the perceived neutrality of the facilitator appeared to allay discord and promote consensus. At the end of the workshops, participants reflected on how successful the workshops had been and how much had been achieved.

### Evaluation Capacity Building Approaches

Evaluation capacity building (ECB) describes intentional initiatives undertaken aimed at increasing motivation, knowledge, and skills to conduct or use evaluative concepts and practices. These may apply in organizational, program, group, and individual contexts (Labin, Duffy, Meyers, Wanderman, & Lesesne, 2012). Within organizations and programs, potential functional benefits of monitoring and evaluation for accountability and planning, as well as learning, have been increasingly recognized, bringing more visibility and support of ECB as a strategy. More broadly, increasing value has been attributed to the development of evaluative thinking so that organizations can actively question and improve practice and learn more readily (Clinton, 2014; Labin, 2014; Labin et al., 2012; Preskill & Boyle, 2008).

The most commonly used strategies for ECB include the provision of training, mentoring, and coaching, as well as supported involvement in the conduct of an evaluation (Labin et al., 2012). Additionally, online resources are increasingly available for self-directed learning about evaluation. Prior to initiating ECB in an organizational or program context, an assessment of readiness for such as activities is advisable (Preskill, 2014). Experience has highlighted a range of factors that can facilitate or hinder the introduction of ECB initiatives. These include the support of organizational leadership, the existence of a culture of inquiry and learning or readiness to develop in this area (Preskill, 2014; Preskill & Torres, 1999), and sufficient financial and human resources allocated to the process (Bamberger et al., 2012).

Areas where ECB support may be required for stakeholders involved in the development and implementation of a Monitoring and Evaluation Framework are identified in Table 3.4.

**Table 3.4** Areas for Evaluation Capacity Building for Involved Key Stakeholders

| *Stage* | *Areas of Knowledge and Understanding* |
|---|---|
| **Initial orientation** | • The purpose and function of Monitoring and Evaluation Frameworks<br>• Reasons for investing in the process<br>• Differences between routine monitoring and periodic evaluation<br>• The stages and steps involved in developing a Monitoring and Evaluation Framework for a program<br>• The importance of scoping the focus and parameters of Monitoring and Evaluation Frameworks against expectations and resources available<br>• The need to identify realistic time frames for the development and implementation of Monitoring and Evaluation Frameworks<br>• The roles played by different types of stakeholders in the process<br>• The need to follow a sequential approach using program theory, program logic, and evaluation questions as the foundation of the Framework |
| **Developing the Framework** | • Results-Based Management and the constructive relationship between planning, monitoring, and evaluation<br>• The role of program theory and program logic<br>• How to approach developing evaluation questions<br>• The complementary roles that monitoring and evaluation play in answering evaluation questions<br>• How to approach designing Monitoring Plans and Evaluation Plans<br>• Developing key performance indicators and setting appropriate targets<br>• The range of appropriate data collection methods and tools and how to appropriately select from that range available<br>• Developing data collection tools and ensuring that accurate data is collected<br>• Identifying data gaps and either remedying these gaps or modifying the approach<br>• How to develop an analytical framework to be applied to data collected<br>• How to deal with issues of attribution when examining results<br>• Ethical issues involved and suitable responses |

# Chapter 3  First Steps: Scoping the Monitoring and Evaluation Framework

| Stage | Areas of Knowledge and Understanding |
|---|---|
| Implementing the Framework | • How to best implement the Monitoring Plan and Evaluation Plan<br>• How to develop and support data collection, management, and analysis processes<br>• Understanding the nature and meaning of results generated and how they can be applied for program improvement and learning<br>• How to best implement learning strategies |
| Managing findings and reporting | • How to use findings generated for internal accountability, decision making, program improvement, and for broader learning<br>• How to identify audiences for results and reports<br>• Best approaches for reporting and dissemination of results |

### Practice Example

**Capacity Building for Participants Involved in Developing a Monitoring and Evaluation Framework**

In the development of a Monitoring and Evaluation Framework for a non-government organization delivering aged care services, several preparatory workshops were scheduled. It became clear during early discussions with program staff that many of the participants attending these workshops would have limited knowledge about monitoring and evaluation and the processes to be followed in designing a Monitoring and Evaluation Framework. Consequently, the evaluator engaged to assist with this process met with several potential participants to ascertain more about their background and interests. The evaluator subsequently designed the first workshop as a training session. A short handout was prepared and circulated outlining the core concepts and steps involved in the development of a Monitoring and Evaluation Framework. The handout also included a list of references and relevant websites for further self-directed learning. Participant feedback indicated that they found both the written material and the presentation to be very useful. On the basis of this preparation, they indicated that when participating in the second workshop, they were better able to engage with the process. Attention to the capacity-building needs of the participants thus enabled a more effective and participatory process to ensue.

### Step 3: Identify Possible and Preferred Approaches

Following on from stakeholder selection and engagement, there is a need to identify the preferred evaluation approaches and associated evaluation methodologies that will underpin the development and operation of the Monitoring and Evaluation Framework. The final selection of evaluation approaches and methods will be confirmed once the evaluation questions have been selected and agreed upon. As part of preliminary scoping, it is worthwhile to canvass the preferred approaches of key stakeholders in order to guide the orientation of the Monitoring and Evaluation Framework to be developed.

The selection of evaluation approaches is informed by the extensive literature, which details different evaluation theories and paradigms and the values associated with each (e.g., Alkin, 2013; House & Howe, 1999; Mertens & Wilson, 2012). Given the depth and breadth of the available literature, the discussion here is necessarily limited to provision of broad guidance for this task.

Figure 3.2 identifies selected examples of broad overarching approaches within evaluation. The approaches summarized next are not definitive but rather are a sample intended to provide direction for monitoring and evaluation activities. It is possible and quite common for more than one approach to be influential in a particular monitoring and evaluation system. Furthermore, many of the approaches overlap with each other in intent or will operate in sequence.

**Figure 3.2** Selected Evaluation Approaches

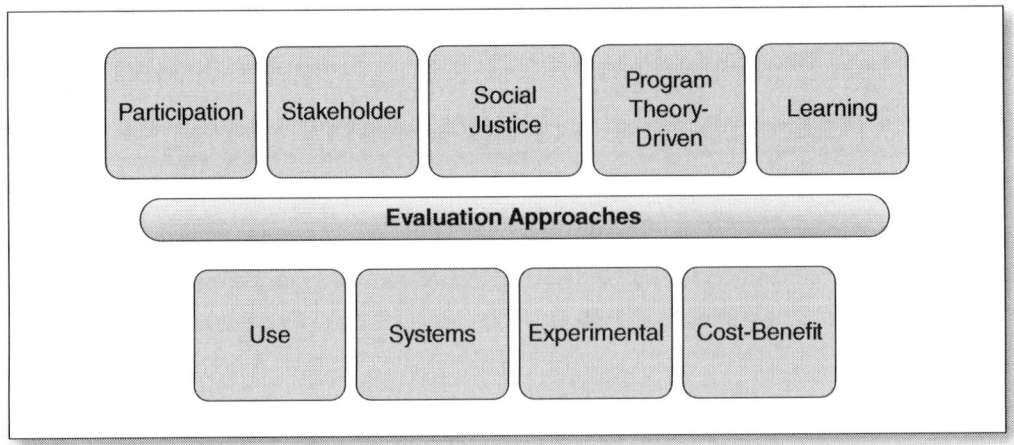

## Chapter 3  First Steps: Scoping the Monitoring and Evaluation Framework

The selected approaches are summarized below and discussed in greater detail in Chapter 7 that deals with the development of the Evaluation Plan.

**Participation:** This refers to a range of evaluation approaches that actively encourage stakeholder participation at critical junctures in the design and implementation of monitoring and evaluation activities. These may include, for example, scoping the focus and contents of the Monitoring and Evaluation Framework, deciding on an evaluation approach, conducting monitoring and evaluation activities, and drawing evaluative findings and conclusions. Empowerment approaches to evaluation provide stakeholders with the knowledge and skills required to become active players in monitoring and evaluating the performance of their own programs. In general, participatory approaches are justified by democratic values and by the value of participation in increasing the reliability and use of the information generated.

In constructing a Monitoring and Evaluation Framework, decisions will need to be made as to the degree of stakeholder participation that is required and acceptable, both for developing the Framework itself and for conducting the monitoring and evaluation activities. Different evaluation approaches vary in the degree to which stakeholder participation is inherent. For example, evaluation approaches that emphasize convening stakeholder forums are likely to generate interchange, provide opportunities for comparing different viewpoints, and build consensus.

**Stakeholder:** Related to the participatory approach discussed earlier, but more general in orientation, are stakeholder-focused approaches. These approaches emphasize gaining an understanding of a program's performance and outcomes by eliciting the perspectives of key program stakeholders and beneficiaries, drawing on their direct experiences of the program or their interpretations of the program based on available data. In the application of a stakeholder-focused approach, for example, the program logic may act as a point of reference, with the views of stakeholders elicited as to the degree to which the program contributed to or achieved change. The change identified may have come about through the direct work of a program or through the program working in partnership with affiliated programs. In this manner, stakeholder approaches may elicit the perspectives of program beneficiaries as to the types of changes they experienced through their direct involvement with the program.

In determining how monitoring and evaluation will be undertaken, consideration needs to be given to the degree to which stakeholder and beneficiary perspectives are to be included in order to generate the required data. If the approach used is stakeholder-focused, then stakeholders need to be identified and engaged early in the process so that their interest in, and cooperation with, monitoring and evaluation activities can be assured.

**Social Justice:** This approach focuses on the highlighting the perspectives and needs of marginalized groups, using evaluation to further social justice, and promote human rights (Mertens & Wilson, 2012). In this approach, an emphasis is placed on producing and using evaluation findings to reduce identified inequalities. Such findings may be employed in advocacy, social policy development, and to inform strategies for social change. In using a social justice approach to evaluation, deliberative, proactive strategies may be employed to locate and elicit the views and experiences of marginalized groups and to encourage their active involvement in evaluation activities, with the aim of best representing their perspectives.

**Program Theory–Driven:** The program theory–driven approach is concerned with developing an understanding as to how and why a program achieved its results and the underlying mechanisms that contributed to these results. In program theory–driven evaluation, a narrative or diagrammatic model is usually developed delineating how the planned program processes (often delineated into inputs, activities, and outputs) will causally lead to a presumed sequence of intended changes (outcomes in the short, medium, and longer term) and the conditions or assumptions under which these changes are expected to occur. Program theory–driven evaluation usually works collaboratively with stakeholders drawing on their understanding of the program.

Program theory–driven approaches, such as Realist Evaluation, also recognize the importance of identifying and understanding the context in which programs operate, as programs may operate differently in different contexts. This is achieved by considering the mechanisms that are applied, the context in which the programs are implemented, and the outcomes produced by the mechanisms in their given context (Pawson & Tilley, 1997). It is the interaction between context and mechanisms that create the outcomes. This approach, rather than concentrating on identifying overall program outcomes, frequently asks the broader evaluative question of what (mechanisms) work (outcome) for whom and under what circumstances (context). In this approach, there is a focus on the identification of those groups that the program benefitted and those it did not.

**Learning:** Evaluation approaches that adopt an explicit learning focus support regular reflective processes, encourage team and stakeholder dialogue, and ensure that decisions made draw from evaluation findings (Torres & Preskill, 2001).

A learning focus also supports evaluation capacity building to ensure that those involved have the knowledge and skills to use evaluation in their work. Learning approaches typically adopt a strengths-based, rather than a deficits-based approach to evaluative inquiry. Such an orientation emphasizes positive features and learning as a basis for further development, rather than focusing on problems that need to be resolved. A learning approach may be applied within a program, the broader organization within which the program is based, and also with stakeholders and beneficiaries who are involved with evaluation activities or their results.

**Use:** This evaluation approach is described as "pragmatic" (Mertens & Wilson, 2012) or "decision-oriented" (Alkin, 2013), and it has a focus on assisting key stakeholders with their decision making and promoting the use of evaluation results in program development and organizational change processes. A utilization-focussed approach (Patton, 2012) emphasizes early identification of the primary users of the evaluation, their needs and expectations, and the uses to be made of the evaluation by the users. A subsequent emphasis of this approach is on ensuring that evaluation findings generated are useful and used by the program.

**Systems:** These approaches have been developed to facilitate the understanding and practice of evaluation in a systems environment that is typically both complicated and complex. In such systems, relationships and dynamics are frequently nonlinear, uncertain, and unpredictable. Programs are complicated when they rely on multiple components implemented by multiple partners with no linear causality able to be established between the program's methods and its effects or when the effects are separated in time from the program's life span. They are also complex when they are highly context sensitive with the same interventions likely to result in different behaviors. Predictability of outcomes is not easily established (Funnell & Rogers, 2011; Williams & Hummelbrunner, 2011).

To be useful in such environments, evaluative approaches need to be sensitive, adaptive, and responsive. Developmental Evaluation (Patton, 2011) is one example of an approach that responds to the realities posed by evaluating complicated and complex programs, emphasizing the role of the evaluator both as an active player in the conceptualization and design of the program and contributing to its adaptation and continuous development. The application of evaluative thinking and reflection to guide program development is a key feature of this approach.

**Experimental:** These approaches are focused on determining causal relationships between a program's interventions and its results with a largely quantitative orientation and an emphasis on proof and measurement. The experimental and quasi-experimental approaches follow the classic research principles involved in conducting an experiment. In a true experimental design, there is randomization between one context that receives the program intervention and the context that does not, whereas in a quasi-experimental design, there is a matched comparison made between the program intervention and a context that is without the program intervention.

The quasi-experimental approach is more likely to be encountered in program evaluation than the experimental approach with its use of Randomized Control Trials (RCTs), given that it is often not practical, ethical, or possible to randomly assign people to experimental and control groups (Alkin, 2013). The quasi-experimental approach may be considered, for instance, when it is appropriate to compare contexts with or without the said program intervention, such as examining the differences between the academic results for students in schools that received the new curriculum compared to those that did not.

**Cost-Benefit:** Approaches such as Social Return on Investment are one amongst many that attempt to assess value-for-money, establish cost-effectiveness, or identify a program's cost-benefits. These approaches may be used to identify and quantify the financial benefits derived from a program in relation to its results. While they are entirely different to the experimental approach, they have a shared objective of measuring program results in a quantifiable way with a level of assumed internal validity.

>Following discussion of preferred and applicable evaluation approaches, the range of methodologies to be employed can be considered. Historically, a dichotomous distinction has been made between positivist and constructivist methods. The former are often linked to concerns with quantitative measurement and the latter with interpreting different values and perspectives qualitatively. Mixed-methods approaches that combine the use of different methods are becoming increasingly used in evaluation as a means for reducing the limitations inherent in the use of any one method on its own (Creswell, 2015; Mertens & Wilson, 2012).

The two paradigms, together with examples of methods associated with each are highlighted in Table 3.5.

While the "paradigm wars" evident in evaluation debate and literature have settled somewhat, differences of opinion remain about the merits of various approaches and methodological options. Moreover, the landscape of different approaches and values that characterize evaluation practice is more complex than the bipolar schema presented in making quantitative and qualitative distinctions.

## Chapter 3  First Steps: Scoping the Monitoring and Evaluation Framework

**Table 3.5** Methodological Paradigms

| *Paradigm* | *Focus* | *Methods* | *Examples of Method* |
|---|---|---|---|
| Positivist | Program effectiveness through measurement | Quantitative | • Experimental designs<br>• Quasi-experimental designs<br>• Onetime, interval, or panel questionnaires<br>• Pre-post rankings<br>• Testing<br>• Cost-benefit analysis<br>• Observation (with checklists) |
| Constructivist | Interpretation of multiple values and perspectives | Qualitative | • Semistructured interviews<br>• Focus groups<br>• Observation<br>• Stories of change<br>• Visual records<br>• Workshops and meetings<br>• Case studies<br>• Stakeholder and network analysis<br>• Phenomenological, ethnographic, and narrative studies<br>• Social and economic assessments<br>• Community scorecards |
| Mixed Methods | Triangulation of data through use of different methods | Concurrent | • Performance data, questionnaires, focus groups, and case studies |

A range of different approaches that influence evaluation, and more broadly the field of social research, are likely to be at play and will be reflected in views and preferred methods of evaluators and other stakeholders alike. Eliciting and discussing these different options and reaching some consensus are important to the process of developing the Monitoring and Evaluation Framework.

## Step 4: Review Resource Parameters

In developing the Monitoring and Evaluation Framework, early consideration should be given to assessing the capabilities of the system to generate the requisite monitoring and evaluation data. There will be a number of iterations of the Monitoring Plan and Evaluation Plan required before there is general agreement reached that they are realistic and achievable in view of the available data, timing issues, budget, and other resources available. It is important therefore to scope the availability of funds and human resources so the breadth and depth of the Monitoring and Evaluation Framework can be more accurately predetermined.

In constructing Monitoring and Evaluation Frameworks, a frequently noted risk is to be overambitious. Such tendencies are understandable given the level of demands and expectations placed on evaluation practice but are ill advised. It is important to consider the realities of context and the constraints commonly experienced in terms of budget, time, and data availability. As a pragmatic response, Bamberger et al. (2012) have advanced a "Real World Evaluation" approach. Such an approach balances sensitivity to inevitable constraints, while striving to maximize rigor in evaluation. Figure 3.3 identifies a set of strategies that may be employed to respond to challenges commonly experienced in the development of Monitoring and Evaluation Frameworks.

In negotiating concessions to the scope of a Monitoring and Evaluation Framework, including narrowing its focus or rationalizing the methodology used, it is important to keep in mind the minimum standards required for credible and defensible evaluation practice and ensure that these are not compromised. Guidance to this area can be obtained from professional associations, as reflected, for example, in the American Evaluation Association's (2004) *Guiding Principles for Evaluators*.

## Step 5: Confirm Purpose and Parameters of the Framework

The final step involves confirmation of the purpose, focus, and scope of the Framework and planning for the events involved in designing the Framework. This confirmation will likely involve a final round of consultation (either directly or remotely) with key stakeholders, possibly based on a draft outline, and any refinements made as a response. Once agreed, understandings can be subsequently incorporated into the introductory paragraphs of the Monitoring and Evaluation Framework document. These understandings provide a foundation upon which the rest of the Framework can be developed. Over time, however, some flexibility and revision may be required in response to events such as turnover in key personnel and organizational and policy changes. The identification of an agreed review process for the Framework is likely to be of assistance with such factors. This could entail, for example, undertaking a review after 12

**Figure 3.3** Possible Responses to Expectations and Constraints in Developing a Monitoring and Evaluation Framework

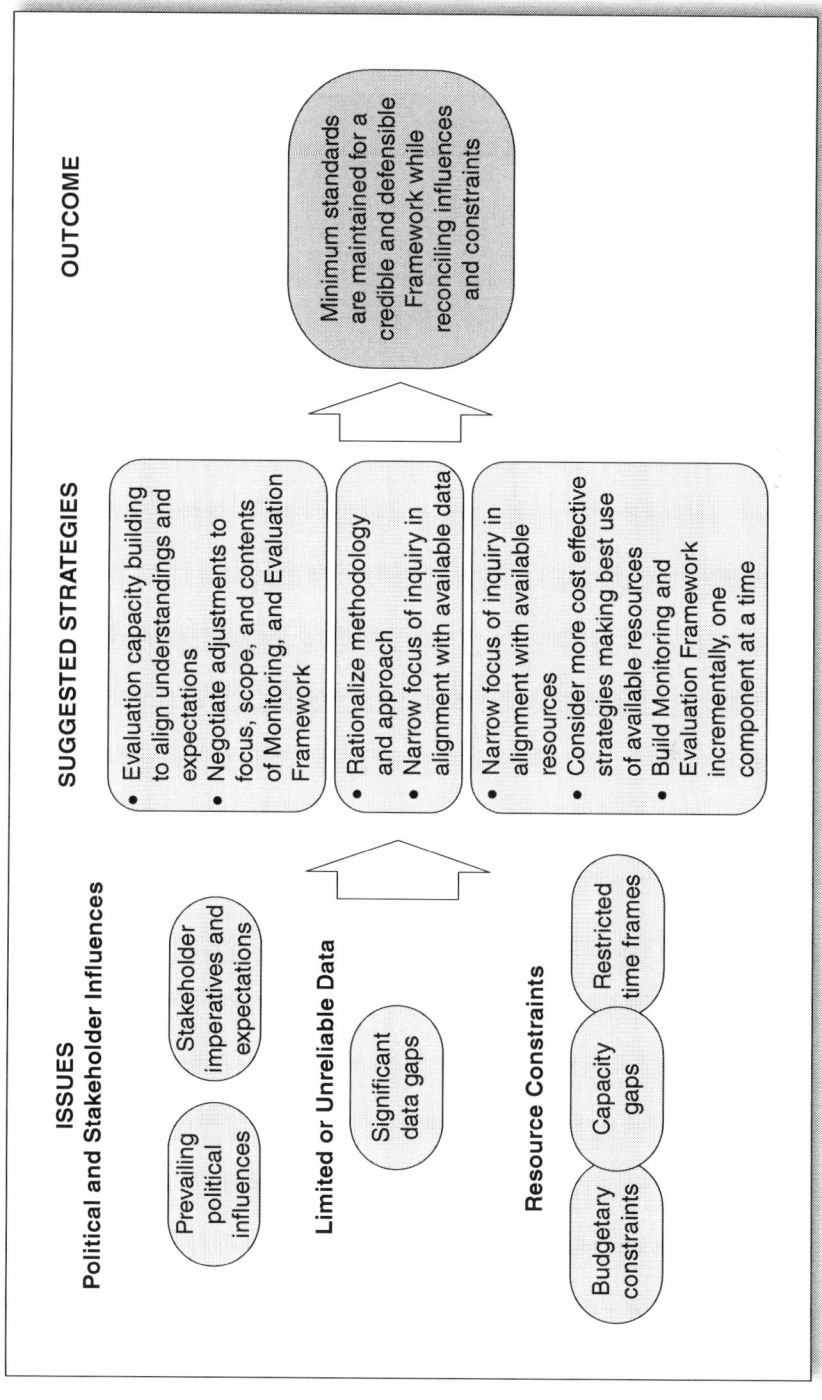

to 24 months involving assessment of the focus and effectiveness of the Framework based on internal program reflection and stakeholder input.

## 3. FROM FIRST STEPS ONWARD

Having undertaken thorough preparation and reached agreement as to the purpose, focus, and scope of the Monitoring and Evaluation Framework, the evaluation team should now be well positioned to move into the next stage of developing the foundational constructs of program theory, program logic, and evaluation questions in a participatory manner. Chapters 4 and 5 outline how stakeholders can become actively involved in developing these foundation steps, ideally through their participation in a stakeholder workshop where they can have the opportunity to exchange and debate their ideas and perspectives and reach an adequate level of consensus.

Organizing and facilitating a stakeholder workshop requires a level of skill and confidence in managing disparate views and moving participants toward constructive agreement. When handled well, a participatory workshop provides a valuable opportunity for stakeholders to appreciate their respective positions and view these in relation to the Monitoring and Evaluation Framework under development. When not handled well, a participatory workshop can leave behind a string of unanswered issues and dilemmas that can then work to stall the process of developing the Framework for some time. Therefore, consideration should be given to the facilitation skills of those tasked with running the workshop to ensure that there is the best chance of reaching consensus.

Subsequent chapters provide guidance for development of these foundation steps followed by the development of the Monitoring Plan and the Evaluation Plan.

## SUMMARY CHECKLIST

- Has the purpose of the Monitoring and Evaluation Framework been specified?

- Have key stakeholders and their various interests been identified?

- Has a stakeholder engagement strategy been developed with an associated plan for capacity development in monitoring and evaluation, as required?

- Have the requirements, expectations, priorities, and preferred approaches of key stakeholders been canvassed?

# Chapter 3   First Steps: Scoping the Monitoring and Evaluation Framework

- Has an assessment of data collection capabilities been undertaken?
- Has the scope and timeframe of the Monitoring and Evaluation Framework been adequately tailored to available resources, as well as to predicted data availability?
- Are the time frames identified for the development and implementation of the Monitoring and Evaluation Framework realistic and achievable?
- Has the purpose and scope of the Monitoring and Evaluation Framework been confirmed with key stakeholders?

## CHAPTER REVIEW QUESTIONS

1. Think of a program that you have worked with or are familiar with. How would you map and select stakeholders for involvement in the development of a Monitoring and Evaluation Framework for that program?

2. For the Framework to be developed in a participatory manner, what would be the ideal ways to involve stakeholders? How many and what types of stakeholders should be involved?

3. If some of the selected stakeholders had limited knowledge about monitoring and evaluation but were keen to learn, how would you respond to their needs?

4. How would you clarify and reach consensus as to the purpose and scope of the Monitoring and Evaluation Framework?

5. How would you go about identifying stakeholder requirements and their preferred approaches to developing a Monitoring and Evaluation Framework?

6. How would you go about scoping the resources and time frames required for developing and implementing a Monitoring and Evaluation Framework?

7. How would you establish a program's capabilities for data collection?

8. How would you respond to stakeholders holding unrealistic or different expectations as to what could be achieved from a Monitoring and Evaluation Framework given limitations in resources available for its development and implementation?

# CHAPTER 4

# Program Theory and Program Logic as Foundations for the Monitoring and Evaluation Framework

# Chapter 4  Program Theory and Program Logic as Foundations

*The approach adopted for the development of a Monitoring and Evaluation Framework in this text is program theory-driven. Accordingly, it uses program theory and program logic at its foundation.*

*Program theory outlines the theory, reasoning, and assumptions as to how and why the strategies employed by a program will work to produce the intended results. This is represented in a narrative or visual presentation of a causal model.*

*Program logic visually maps the steps involved in progressing from a program's actions to its intended results by identifying its expected sequence of inputs, activities, outputs, outcomes, and impacts. This is presented in diagram, frequently appearing as an arrangement of connected boxes or columns.*

## 1. INTRODUCTION TO DEVELOPING PROGRAM THEORY AND PROGRAM LOGIC

The use of program theory and program logic in evaluation encourages evaluators to make explicit the causal relationships that exist between what a program does and the results it is expected to achieve. Consistent with a Results-Based Management approach, the use of program theory and program logic reinforces the identification of expected results based on appropriate analysis and clear communication (UNDP, 2009). Program theory and program logic represent core understandings of a program's intent and mode of operation. As such, they are powerful tools for use in both evaluation and in broader program communications. Participation of stakeholders in the process of development of program theory and program logic strengthens stakeholder ownership of evaluative processes and increases the validity and usability of evaluation (Donaldson, 2007).

It is important to ensure that the program theory and logic are articulated and in place before monitoring and evaluation activities commence as they contribute to forming hypotheses of cause and effect and identifying key variables to be tested. Correspondingly, the development of program theory and logic encourages choice of evaluation methods that are relevant to the concerns, issues, and challenges which have been highlighted in the process. This contrasts with a less than desirable "one size fits all" approach to the selection of evaluation methods (Donaldson, 2007). While the use of program theory and logic is commonplace in evaluation practice, there is a significant lack of clarity as to the meaning of each practice, and how they are differentiated from each other.

### Program Theory

Theory-based approaches to evaluation emerged in the 1970s through the work of Carol Weiss, Peter Rossi, Huey Chen, and others, but they took time to gain traction in evaluation practice (Alkin, 2013; Knowlton & Phillips, 2013). This foundation work achieved more visibility in the 1980s, and the approaches gained popularity in the mid-1990s (Frechtling, 2007). There are a range of different perspectives and terminology used in theory-based approaches. A common and unifying concern identified across these approaches involves attempting to unpack the "black box" that exists between a program's efforts and its intended results. Such a process makes explicit the causal linkages that operate between these two areas, identifying how and why change is expected to occur. In doing so, the program theory identifies and articulates the program's assumptions about the sequence of expected change over which it has influence. A significant role of evaluation is to test the validity of these assumptions, that is, the causal model that is identified (Astbury & Leeuw, 2010; Chen, 2013, 2015).

A program theory may be represented as a narrative, but it is commonly summarized and depicted in diagrammatic form. For example, Figure 4.1 contains

**Figure 4.1** Program Theory for School-Based Anti-Smoking Program

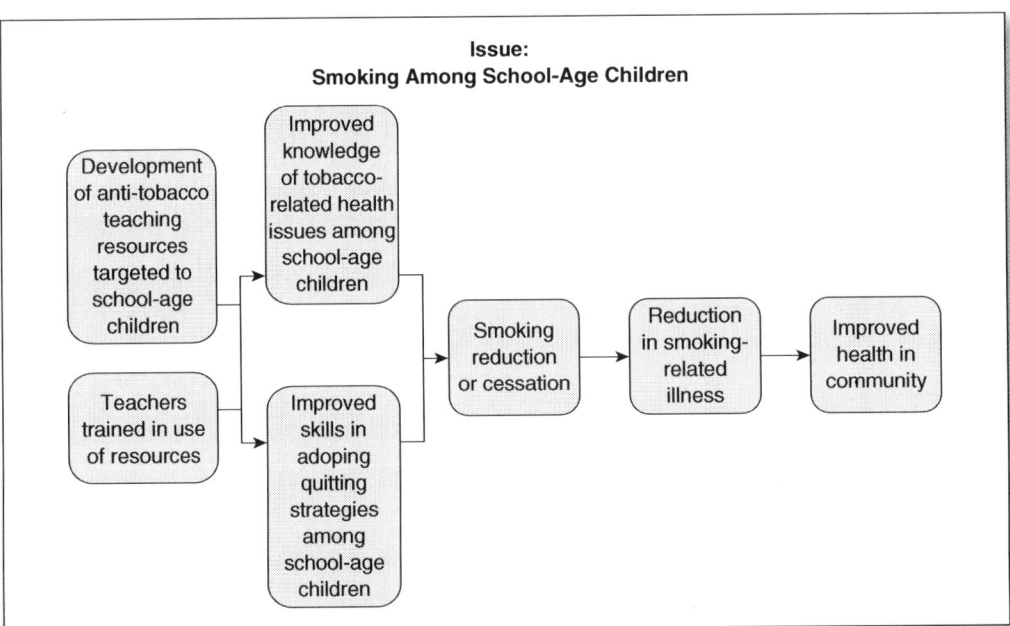

## Chapter 4  Program Theory and Program Logic as Foundations

the program theory for a hypothetical intervention designed to reduce the rate of smoking among school-age children. It uses a common form of visual representation, among many available (Funnell & Rogers, 2011).

A program theory will typically be based on views, experience, and literature about what works in a specific context. This will include drawing on the views of a range of stakeholders. The challenge for an evaluator is to mediate these perspectives and develop a program theory that is coherent, informed by evidence, and plausible. An evaluation will typically test the program theory through assessing whether the specific steps and sequence involved, in fact, lead to identified results. For example, in practice, an evaluation would examine whether improving knowledge of school-age children about tobacco-related issues and developing their skills in applying quitting strategies leads to a reduction in smoking. It is possible that provision of information alone will not be sufficient to yield the desired result. A program theory and associated program logic may be progressively updated as understandings about the program's intent and results are refined over time.

An evaluation may identify that the theory was valid or incorrect either as a whole or at a particular step. In the latter situations, it is most common for expected outcomes not to be achieved or be altered or limited. In some contexts, it is possible for results to still be produced but be attributable to unexpected external influences, such as a similar program in operation, with little or no attribution to the program in question.

It is important to note that the program theory as depicted in Figure 4.1 is presented as a condensed summary. A program theory incorporates not only expected changes but also the reasons and specific factors that lead to such change. Therefore, in addition to actual outcomes, a program theory is concerned with the mechanisms that promote such change. Mechanisms are not the same as program activities and require a greater level of explanation than the causal arrows that are depicted in Figure 4.1. Mechanisms may be regarded as the "underlying entities, processes, or structures which operate in particular contexts to generate outcomes of interest" (Astbury & Leeuw, 2010, p. 368). Therefore in relation to Figure 4.1, mechanisms operating between the variables of school-aged children increasing their awareness and reducing their smoking might include increased motivation instilled for better health and the influence of fears instilled about smoking-related disease that may occur in later life. Mechanisms are often hidden and need to be made explicit. Mechanisms are also sensitive to context in the way that they generate outcomes (Astbury & Leeuw, 2010). Evaluation will therefore test the causal pathways contained in program theory and the mechanisms that mediate whether, and in what ways, change occurs.

### *Differences Between Program Theory and Program Logic*

Program theory and program logic describe separate but related approaches for understanding the causal associations that underpin a program. Program theory makes explicit the reasoning as to how and why it is believed that program actions will produce the intended results. In contrast, program logic is more operational in nature in identifying an intentional and sequential progression from a program's actions to its results over time. Knowlton and Phillips (2013) provide a useful distinction between program theory and program logic with the former described as providing "a general representation of how you believe change will occur" and the latter detailing the "resources, planned activities, and their outputs and outcomes over time that reflect intended results" (p. 5). Chen (2005) distinguishes program theory as "a systematic configuration of prescriptive and descriptive assumptions underlying a program, whereas the logic model stresses milestones like components" (p. 34).

Both program theory and program logic draw on the same evidence base, but they differ in their purpose. Program theory is conceptual in orientation and concerned with testing the plausibility of a program's design and establishing the elements that make the program sound or otherwise. The intent is largely to inform the development of better program models and approaches. The operational orientation of program logic, by contrast, is largely concerned with how a program is delivered and linked to its results. The program logic is a tool used to portray and promote understanding and analysis of a program's intended sequential progress and development. It thereby supports assessment of a program's feasibility. Its broader purpose is to assist with the development of improved and better managed programs (Chen 2005; Knowlton & Phillips, 2013).

### *Program Logic*

Program logic is a visual means to depict a program's pathway from action to results. Many forms of visual representation are used including chains of boxes similar to the program theory shown in Figure 4.1, circular formats, and so on (Funnell & Rogers, 2011; Knowlton & Phillips, 2013). One common form of presentation is known as the "pipeline logic model," which uses a series of connected columns representing different elements of the logical progression. Well-known, early examples of the pipeline logic model are those developed by the extension service of the University of Wisconsin (University of Wisconsin—Extension, 2003) and the W.K. Kellogg Foundation

(W.K. Kellogg Foundation, 2004). This model groups together individual items under broader categories. It shows causative relationships between the categories as a whole rather between individual entities and is therefore relatively straightforward to construct. It represents a useful means to communicate a logic to stakeholders especially when they may be unfamiliar with the approach. The model has also been subject to critique for possibly oversimplifying the nature of program and the causative relationships that operate between individual entities within it (Funnell & Rogers, 2011). The six main elements in the model are as follows:

**Inputs:** The financial, human, and other resources available to deliver program activities and produce program outputs

**Activities:** Specific actions taken by the program (tasks and processes) that contribute to the identified outputs

**Outputs:** The products or services delivered by the program that reach people who participate or who are targeted by the program

**Outcomes:** Changes for individuals, groups, communities, organizations, or systems over time; they involve changes in knowledge, values, motivation, and skills (usually in the shorter term); changes in behavior and the way that organizations operate (usually medium term); and changes in the conditions that people experience (usually in the longer term).

**Assumptions:** Statements or hypotheses that are believed to be true and from which a conclusion can be drawn; these statements concern how and why we think the program will work in its context. Assumptions are often unstated or implicit and made explicit through the program theory and the program logic.

**External Factors:** The environment in which a program exists includes a variety of external factors that interact with and influence the program, either positively in supporting or advancing it or negatively in potentially detracting from its success.

The activities that contribute to the identified outputs are often numerous and, for the sake of brevity, are not always included in logic models. Otherwise, their inclusion can result in a diagram that is too cramped to be easily understood and accessed. While depicted in this text in summary form, they may also be attached to the program logic diagram as an appendix. Another means of addressing this issue is to use computer-based program logic mapping software that can optionally display the full range of activities which lie behind the outputs.

The use of assumptions is refined in this text in distinguishing between assumptions which are "preconditions" to the success of the program and those concerning "connections," that are the causative links between what the program does and its results (Morra Imas & Rist, 2009). The common factor shared by these two categories is that they are assumptions internal to the logic and operations of the program. They stand in contrast to external factors that influence the program from outside. Assumptions are typically derived in the process of developing both the program theory and the program logic and apply across both contexts. For the sake of clarity and brevity, in this text, the assumptions are recorded under the program logic, rather than with the program theory.

Using the preceding elements, Figure 4.2 shows a hypothetical program logic for the intervention designed to reduce the rate of smoking among school-age children. The program theory for this intervention was detailed previously.

Effective logic models, no matter which style of visual representation adopted, should depict coherent causal relationships rather than a simple flowchart of activities. As a point of emphasis, logic models need to be logical, that is, based on correct and valid reasoning. They also need to communicate clearly and avoid including any elements that do not add meaning (Funnell & Rogers, 2011).

## *Program Theory and Program Logic for a Community Education Program*

A further example of a program theory and program logic is provided below for a community education program. This program is used throughout the text as a case study against which to illustrate various steps involved in developing a Monitoring and Evaluation Framework. The hypothetical program is targeted to families in a disadvantaged community where the rates of school attendance of children are low. The program goal, which follows, broadly suggests areas of expected longer term change, while the objectives broadly align with expected medium-term changes.

### Community Education Program: Goal and Objectives

**Program Goal:** To improve the pathways of children from the completion of their basic education to further education, training, and employment so that they achieve a sustainable livelihood.

**Objective 1:** To increase the enrolment rate of children in school

**Objective 2:** To increase school participation and reduce absenteeism

**Figure 4.2** Program Logic for School-Based Anti-Smoking Program

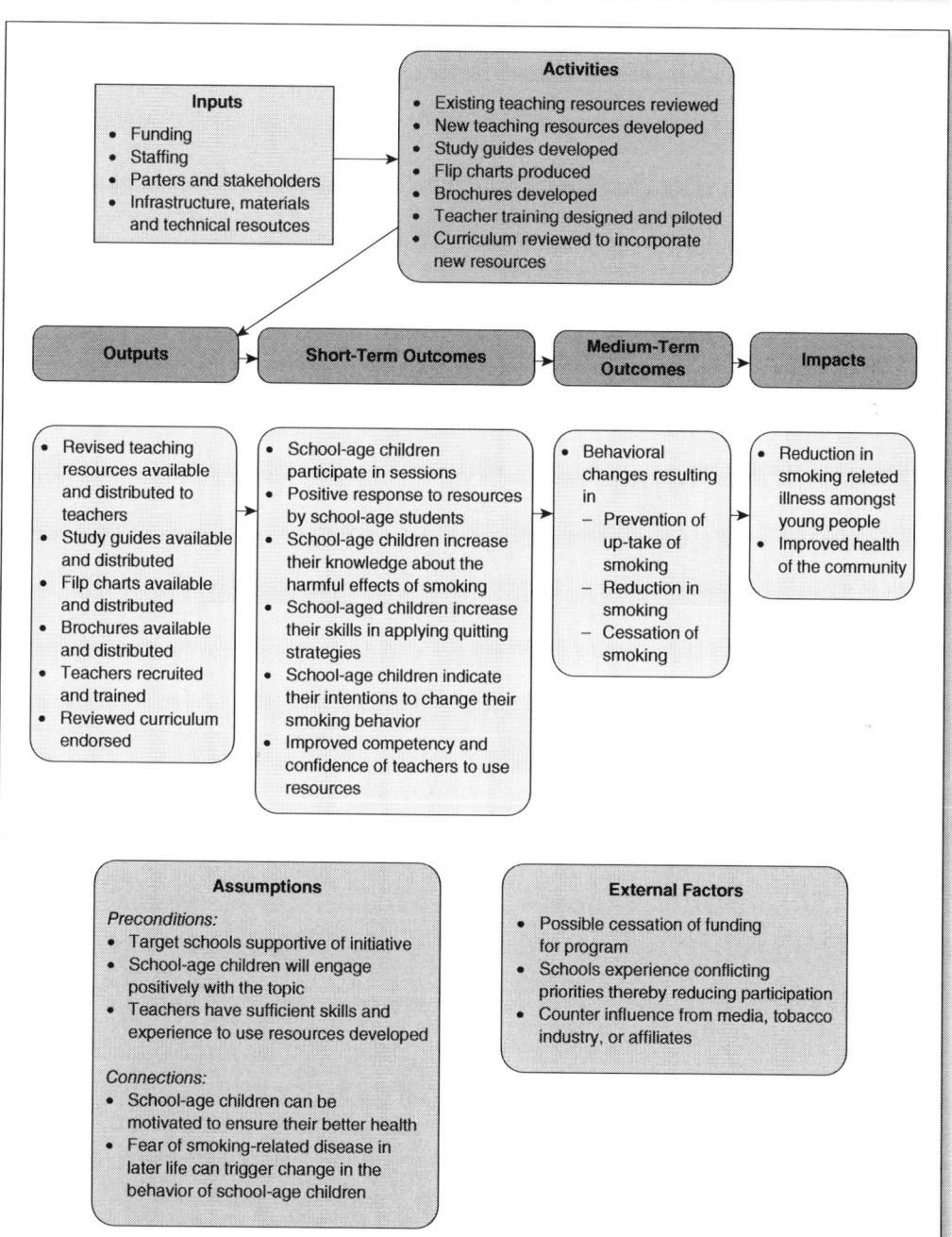

**Objective 3:** To increase the number of children who complete their basic education

**Objective 4:** To increase the number of children moving from basic education onto further education, training, and employment

The development of a program theory as presented in Figure 4.3 would typically draw on the program goal and objectives and other information to identify the detailed and precise sequence of causal linkages involved with the program. In this case, the theory shows a causal pathway showing linkages stemming from information provided to families through to expected broader impacts on the lives of children.

Assumptions that underlie the operation of this program include both preconditions and those pertaining to causal connections. For example, as a precondition it is assumed that parents are in a position to send their children to school. An example of an assumption relating to a causal connection is that provision of information to parents will lead to changes in parental behavior in sending their children to school. While all key assumptions should be tested, the literature and experience are likely to highlight areas where validation of assumptions is particularly important. The observations of Rossi, Lipsey, and Freeman (2004) are pertinent in this regard. They caution that many programs that attempt to address negative social behaviors through the provision of educational services and counseling encounter resistance from participants. Programs of this kind that fail to test such assumptions about behavior change are also likely to fail to recognize the strengths and limitations of the program approach. The program logic for the community education program, which includes its key assumptions, appears in Figure 4.4.

**Figure 4.3** Program Theory for Community Education Program

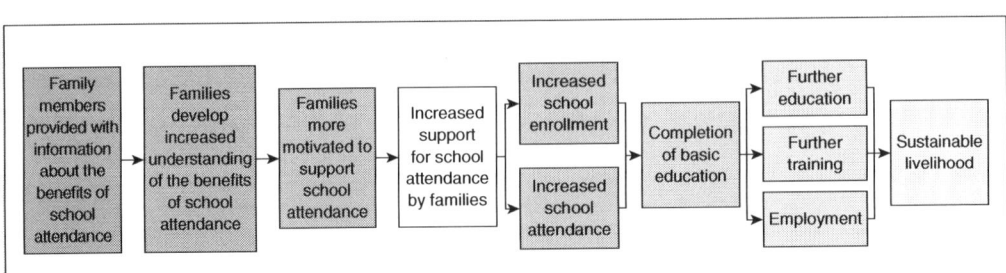

**Figure 4.4** Program Logic for Community Education Program

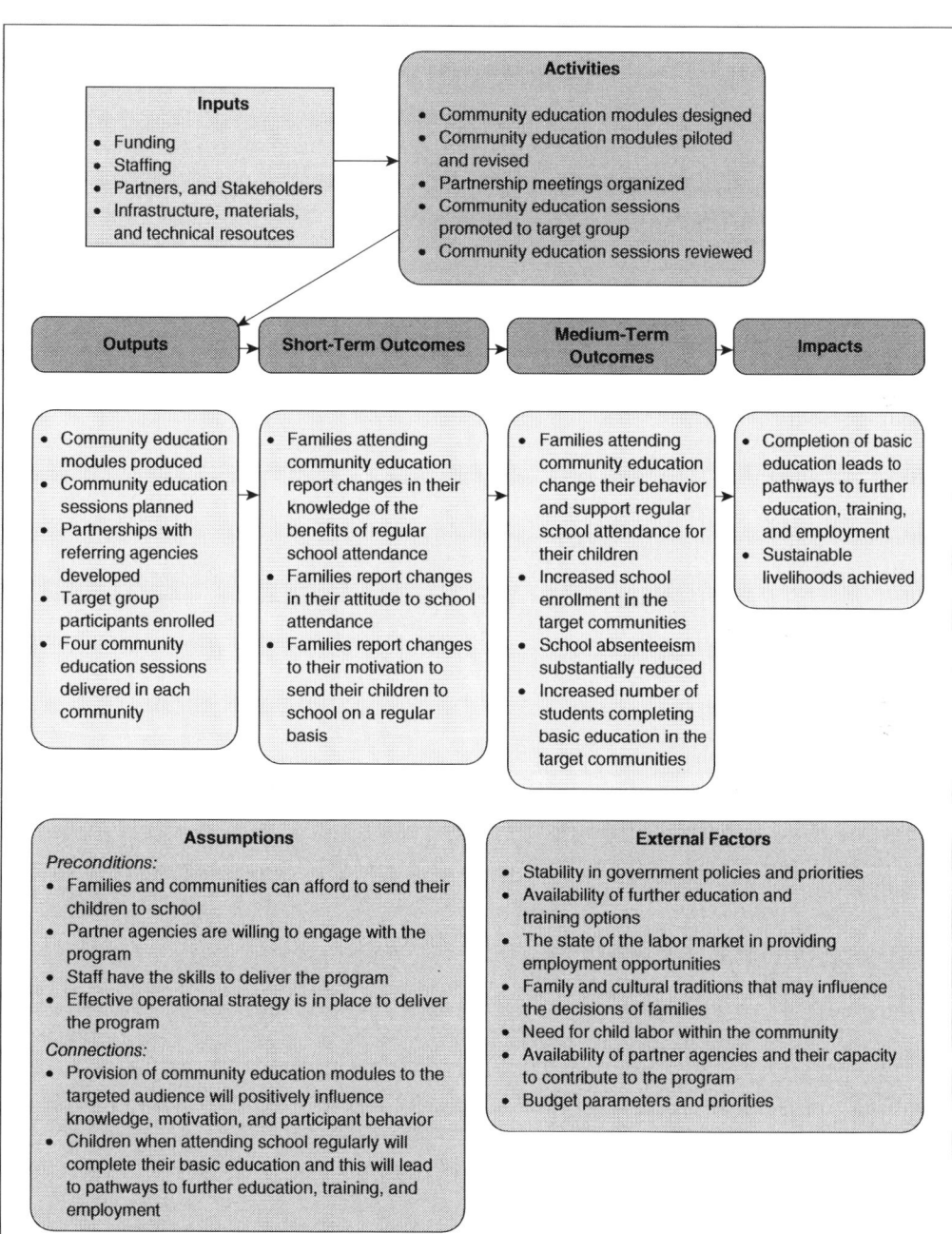

## 2. STEPS INVOLVED IN DEVELOPING PROGRAM THEORY AND PROGRAM LOGIC

Program theory and/or program logic may be in place prior to the development of the Monitoring and Evaluation Framework or possibly developed during the initial program design stage. Most commonly, the program theory and the program logic are developed, or at least updated, as part of the generation of the Monitoring and Evaluation Framework. Active involvement of stakeholders in this process is a positive feature and should add to the quality and utility of what is developed.

In an iterative and interconnected process, the program theory informs the subsequent development of the program logic. Underpinning both the program theory and the program logic and the causal linkages identified, are mechanism which represent the fine-grained factors that influence and mediate why, when, and how change occurs (McDavid et al., 2013). Assumptions are also identified as pertaining to both the program theory and logic and, in this text, recorded as part of the program logic. Both the program theory and the program logic are used as part of the identification of evaluation questions.

The following are the key steps involved in developing the program theory and the program logic as part of the Monitoring and Evaluation Framework. They involve initial planning for stakeholder engagement, followed by two steps focused on working with stakeholders to develop the program theory and the program logic respectively. The final step has a focus on final review and confirmation of the models by the program's key stakeholders.

**Table 4.1** Steps Involved in Developing Program Theory and Program Logic

| *Stage 2: Foundations for the Monitoring and Evaluation Framework* <br> *Develop Program Theory and Program Logic* | | |
|---|---|---|
| *Steps* | | |
| 1 | **Plan stakeholder engagement strategy** | • Establish process for engaging key stakeholders in development of the program theory and the program logic, such as convening a stakeholder workshop, forum, or other arrangement. |
| 2 | **Develop or review program theory** | • Convene appropriate participatory arrangements with key stakeholders. |

# Chapter 4  Program Theory and Program Logic as Foundations

|   |   | |
|---|---|---|
|   |   | • Identify sources of information to be used in developing the program theory such as literature, research, studies, practice experience, and other evidence.<br>• Identify key assumptions to be tested during the evaluation.<br>• Develop draft program theory in conjunction with key stakeholders. |
| 3 | Develop or review program logic | • Convene appropriate participatory arrangements with key stakeholders.<br>• Identify the key assumptions and outcome areas to be tested during the evaluation.<br>• Develop program logic with key stakeholders and with reference to the program theory. |
| 4 | Confirm program theory and logic with key stakeholders | • Present the program theory to key stakeholders to determine its plausibility and consistency with the evidence base, coherence, logical flow, and the clarity of its communication.<br>• Confirm the program theory and the program logic as key reference points for developing the evaluation questions for the Monitoring and Evaluation Framework. |

## *Step 1: Plan Stakeholder Engagement Strategy*

Promoting participation of key stakeholders in the development and confirmation of core elements of the Monitoring and Evaluation Framework was emphasized in Chapter 3. Elements highlighted were the program theory, program logic, and evaluation questions. The need for capacity building of key stakeholders to support this process, as required, was also discussed.

Convening a workshop, forum, or other consultative mechanism is an appropriate means to promote stakeholder engagement in the development of program theory and program logic. The format and the process involved need to introduce stakeholders to the purpose and constructs of the program theory and logic and draw on their prior knowledge and understandings of the program, how it is intended to operate, and its expected results. This process will need to consider formal program documentation including the program objectives. In the case of a program that has already commenced, there is a higher likelihood of divergence between the formal design, the manner in which the program has evolved, and the understandings of stakeholders. A workshop or similar process would need to make explicit and moderate such differences where they exist.

Consideration may also be given to research and other forms of evidence that would inform the development of the program theory and program logic. The degree to which this investigation occurs would need to consider the priorities, capacity, and interest of key stakeholders. The precise format for a participatory process will therefore vary according to the characteristics and expectations of the stakeholders involved and resources available. There are many options and guides to participatory practice available (e.g. International HIV/AIDS Alliance, 2001; Seeds for Change, n.d.; Slocum, 2003). For a smaller group of stakeholders, a round table discussion may more apt, as opposed to a workshop. Consideration could be given to a two-stage process, involving initial broader consultation, followed by convening a smaller working group that discusses material in detail. A panel of reviewers could be assembled to assess the coherence and plausibility of the program theory and/or program logic. Such a panel may include representation from program staff, program stakeholders, and outside experts (Rossi et al., 2004).

The use of participatory methods can involve stakeholders building drafts of the program theory and the program logic. This may involve use of sticky notes or cards to identify concepts that are then repositioned or amended until consensus is reached. Alternatively, the models can be built using one of the software packages available that is then projected onto a screen and amended in real time. Whatever approach is used, the facilitation skills of the evaluator are important to encourage dialogue and debate and to move stakeholders to consensus in a timely fashion.

> **Practice Example**
>
> ### Undertaking Wide Consultation for Developing Program Logic
>
> In a developing country context in South Asia, a program aimed at upgrading urban slum settlements engaged an evaluator to develop program logic for the initiative. The evaluator undertook a range of consultations to develop a clearer understanding as to how the affected communities viewed the potential results of the program and what would typify positive outcomes. Working with local facilitators, the evaluator met with members of the communities. In these meetings, community members identified their expectations of improvements to be derived from the program. These included placing priority on improved sanitation in order to reduce disease and improve the health of the community. These meetings also identified

a range of barriers to improvement such as inefficient local government agencies, flooding, and exploitation by landowners. The evaluator was encouraged by the level of insight shown by community members attending the meetings. Using sheets of paper and pens, the facilitators identified the different types of results participants expected from the program. These were identified by pictures rather than words, given the low literacy levels of participants. In discussion with the group, these results were then sequenced, developing a simple results chain with issues that may affect such change also identified.

The findings from community consultations were then brought to a meeting with stakeholders including urban planning authorities, local government authorities, and funding organizations. Several community representatives were present to explain what had been developed. This input proved to be both influential and useful in increasing stakeholder awareness of community perspectives and aspirations about anticipated change. Many of the ideas shared were then incorporated in the subsequent program theory and logic developed for the program. Issues identified by the community were included in the program logic as assumptions or external factors influencing change. Several community representatives participated in further meetings with the other stakeholders to further develop the program logic and other parts of the Monitoring and Evaluation Framework. Efforts to gain the insights of community-level stakeholders brought their perspectives into planning for monitoring and evaluation in a way that otherwise may have been overlooked. Active engagement with disadvantaged groups also contributed to their empowerment, which appeared critical to affect change in a very challenging environment.

## *Step 2: Develop Program Theory*

An initial step in convening a stakeholder forum is to assemble the known evidence base and to consider how to facilitate a process that will make explicit the implicit theory held by stakeholders. Program theory is usually derived from an evidence base comprised of more formally recorded research and evaluation findings and the less formal implicit theory, practice knowledge, and direct experience of key stakeholders. Program theory should potentially be based on, or consistent with, behavioral or social science theories and embrace the beliefs and practical experiences of the concerned stakeholders (Bamberger et al., 2012; Donaldson, 2007; Rossi et al., 2004). This is particularly important if the program is trying to achieve behavioral change in an area that has received prior research or evaluation focus or has been the subject of stakeholder investigation. Both formal and informal theories thus need to be drawn out and discussed during the stakeholder forum.

The next step in the process is to involve key stakeholders in the identification of the assumptions that are relevant to their program and that need to be tested. For example, a significant assumption in the case study involving community education is that raising awareness of parents triggers positive parental aspirations for improving their children's future. Gathering an evidence base to justify these underpinning program assumptions is thus important in order to argue their validity and therefore that of the program theory as a whole. Assumptions also need to be tested. As Funnell and Rogers (2011) state, "the very act of articulating the assumption makes it fair game for investigation as part of an empirical evaluation, a research study or perhaps a literature review" (p. 303). The assumptions in this scenario can be interrogated through evaluation questions such as the following:

- To what extent will increasing understanding by parents of the benefits of school attendance be sufficient to trigger positive aspirations for their children's future that will result in regular school attendance?
- What level of dose (community education) will be sufficient in its breadth and depth to generate the desired response (attitudinal and behavioral change)?
- To what extent will the mechanisms that trigger change differ in quantity and type for different family groups?

Engagement with stakeholders will assist in clarifying the major areas that require examination in relation to the program theory including which key assumptions should be investigated. Determining the program theory can also highlight other kinds of issues in a specific program, such as whether the program objectives are consistent with the expected outcomes.

The assessment of program theory through the evaluation process can potentially inform like programs and build the evidence base across a range of common problem areas. In relation to behavior change stemming from community education, for example, there are many lessons that can be learned about the characteristics of a successful intervention and what groups are most likely to benefit from which type of program activities. It is possible that some families will respond positively, but others may require a different type of approach in order to generate behavioral change, especially when the benefits of not changing may outweigh the risks or costs associated with making that change (Funnell & Rogers, 2011).

The final step is to develop a draft program theory based on the consultations undertaken. The circulation of such documentation will benefit those stakeholders who were not able to directly participate in the forum but who would still appreciate the opportunity to respond. A draft document also enables participants who did attend the forum to review their contribution and ensure that their input was reflected in the recording process.

### *Step 3: Develop Program Logic*

The same consultative arrangements that brought key stakeholders together to develop a program theory should also serve the development of program logic. The program theory should provide the conceptual background required for development of the more operationally focused program logic with its sequence of outputs and outcomes delivered over time. When put together, the two models provide a strong foundation of shared meaning in relation to the intent and delivery of the program (Knowlton & Phillips, 2013). The interconnection between program theory and logic is illustrated in Figure 4.5.

As detailed earlier, this text has selected the pipeline logic model approach to represent the program logic, which has value in its accessible communication features. Program theory and program logic diagrams can be drawn using standard software or using specific drawing software packages. Despite risks of oversimplification, the pipeline model does allow for the representation of the progression from outputs to impacts that can get lost in more complex mapping approaches (Bamberger et al., 2012; Frechtling, 2007; Funnell & Rogers, 2011). Where greater detail is required, use could be made of web-based program logic mapping programs, which allow both a simplified representation and the details behind different sections to be recorded and subsequently investigated. Furthermore, the details of the program (such as the range of program activities that precede the outputs) can be included as attachments to the main program logic diagram without crowding out the main graphic representation that provides the central focus for discussion.

**Figure 4.5** Program Theory and Program Logic

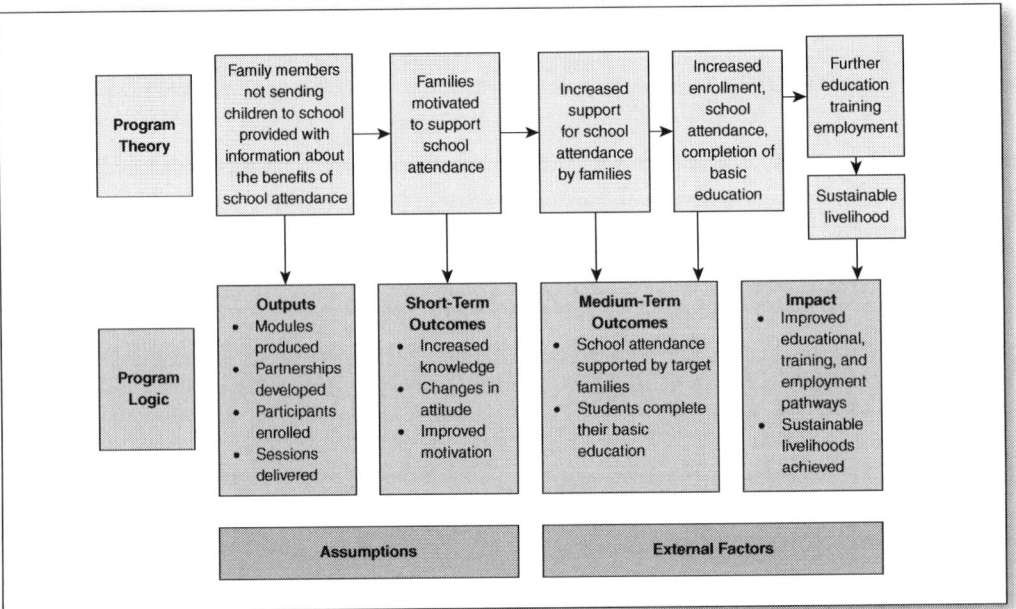

Through active facilitation, stakeholders can be supported to develop a program logic that is coherent, logical, and clear in its communication. In addition to identifying the consecutive steps that make up a program logic, stakeholders should also be involved in the specification of assumptions and external factors. Assumptions include those that relate to preconditions, such as that families can afford to send their children to school, and connections, such as that community education will positively change behavior.

External factors, the influences from outside the program that could affect its operations, commonly include changes in government policies and priorities and adverse climatic events. In the most extreme scenario, these could derail the program. Identification of external factors can draw on research undertaken, comparison with similar programs, and elicit stakeholder views. External factors may include, but are not limited to

- significant political changes (e.g., political unrest, changes in government policy directions, new legislation, changes in government priorities and directions, major restructures in government organizations),

- economic conditions (e.g., strength of the economy and state of the labor market),
- climatic and environmental conditions (e.g., effects of the wet season in the tropics) and natural disasters (e.g., floods, bushfires, earthquakes, hurricanes),
- security conditions (e.g., war, conflict, terrorism),
- health conditions (e.g., outbreaks of infectious diseases),
- demographic changes (e.g., population mobility),
- community issues (e.g., internal dissent and unrest, factional infighting, changes of leadership and representation, community withdrawal of cooperation and support),
- public perceptions (e.g., ill effects from stigma, discrimination, marginalization, racism, sexism, homophobia),
- continuity of funding (funding priorities or the terms and conditions of funding),
- continuity of partnership arrangements (including changes of funding, policies, practices, or leadership that affect cooperation), and
- access to required resources (e.g., availability and retention of skilled personnel to deliver the program, availability of required infrastructure, access to affiliated support services).

The external factors, once identified, can be further developed into a risk matrix, with risks detailed, graded in terms of their likelihood and potential severity, and possible strategies identified to mitigate their effects (UNESCO, 2010). While risks and assumptions are related, there are important differences between them. An assumption refers to a condition that should be in place for the program to proceed, with a high probability identified of this occurring. Risks relate to the possibility of external negative events occurring that could jeopardize the success of the program. The related assessment for risks can range from a low to a high probability of the event occurring (Centers for Disease Control, 2006; UNDP, 2009).

The evaluation literature is characterized by debate about whether to include SMART (specific, measureable, achievable, realistic, and time-bound) measures and also indicators as part of the program logic diagram. SMART measures may be incorporated, for example, by detailing numbers of outputs and outcomes produced by a certain time. Some authors (Knowlton & Phillips, 2013) advocate for SMART principles and indicators in a program logic to add precision in program evaluation. Others (Funnell & Rogers, 2011) caution that determining performance indicators at this stage is premature and potentially distracting from the core task of identifying the sequence of causal linkages that characterize the program. The position of this text supports the latter view. In this approach, performance indicators are generated subsequent to the program logic and the identification of evaluation questions and included as part of the Monitoring Plan.

> **Practice Example**
>
> ### Facilitating a Program Logic Workshop for a Complex Program
>
> A full-day workshop was held with around 20 personnel drawn from a range of government departments and nongovernment agencies in order to develop program theory and program logic for a national initiative focusing on labor issues. Specifically, the program was concerned with ensuring fair work practices in a range of employment contexts. The process commenced with a planning meeting involving a smaller group of around six key stakeholders. The meeting confirmed that preparatory materials to be produced and circulated to all participants ahead of the workshop would be at an introductory level. A link to an introductory video and presentation about the program was also forwarded. This approach was particularly useful given the technical nature of the program and its complex context. During the workshop, the draft materials produced, including an outline of the program theory and the program logic diagrams, were projected onto a screen and the evaluator proceeded to facilitate a step-by-step discussion of their contents. A significant number of enhancements to the diagrams were made by the evaluator in response to the discussions between participants. The capacity to alter the contents in real time appeared to engage the stakeholders who could see the evolution of the diagrams in response to their contributions. The draft program theory and program logic were then circulated to participants after the workshop and to others who were unable to attend or who were not included in the workshop but were considered to be interested parties. Following further minor amendments, the documents were accepted. These then provided the basis for generation of evaluation questions and the further development of the Monitoring and Evaluation Framework for the program.

**Chapter 4** Program Theory and Program Logic as Foundations 89

> **Practice Example**
>
> ### Facilitating Interactive Program Logic Workshops
>
> A series of workshops was held to develop program logic for a regional program operated by a nongovernment agency. The agency was focused on providing emergency relief services following natural disasters. The agency requested that the evaluator adopt a highly participatory and inclusive approach. The first workshop involved 15 personnel from the agency and commenced with a brainstorming session regarding the program intent and strategies, which then led to a review of the program goal and objectives. The process identified that the program had evolved since the goal and objectives were determined, and that participants held different perspectives as to the purpose of the program in providing emergency relief and its expected results. During the second workshop, the different types of results expected of the program were elicited from the participants. Large sheets of paper were posted around the room and titled according to the different columns of a program logic diagram. Participants then used sticky notes to build the program logic in an interactive manner. Sticky notes were shifted around between sheets of paper and ordered on each individual sheet. An emphasis was placed on discussion and building consensus as to the intent of the program. Participants commented that the approach used was interactive and dynamic, while also being enjoyable. During the third workshop, the draft program logic was translated to a more formal diagrammatic style. The program logic diagram was then circulated to a broader group of stakeholders for their comments and input. As a result of the workshops, program management negotiated with the agency funding the program, with agreement reached to refine the program goal and objectives accordingly.

As with program theory, the final step is to develop a draft program logic for review by both the key stakeholders who directly participated in its construction and by other stakeholders who would like to be able to contribute their ideas.

## Step 4: Confirm Program Theory and Program Logic With Key Stakeholders

Following development of the draft program theory and program logic, a review process with key stakeholders will enable any fine-tuning to be undertaken and to confirm understandings. This may be undertaken directly in a group setting or remotely. For the process of review, prompt questions can be used to generate dialogue and debate amongst the stakeholders. These may include the following (Knowlton & Phillips, 2013; Rossi et al., 2004):

- Does the program theory have a firm grounding, and is it sufficiently well-justified in terms of available evidence and practice experience?
- Does the sequence of changes in the program theory appear plausible?
- Have the underlying assumptions pertaining to the program theory been appropriately identified?
- Is there a reasonable degree of correlation between the program goal and objectives and the impacts and outcomes identified in the program logic?
- Is there a plausible chain of causation between the outputs, outcomes, and impacts in the program logic?
- Have the more operational underlying assumptions pertaining to the program logic been appropriately identified?
- Is there reasonable correspondence between the resources allocated to the program and the degree of its intended results?

The aim is to develop the program theory and the program logic to the point of achieving the best level of consensus possible so that they adequately represent a program's intent and provide a valid, but simplified representation of real-world complexities (Knowlton & Phillips, 2013). These agreed constructs are then used as a platform or "scaffolding" (Frechtling, 2007) for the development of a relevant set of evaluation questions and an approach to both monitoring and evaluation of the program.

The program theory and the program logic are important documents and need to be of good quality. It is important, however, to remember that they also are likely be modified over time as understandings about the program are further refined. As Funnell and Rogers (2011) indicate, "When we conduct a critique or desk review of program theory, our objective is to ensure that it will be useful rather than perfect" (p. 293). There is a risk of spending too much time in perfecting the diagrams at the expense of the range of other tasks that are involved in developing a Monitoring and Evaluation Framework.

Once an evaluation is conducted and completed, deficiencies in the program theory and logic may well be revealed, necessitating stakeholder involvement in program review and redesign. In this case, evaluation team members can assist with the further review of the program theory and logic in order to inform a revamped program design that is grounded in the insights that have been attained through the monitoring and evaluation process.

## SUMMARY CHECKLIST

- Have the program theory and the program logic already been developed for the program, and if so, do they require review as to their relevance, structure, and currency?
- If a program theory or a program logic is not in place, is there an opportunity to develop it as part of the Monitoring and Evaluation Framework?
- Has the review or development of the program theory and the program logic referred to the program goal and objectives as a starting point?
- Have the differences and interrelationships between the program theory and the program logic been well understood, and are the concepts able to be clearly communicated to program stakeholders?
- Has a method for developing the program theory and program logic been identified and agreed to, involving meaningful participation from relevant program stakeholders?
- Has the evidence base for the program theory been identified and reviewed?
- In constructing the program theory, have justifiable connections been made between the sequential steps that it depicts, and have the underlying assumptions been identified?
- In constructing the program logic, have justifiable connections been made showing the transition from outputs to outcomes over time (short/medium/long term)?
- Have relevant external factors that may help or hinder the changes identified in the program logic been identified?
- Has agreement been reached with stakeholders as to the best approach for representing the program theory and the program logic and the level of detail required for each?
- Is there reasonable correspondence between the resources allocated to the program and the scope of the program theory and the program logic developed?
- Is there a process for ensuring that stakeholders review and confirm the program theory and the program logic prior to further development of the Monitoring and Evaluation Framework?
- Will the program theory and the program logic usefully inform the identification of relevant evaluation questions to guide the Monitoring and Evaluation Framework?

## CHAPTER REVIEW QUESTIONS

1. How would you go about stakeholder engagement and the organization of a participatory workshop to develop the program theory and the program logic for a program?

2. What are the preparatory tasks involved in doing so?

3. How many steps do you anticipate would be involved in the process, from early conceptualization of the program theory and the program logic to their final endorsement?

4. How would you approach the identification of the underlying assumptions about change and how it is brought about?

5. How would you approach the identification of relevant contextual external factors that may impinge on the logic?

6. What would you identify as the features of a good program theory?

7. What would you identify as the features of a good program logic?

8. Think of a program with which you are familiar, and outline the program theory and the program logic for that program.

# CHAPTER 5

# Evaluation Questions—Determining What We Want to Know

*A Monitoring and Evaluation Framework needs to adopt a primary focus on what we want to know, rather than simply on what we can readily measure. Matching this intent, significant emphasis is placed on the role of evaluation questions in the development of the Monitoring and Evaluation Framework to provide focus for the complementary processes of monitoring and evaluation. Well-crafted questions, clearly linked to the purpose of monitoring and evaluation will reinforce both the relevance and usefulness of our investigations. Evaluation questions are critical in the formulation of both the Monitoring Plan and the Evaluation Plan that are key operational sections of the Monitoring and Evaluation Framework. This chapter examines both the purpose of evaluation questions and the process of their development.*

## 1. INTRODUCTION TO DEVELOPING EVALUATION QUESTIONS

Evaluation questions are considered by many evaluation theorists to provide an essential means to focus and structure program evaluations, and program evaluation is fundamentally about answering these questions (Owen & Rogers, 1999; Rossi et al., 2004). Evaluation questions have a similar function in the Monitoring and Evaluation Framework by identifying what we want to know and providing the rationale for decisions about the data needed from routine monitoring and from periodic evaluation. However, as Patton (2012) states, "formulating appropriate and meaningful evaluation questions demands considerable skill and insight." This chapter provides guidance as to how to approach this task with a view to developing an agreed set of practical and useful evaluation questions.

### Answering Evaluation Questions: A Complementary Role for Monitoring and Evaluation

The approach adopted in this text is to use the same set of evaluation questions in order to develop both the Monitoring Plan and the Evaluation Plan for inclusion in the Monitoring and Evaluation Framework. This approach provides a unifying purpose for monitoring and evaluation and promotes integration. It still provides sufficient flexibility to encompass the different functions of monitoring and evaluation and allows for variation in the data sets that they use.

The complementary nature of monitoring and evaluation functions, which are integrated in the Monitoring and Evaluation Framework, were first discussed in Chapters 1 and 2. In summary, program monitoring involves the routine collection of quantitative and sometimes qualitative performance information with a particular focus on the program's processes and outcomes, usually measured against a set of performance indicators and targets. Evaluation, by contrast, is more periodic in nature and usually involves a deeper form of assessment. It is particularly geared to informing program development and provides a level of judgment of program performance against agreed criteria and standards. Monitoring is more closely aligned to management and accountability functions, while evaluation has a stronger learning and program development focus. Coordination and integration of these functions through a focus on answering evaluation questions provides a holistic perspective that is often missing from evaluation practice.

The Results-Based Management approach, discussed in Chapter 2, aligns with this intent of providing greater holism in evaluation practice and highlights how monitoring and evaluation can be integrated together with planning functions. Chapters 6 and 7 provide more detail on this text's approach to integrating monitoring and evaluation functions.

Table 5.1 illustrates how monitoring and evaluation are used in a complementary manner to answer an evaluation question. Together, the data and analysis generated provide a rich picture in relation to program performance with more routine data collection supplemented by periodic investigation of specific issues and trends. The example used here, first introduced in Chapter 4 and appearing throughout this text, concerns a community education program targeted to families in a particular community who do not maintain a regular regime of school attendance for their children.

Usually, both monitoring and evaluation will contribute to answering an evaluation question. In some instances, however, monitoring will provide the only applicable data, and in other instances, only evaluation data will be applicable. The critical criterion for adequacy is whether the question is answered. Such an approach aligns with giving emphasis to what we want to know (taking a results-driven approach), rather than what we can measure (a data-driven approach; Poister, 2010). These points are discussed further in Chapter 6, "The Monitoring Plan," which includes guidance as to where best to use indicators, which in this approach, are used in monitoring rather than evaluation.

## *Developing Agreed, Practical, and Useful Evaluation Questions*

Generation of evaluation questions is an early stage in the development of the Monitoring and Evaluation Framework. When appropriately developed,

**Table 5.1** Answering Evaluation Questions Through Complementary Use of Monitoring and Evaluation

| Evaluation Question | Monitoring | Evaluation |
|---|---|---|
| *Example:* *Appropriateness* To what extent was the community education program design suitable for addressing the needs of intended participants? | *Key focus: Program processes and outcomes. Involves routine data collection.* *Examples of areas assessed through monitoring:* <ul><li>Numbers and characteristics of participants drawn from the intended target group</li><li>Level of participant satisfaction (as identified in post-training survey)</li><li>Numbers of referrals from participants for new enrollments in the program</li><li>Changes to school attendance patterns by the target group</li></ul> | *Key focus: Program development and learning. Involves deeper assessment.* *Examples of areas assessed through evaluation:* <ul><li>Review of the quality of the community education model against good practice in the literature</li><li>Assessments of the quality and value of the community education program from<ul><li>facilitators</li><li>participants</li><li>funders</li><li>managers</li><li>program partners</li><li>other stakeholders</li></ul></li><li>Extent of application of key principles from the program to changed practices</li></ul> |

they provide a needed focus and direction for the whole Framework. Three criteria distinguish an appropriate set of questions: that they are agreed on, practical, and useful. The developer of the Monitoring and Evaluation Framework should aim to promote these attributes as part of the process used, working closely with stakeholders including the program team. It is critical to

- gain stakeholder endorsement of the guiding questions (Agreed),
- scope data availability and the number of questions that can be accommodated given available resources (Practical), and
- review the usefulness of the questions for assessing program progress, results, and value (Useful).

Without due consideration to the preceding, the Monitoring and Evaluation Framework runs the risk of becoming unimplementable or ineffective.

# Chapter 5  Evaluation Questions—Determining What We Want to Know

Figure 5.1 illustrates the three interconnected attributes of evaluation questions developed for the Monitoring and Evaluation Framework.

This schema broadly aligns with the work of Patton (2012), who proposes a set of criteria for developing utilization-focused evaluation questions. He suggests questions should inform understanding and guide future decision making (*useful*); be answerable in a reasonable time frame, at reasonable cost, with data availability (*practical*); and that users have identified the need for the questions and want them to be answered (*agreed*). He also highlights another useful criterion regarding neutrality in the phrasing of questions so that the answer is not biased or predetermined (Patton, 2012).

**Figure 5.1**  Attributes of Evaluation Questions

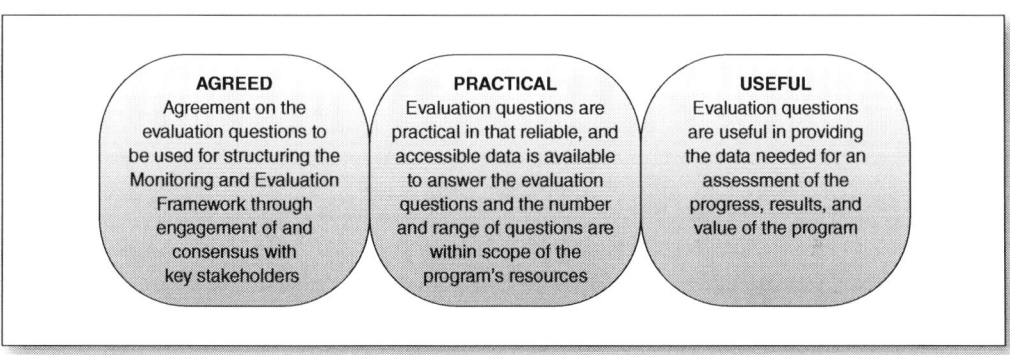

## 2. USING EVALUATION DOMAINS TO GUIDE SELECTION OF QUESTIONS

Evaluation criteria or domains represent areas of investigation or topics under which evaluation questions can be usefully grouped and ordered. Use of domains also serves as a prompt to check that different areas are investigated and receive the appropriate degree of emphasis in the Monitoring and Evaluation Framework. While the evaluation literature and evidence from practice reflects different ways to develop and group evaluation questions, a common approach is to use a set of domains that have been formalized and systemized. A key example, as used in this text, is that promoted by the Development Assistance Committee (DAC) of the Organisation of Economic Co-operation and Development (OECD). The DAC, established in 1991, is composed of 29 member countries and focuses on improving and coordinating international development cooperation including approaches to performance monitoring and evaluation. The five evaluation criteria of relevance, effectiveness, efficiency, impact, and sustainability were first identified in 1991 (OECD DAC, 1991), defined in 2002, reprinted in 2010 (OECD DAC Working Party on Aid Effectiveness, 2010), and are detailed and described in the broader context of evaluating development cooperation (OECD DAC Network on Development Evaluation, 2010).

The five OECD DAC evaluation criteria have been widely adopted in an international development context and noted by Chianca (2008) as "by far the most influential work in the field of development evaluation" (p. 41). Correspondingly, their adoption has been described as important to efforts to improve development assistance and promote a results orientation (Picciotto, 2013). The use of the criteria in an international development context, and increasing adoption in a mainstream context in OECD countries, mirrors convergence in policy debates and issues shared by developed and developing countries. Such trends also reflect more general advances in evaluation theory and practice and rapid dissemination of new ideas. To further reinforce the wide adoption of the OECD DAC criteria, Picciotto (2013) advocates mainstreaming "the well-tested development-effectiveness criteria throughout the evaluation community" (p. 168).

The OECD DAC definitions of the evaluation domains, understandably described in an international development context, are summarized in Table 5.2.

**Table 5.2** DAC Criteria for Evaluating Development Assistance

| Relevance | The extent to which the aid activity is suited to the priorities and policies of the target group, recipient, and donor. |
|---|---|
| Effectiveness | A measure of the extent to which an aid activity attains its objectives. |
| Efficiency | Efficiency measures the outputs–qualitative and quantitative–in relation to the inputs. It is an economic term which signifies that the aid uses the least costly resources possible in order to achieve the desired results. |
| Impact | The positive and negative changes produced by a development intervention, directly or indirectly, intended or unintended. This involves the main impacts and effects resulting from the activity on the local social, economic, environmental, and other development indicators. |
| Sustainability | Sustainability is concerned with measuring whether the benefits of an activity are likely to continue after donor funding has been withdrawn. Projects need to be environmentally as well as financially sustainable. |

*Source*: OECD DAC Network on Development Evaluation (2010)

While the OECD DAC criteria are both enduring and valuable (Picciotto, 2013), for the purpose of this text, the authors have adapted and adjusted the OECD DAC criteria to better suit the broader range of contexts that exist beyond aid activities and to take into account reflection and commentary that have emerged concerning the usefulness of the OECD DAC criteria since their inception over two decades ago.

The authors have replaced the term *relevance* with the term *appropriateness* as the latter term suggests wider accommodation of the interests of all concerned parties. The notion of relevance has been critiqued for being too closely associated with assessing alignment with the priorities of funders and government agencies (Chianca, 2008). *Appropriateness* is considered to be a more inclusive term, additionally encompassing the needs of key stakeholders and program beneficiaries. The notion of appropriateness includes consideration of the degree to which a program's design, implementation, and initial results are adequate to respond to existing needs of a range of stakeholders (Chianca, 2008). The appropriateness domain can also include investigation as to what degree the identified program theory or logic was accurate in capturing program intentionality.

In the OECD DAC definition, the notion of effectiveness applies only to whether a program has met its intended objectives. Although not specified in the OECD DAC definition, the notion of *effectiveness* is more generally associated with bringing about a positive and desirable result. Assessment of this area would be challenged if the objectives were not accurately specified or were overly or underambitious. Moreover, program objectives may be too closely aligned to the needs of donors or governments and thus not reflect the aspirations and needs of program beneficiaries. To overcome these issues, the definition of effectiveness used in this text has been broadened. It retains the assessment of whether a program has met its objectives and adds a complementary and summative assessment of the program's quality and value. The concepts of quality and value are discussed in detail in Chapter 7, "The Evaluation Plan." Determining a program's quality and value requires the setting of agreed criteria and standards for making such assessments. Evaluation rubrics, which specify what makes for excellent to poor rankings, may be applied for this purpose (Davidson, 2005). The use of rubrics is discussed in greater detail in Chapter 8, "Collecting, Managing, Analyzing, and Synthesizing Data to Reach Evaluative Conclusions."

An additional area of assessment that this text adds to the effectiveness domain is that of *fidelity of implementation*. This involves questioning the extent to which the program was implemented as designed and reasons for any variations. Fidelity evaluation is "process evaluation that gauges the degree of congruency between intervention and target groups as planned and intervention and target groups as implemented" (Chen, 2005, p. 165). Program services that were not delivered as planned cannot be expected to produce the intended outcomes, and this is called "implementation failure" (Rossi et al., 2004, p. 79).

The efficiency domain is extended to move beyond assessment of outputs relative to inputs to focus on the way that resources available were used to deliver the outputs. Rather than simply focusing on whether a program was implemented in the least costly manner, the definition is broadened to consider the relationship between costs and benefits achieved. Assessment of the efficiency domain will draw on process monitoring, which will typically count resources used and numbers of activities, outputs, or other benefits received. This assessment will be extended through process evaluation. The latter will look more deeply into the reasons behind trends observed in monitoring, such as variations in the quality of outputs delivered (Chen, 2005). Further considerations are involved when assessing efficiency from the perspective of how things are done, that is the factors that led to successful, or less successful, program implementation. These include the quality of governance, management, and personnel management arrangements.

The impact domain deals with change, and as per the OECD DAC definition, covers intended and unintended and direct and indirect change. For assessment of intended change, the program theory and/or logic will be the key reference point. The program logic provides a categorization of different types of change in terms of time. The impact domain refers to change in general, but the term is also used technically to specifically refer to long-term change. Impacts (long-term changes) are distinguished from short- and medium-term changes, which in this text, are both categorized as outcomes. While the impact domain covers all change, the domain is particularly concerned with the more enduring effects of the program, and therefore, assessment of medium and longer term change is the critical focus.

In practice, there is some overlap and frequently some confusion in distinguishing between the impact and effectiveness domains. Both domains involve assessments of change, although, as discussed earlier, effectiveness has been extended to include assessment of program quality, value, and fidelity of implementation. In relation to the change dimension, for the effectiveness domain, the assessment is made in relation to the change stated or implied in the program objectives only. The impact domain encompasses a much broader range of change, intended and unintended, that is produced by the program. In relation to intended change, the program theory and/or logic may have been generated after the program objectives were specified, and by this time stakeholders may have developed a clearer idea of the changes envisaged by the program. The breadth and specificity of change considered in the impact domain are reinforced through the use of a program logic that involves determination of various subcategories of change. The impact domain also strongly focuses on issues of attribution, testing the validity of the results chain specified in the program theory and/or logic and assessing causal links for each type of change specified.

The OECD DAC sustainability criterion includes environmental and financial aspects of sustainability, but there are other recognized dimensions of this domain. First, the more encompassing term *economic* is commonly used to cover not only financial aspects in relation to available resources but the broader economic conditions which enable human and organizational activity. Social sustainability is commonly included as a dimension of sustainability and refers to the processes, systems, structures, and relationships that actively support continuation of benefits associated with an initiative. Principles of democracy and good governance, equity, diversity, social cohesion, and quality of life are associated with social sustainability (Magis & Shinn, 2009; United Nations, 2012). A further identifying feature of social sustainability is the notion that an initiative should promote the capability of present people without compromising the capabilities of future generations (Anand & Sen, 2000).

Table 5.3 provides the definitions of domains for classifying evaluation questions are based on the authors' review of the OECD DAC Evaluation Criteria.

**Table 5.3** Domains for Organizing Evaluation Questions

| Appropriateness | The extent to which a program's design and approach was suitable in terms of achieving its desired effect and working in its given context. This includes assessment of whether the program was of a suitable type or style to meet the priorities and needs of all identified major stakeholder groups. In this domain, there is questioning as to whether the program theory/program logic was correct in being able to envisage the causal relationships that were predicted between program outputs, outcomes, and impacts. |
|---|---|
| Effectiveness | The extent to which the program and broader stakeholder objectives were achieved, or are expected to be achieved, taking into account their relative importance. This domain includes an overall assessment of the quality and value of the program and the fidelity of its implementation. |

*(Continued)*

**Table 5.3** (Continued)

| | |
|---|---|
| Efficiency | A measure of the outputs delivered and how economically resources/inputs (funds, expertise, time, etc.) have been converted to outputs and outputs to results. It includes the extent to which the program was implemented well with regard to its governance, management, personnel management, and other process dimensions. |
| Impact | Positive and negative, medium to longerterm changes produced by a program, directly or indirectly, intended or unintended, with reference to its articulated program theory/program logic and considering issues of attribution. |
| Sustainability | The continuation of benefits associated with a program. It includes consideration of economic, environmental, and social aspects of sustainability. |

The relationship between the five domains and the development and implementation of a program is illustrated in Figure 5.2.

**Figure 5.2** Relationship Between the Five Domains

| | |
|---|---|
| **PROGRAM PLANNING AND DESIGN** | Assessing the *appropriateness* of the program's design |
| **PROGRAM IMPLEMENTATION** | Examining *efficiency* and fidelity in program implementation |
| **PROGRAM OBJECTIVES** | Assessing program *effectiveness* in meeting its objectives, its value and quality |
| **PROGRAM RESULTS** | Establishing *impact*: intended and unintended, and the degree to which change is attributable to the program |
| **SUSTAINABILITY OF RESULTS** | Identifying ongoing *sustainable* benefits from the program |

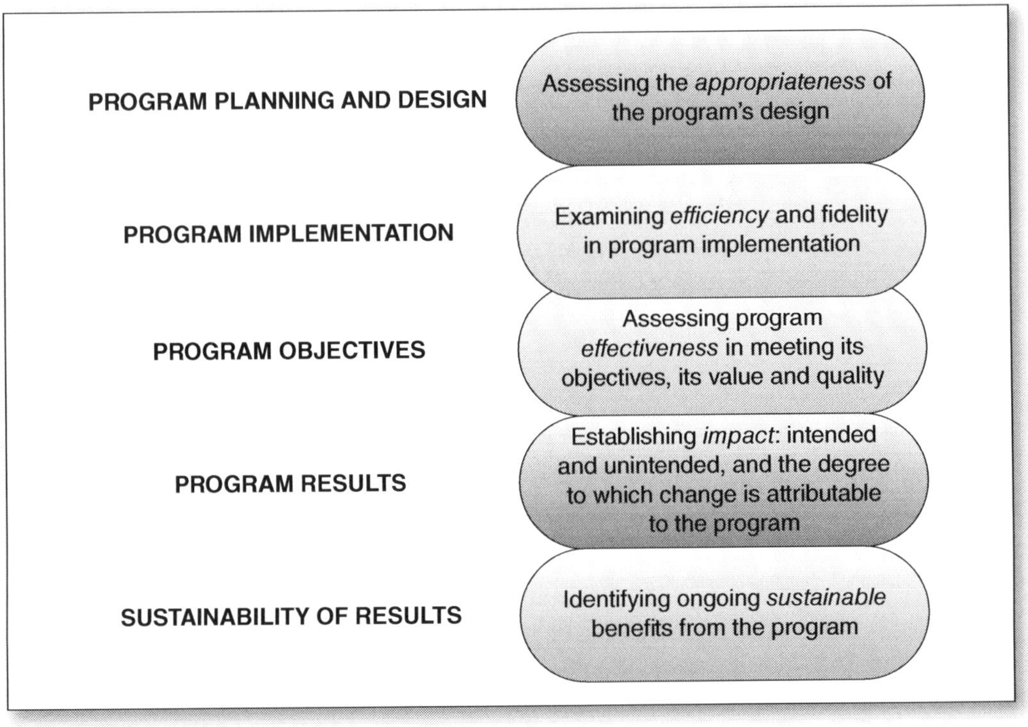

**Chapter 5** Evaluation Questions—Determining What We Want to Know

The five domains, representing areas of investigation and grouping of evaluation questions, have a high level of congruence with what Rossi et al. (2004, pp. 53–54) identify as recognizable types of evaluation questions. These are

- needs assessment (questions about the social conditions a program is to address and the need for the program),
- assessment of program theory (questions about program conceptualization and design),
- assessment of program process (questions about program implementation and service delivery),
- impact assessment (questions about programs outcomes and impact), and
- efficiency assessment (questions about program costs and cost-effectiveness).

An alignment can be identified between the domain of appropriateness, which coincides with needs assessment, and assessment of program design and program theory. The efficiency domain covers program processes and cost effectiveness, while both the impact and effectiveness domains overlap with impact assessment, which involves assessment of change. Some dimensions such as sustainability and assessment of program objectives are not covered. These relationships are illustrated in Figure 5.3.

**Figure 5.3** Rossi, Lipsey, and Freeman (2004): Five Types of Evaluation Questions and Relationship to Five Domains

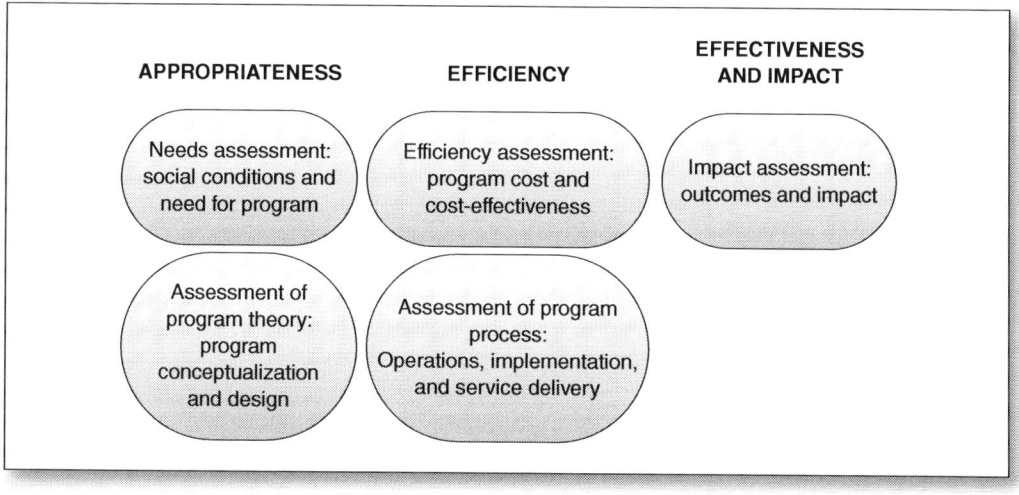

Other constructs are also available for developing and ordering evaluation questions. Davidson (2005) has built on Scriven's Key Evaluation Checklist, for example, and includes 15 main areas for evaluative inquiry. The areas of process evaluation (looking at design, implementation, and delivery issues), outcome evaluation (looking at intended and unintended impacts), and comparative cost effectiveness are amongst those identified as critical to answer evaluation questions. These areas have a high level of correspondence with the five domains.

Morra Imas and Rist (2009) suggest grouping evaluation questions into three categories, these being descriptive questions that depict the status of a process or condition, normative questions that compare what is with what should be, and cause-and-effect questions that attempt to determine the differences the program has made. They suggest that formative evaluations will use more descriptive and normative questions while impact evaluations will ask more cause-and-effect type questions. The preceding reinforces a principle of consideration of the focus, purpose, and priorities in evaluation in determining the balance of evaluation questions used. Such consideration will therefore be also reflected in the relative weighting of evaluation questions across the five domains in the Monitoring and Evaluation Framework. While coverage of all domains would be usual in an evaluation, a particular kind of evaluation, with a specific emphasis, such as an impact evaluation, may result in some domains not being covered. This issue is discussed further in Chapter 7, "The Evaluation Plan."

For the five evaluation domains, there is no rule as to how many questions to use overall, nor how many to be included in each of the five domains. This decision will vary according to the intent and emphasis of the Monitoring and Evaluation Framework being developed and the size and scope of the program. Given this context, it would not normally be expected to have an equal number of evaluation questions included in each domain. One working principle and useful reminder is the need for parsimony in setting evaluation questions. For every evaluation question posed, data will need to be acquired and analyzed either through routine monitoring or through periodic evaluation, or through both.

Grouping of questions into headline and subsidiary evaluation questions, where applicable, is likely to promote an efficient approach. Addressing and reporting on the headline questions will be most critical and may allow incorporation of responses from subsidiary questions. This approach is demonstrated in the context of an effectiveness question:

**Headline Evaluation Question**: To what degree was the program able to achieve its intended objectives?

**Subsidiary Evaluation Questions**:

- To what extent was the program able to [area of intent in Objective A . . . ?]
- To what extent was the program able to [area of intent of Objective B . . . ?]

- To what extent was the program able to [area of intent of Objective C . . . ?]
- To what extent was the program able to [area of intent of Objective D . . . ?]

Headline and subsidiary evaluation questions that are commonly used in evaluation appear in Table 5.4.

**Table 5.4** Common Headline and Subsidiary Evaluation Questions

| Appropriateness<br><br>- Suitability of program design in context<br>- Fit of program with program theory and/or logic<br>- Testing of underlying assumptions<br>- Extent program meets the priorities and needs of key stakeholders | *To what extent was the design of the program suitable in meeting the needs of key stakeholders and beneficiaries?*<br><br>- To what extent was the nature and scope of the need or problem to be addressed clearly articulated?<br>- Within the parameters of the program design, to what extent were the intended target group or program beneficiaries clearly identified?<br>- Was the program theory and/or logic correct in capturing program intent?<br>- Were the underlying assumptions about how change occurs clearly identified?<br>- To what degree was the program design suitable for the cultural context?<br>- To what extent did the program design meet funder priorities and policies?<br>- To what extent did the program design meet the needs of the broader stakeholder community?<br>- To what extent did the program design meet target group and beneficiary needs? |
|---|---|
| Effectiveness<br><br>- Fidelity of implementation<br>- Achievement of program objectives<br>- Assessment of the quality and value of the program | *To what degree was the program implemented as intended? If it wasn't, why not?* |
| | *To what degree was the program able to achieve its stated objectives?*<br><br>- To what degree were benefits of the program available to the intended target group and beneficiaries?<br>- What factors contributed to, or prevented, achievement?<br>- To what degree can we attribute any outcomes achieved to the program or to its effects? |
| | *To what degree can the program be assessed as being of value to its key stakeholders and beneficiaries?* |
| | *To what degree can the program be assessed as being of good quality?* |

*(Continued)*

**Table 5.4** (Continued)

| | |
|---|---|
| Efficiency<br><br>• Conversion of inputs to outputs and outputs to results<br>• Governance and management | *To what extent was the program implemented in an efficient manner?* |
| | • To what extent were the intended outputs delivered?<br>• To what extent were the costs of program delivery justifiable against its results?<br>• To what degree was the program cost-effective when compared with other like programs or other options that address the same needs?<br>• To what extent was the available budget sufficient to cover program costs?<br>• To what degree were available resources (budget, staff, time) used to best effect?<br>• To what degree was there good governance and management of the program? |
| Impact<br><br>• Changes (results) produced by the program, intended and unintended, direct and indirect | *What results, expected and unexpected, and direct and indirect, were produced by the program?* |
| | • To what extent did the program achieve its intended changes?<br>• What factors led to change or contributed to lack of change?<br>• To what extent were changes identified attributable to the program or its effects?<br>• Which changes were intended, and which were unintended? |
| Sustainability<br><br>• Continuation of program benefits | *To what degree was there an indication of ongoing benefits attributable to the program?* |
| | • To what degree did the program develop capacity (in individuals and organizations) to produce ongoing benefits?<br>• What factors contributed to or prevented the achievement of ongoing benefits?<br>• To what extent can and should the program model be replicated to other settings? |

Evaluation questions that seek to determine relative value will be the most commonly posed and are consistent with the notion of evaluation used in this text. These *evaluative* questions are typified by a preface that involves terms such as *to what extent* or *how well*, which will prompt assessment against agreed criteria and standards. Absolute questions have a more limited use and will typically prompt a yes or no answer or involve ranking against a scale. Examples include "Was the service delivered consistent with standard X?" "Which pilot activity was most cost effective" (Davidson, 2005, pp. 18–19). An absolute question such as "Did the program achieve its objectives?" would, in literal terms, prompt an answer with no explanation and therefore be of very limited use. Additionally, questions should have a single focus and not be "double-barreled." This type of question can cause difficulty due to its complexity and the range of data required to answer the multiple parts that are involved.

## 3. USING PROGRAM THEORY AND LOGIC TO DETERMINE EVALUATION QUESTIONS

Establishing the program theory is a critical process to clarify the program intent and how the expected results will be generated. As Funnell and Rogers (2011) describe, the clarification process involved helps to establish specific areas of examination, such as which outcomes should be investigated. Determining the program theory can also highlight broader critical questions and related issues in a specific program, such as whether program objectives are consistent with expected outcomes and whether the inherent logic of the design was correct. As described in Chapter 4, the program logic depicts the program theory from a more operational and technically detailed viewpoint. As such, it has been represented as a framework or "scaffolding" from which to position a range of evaluation questions (Frechtling, 2007). These include, for example, formative, process-orientated questions about the implementation of activities and outputs and more summative questions relating to the achievement of specific outcomes.

The program logic may be directly applied to assist with the generation of evaluation questions for the evaluation domains. The connective assumptions that were outlined in the process of developing the program theory and the program logic should provide guidance for the types of questions that can be considered under the appropriateness domain. For example, the assumption identified in Chapter 4 that "the provision of community education will positively influence participant behavior," leads to formulating an appropriateness question phrased as "To what extent did the program design facilitate positive behavioral changes in participants from the target community?" The outcomes (shorter term and intermediate) specified in the program logic can be used to inform the types of questions considered under the effectiveness domain. The outputs identified in the program logic can lead to questions under the efficiency domain that are concerned with the connection between resource use (inputs), implementation (activities and outputs), and results. The impacts identified in the program logic directly inform the questions included under the impact domain. The sustainability domain provides a focus on enduring results or program continuity. The sustainability domain does have an associational connection with that of impact, with longer term effects being more inherently sustainable. Determining the impacts of a program will assist in illuminating which of its effects are more sustainable. The relationship between program logic, the five domains for classifying evaluation questions, and the development of evaluation questions is illustrated in Figure 5.4.

**Figure 5.4** Relationship Between Program Logic, Evaluation Domains, and Development of Evaluation Questions

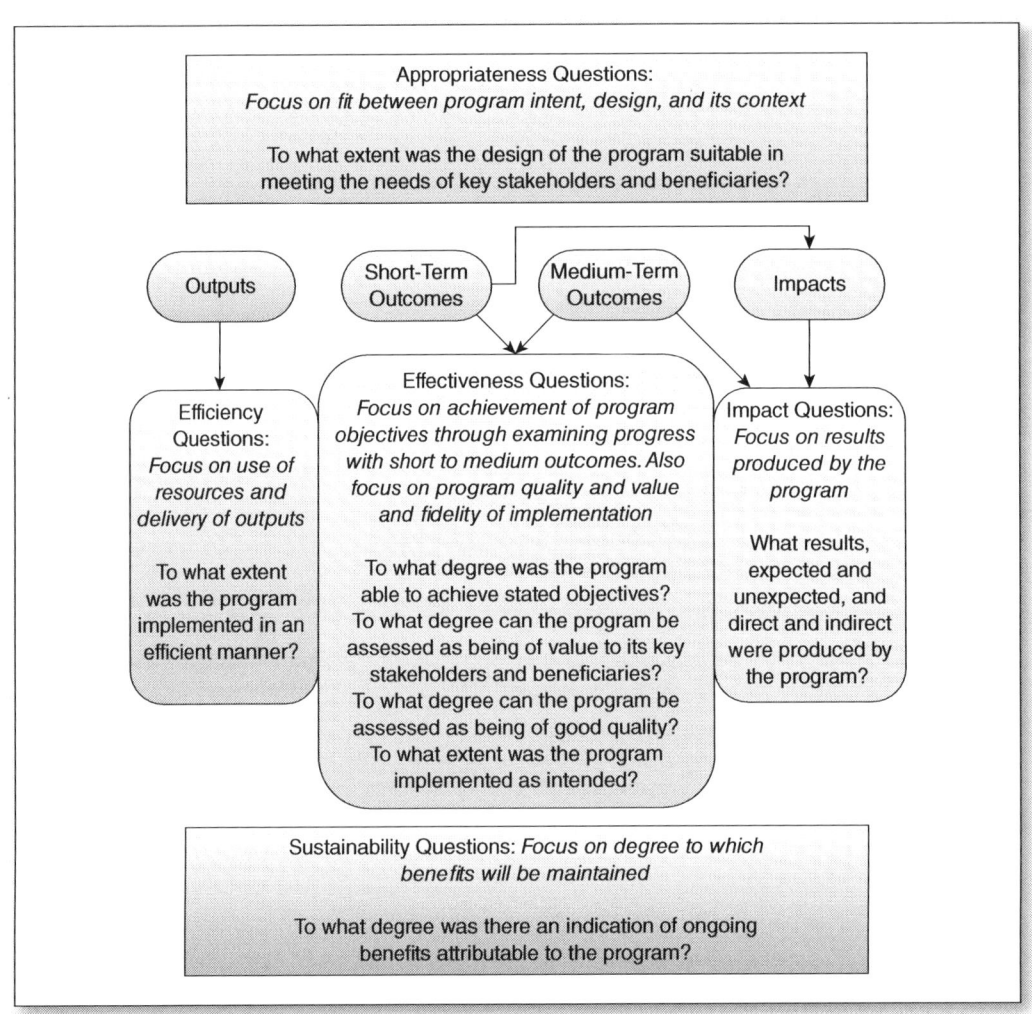

> **Practice Example**
>
> ### Using Program Logic to Generate Evaluation Questions
>
> The process of developing a Monitoring and Evaluation Framework for a youth support program used program logic as a major guide to the development of evaluation questions. The program was delivered by a nongovernment organization located in a particularly disadvantaged community. Previously, program staff, a representative from the governing body, and two external stakeholders involved with program delivery had worked with the evaluator to develop the program logic for the program. They had transferred this to a large format presentation and referred to this when developing the evaluation questions. They first considered the major areas of change as identified in the program theory and the related connective assumptions upon which such change relied. The assumptions particularly focused on whether the program model would trigger positive change in young people who were displaying risky behaviors in the community. Another important assumption was that the program could operate in a culturally appropriate manner and thereby engage with and motivate young people to consider change. These assumptions were translated into appropriateness questions designed to test whether the assumptions were valid. An example question included, "To what degree did at-risk young people in the community use the available support services provided by the agency?"
>
> Stakeholders then identified the short-term and intermediate outcomes in the program logic that most closely related to the program objectives. These were used as the basis of effectiveness questions designed to investigate whether such change eventuated. The stakeholders agreed to use a headline effectiveness question focusing on the degree to which the program had met its stated objectives. Subsidiary effectiveness questions examined specific areas of program performance. Several effectiveness questions were also generated that involved examination of issues relating to quality and value. Specifically, these involved assessment of the quality of the program's work in engaging with at-risk young people and their families and the value of different types of services as perceived by young people from the target group, their families, and program partners. In considering the domain of efficiency, the stakeholders identified questions, such as "To what extent were services delivered within budget, and if not, why not?" They also considered issues of governance and management,
>
> *(Continued)*

> (Continued)
>
> generating questions, such as "To what degree were program personnel sufficiently trained to undertake their roles?" The impact areas that were identified in the program logic were translated into impact questions. These focused on assessing the contribution of the program to longer term, system-level changes, while also identifying any unintended results. Such questions included, "To what degree did the program contribute to improvements in the overall health and well-being of at-risk young people in the community?" Sustainability questions particularly examined whether ongoing benefits for the targeted community were likely to be maintained. Sustainability questions included, "How likely was it that affiliated services would provide ongoing support to maintain and further improve the health and well-being of at-risk young people in the community?" At the end of the process, a set of evaluation questions had been developed, organized under the five domains, covering the main areas of program performance.

## 4. STEPS INVOLVED IN DEVELOPING EVALUATION QUESTIONS

Prior to development of the evaluation questions, it is assumed the purpose of the Monitoring and Evaluation Framework has been clarified and that that preferred evaluation approach has been identified. These points were introduced in Chapter 3 as initial steps involved in the development of a Monitoring and Evaluation Framework. Focusing on the purpose of the Monitoring and Evaluation Framework, and initial thinking on the approach to be used (e.g., more or less qualitative or quantitative), will influence the types of evaluation questions that are selected. It is also possible that expectations in relation to the Monitoring and Evaluation Framework have also been formally specified such as in a program design document or funding agreement.

Generation of evaluation questions and the reflection intrinsic to this process may prompt refinement of the purpose of the Monitoring and Evaluation Framework. This may occur, for example, if reflection leads to a higher priority accorded to a particular area of investigation, such as program impact. Similarly, initial thinking about the evaluation approach is likely to be further refined during the generation of questions. Such a process is itself influenced by reflection on the preferred and possible means to answer them. In general, development of the Monitoring and Evaluation Framework is expected to be an iterative process with thinking involved in the generation of one section possibly prompting refinement of another.

# Chapter 5   Evaluation Questions—Determining What We Want to Know

The evaluator is usually responsible for developing a first draft of suitable evaluation questions upon which the Monitoring and Evaluation Framework will then be based and developed. The term *evaluator* describes the person or team members tasked with the development of the Framework. Specifically, this means the person or team responsible for both facilitating the process and coordinating the product. The evaluator, whether internal or external to the program, plays a crucial role in framing the evaluation questions. While key stakeholders provide expertise grounded in the reality of the program, the evaluator holds particular expertise in the development of a robust and implementable Monitoring and Evaluation Framework (Rossi et al., 2004).

In some instances, the entire process of developing evaluation questions may be undertaken in a participatory way with key stakeholders in a workshop or other forum in order to build stakeholder engagement and capacity from the outset. The guidance below can thus be applied either to an approach where the facilitator develops the initial set of evaluation questions or where the facilitator works alongside other key stakeholders to develop the initial evaluation questions.

The suggested steps for developing a set of evaluation questions are listed in Table 5.5.

**Table 5.5**   Steps in Developing Evaluation Questions

| *Stage 2: Foundations for the Monitoring and Evaluation Framework* <br> *Develop Evaluation Questions* | | |
|---|---|---|
| *Steps* | | |
| 1 | **Develop draft evaluation questions** | • Draw on prior clarification as to the purpose of the Monitoring and Evaluation Framework. <br> • Review documentation that provides context and background to the Monitoring and Evaluation Framework. <br> • Develop an initial set of evaluation questions using the five evaluation domains to prompt areas of investigation, and categorize questions generated. <br> • Consider the relative significance of each domain given the purpose of the Framework. <br> • Use the program theory, program logic, and other available materials to assist in identification of the evaluation questions, including those that focus on achievement of critical results areas. |

*(Continued)*

**Table 5.5**  (Continued)

| 2 | Facilitate stakeholder participation | • Facilitate broad stakeholder engagement in selecting and agreeing on evaluation questions. This ideally will involve a Monitoring and Evaluation Planning Workshop held at an early opportunity. |
|---|---|---|
| 3 | Scope number and range of questions against data and resources available | • Scope data availability to respond to proposed evaluation questions.<br>• Scope the number and range of questions proposed against the resources available, including budget, staff availability, and capacity for monitoring and evaluation. |
| 4 | Present questions to stakeholders for final endorsement | • Re-present evaluation questions to the key stakeholders involved in Step 2 for final endorsement. |
| 5 | Finalize evaluation questions | • Develop a final agreed set of evaluation questions for inclusion in the Monitoring and Evaluation Framework. |

### *Step 1: Develop Draft Evaluation Questions*

As preparation for the development of evaluation questions, the evaluator should draw upon prior planning and documentation regarding the program intent and design and the purpose and approach of the Monitoring and Evaluation Framework. This involves discussions with key personnel such as program designers and funders and drawing on key documentation.

Care should be exercised in relation to using documentation, which although having an important formal status, may contain outdated understandings of program intent or expectations of evaluation. For this reason, consultations with key personnel are critical, with attention focused on developing evaluation questions and the broader Monitoring and Evaluation Framework so that they are both understood and accepted.

Source documents likely to inform the initial drafting of evaluation questions can include the following:

- Program design documentation, including specification of the program aims and objectives and evaluation purpose
- Program funding agreements or funding guidelines in relation to monitoring and evaluation
- Other relevant guidelines to monitoring and evaluation, such as from implementing organizations or sectoral organizations

- Documented program theory or program logic for the program (if in place)
- Higher level evaluation questions, performance indicators, and targets that the program may be required to align with; such requirements may be in place, for example, where the program is part of a coordinated approach in a particular sector. Higher level (e.g. national, sectoral, or organizational) Monitoring and Evaluation Frameworks may already be in place and represent important points of reference.
- Research and evaluation findings drawn from available relevant literature. Such literature is likely to highlight key learnings, issues and knowledge gaps in the area of program operation and thereby inform selection of questions.

The next step in the process is to develop an initial set of evaluation questions using the five evaluation domains to prompt areas of investigation and categorize the questions generated. In doing this, consider the relative significance of each domain given the purpose of the Monitoring and Evaluation Framework. It is usual, but not essential, that all the evaluation domains are addressed.

It is important to use the program theory and the program logic (if in place) to assist with the identification of the evaluation questions, including those that examine whether the design can reasonably be expected to support the program's formal objectives, expectations of program implementation, and achievement of critical results areas.

Care should be taken to produce a streamlined initial list of questions, highlighting the most important areas of investigation. Headline and subsidiary questions can be used. The purpose of the initial list is for clarification and as a point of reference and response by stakeholders who are likely to identify other significant priorities for examination.

## *Step 2: Facilitate Stakeholder Participation*

The involvement of key stakeholders is central to establishing an agreed set of evaluation questions. As detailed in Chapter 3, stakeholder engagement and participation is justified from the perspective of empowering and building the capacity of those who have a stake in the evaluation. Stakeholder engagement is also necessary to ensure that the questions developed are clear, answerable, and utilization focused. The use of the information and analysis generated is promoted through direct engagement with the intended users in the evaluation planning process (Patton, 2012). Key stakeholders who should become involved in the development of evaluation questions broadly include program funders and policy makers; program managers and implementers; and program consumers or beneficiaries (Fitzpatrick et al., 2011). A stakeholder mapping exercise is likely to be of assistance to identify stakeholders and their type of involvement (see Chapter 3).

Organizing a Monitoring and Evaluation Planning Workshop is usually an effective means to promote stakeholder consensus and support for the set of evaluation questions. Such a workshop would usefully involve an educative function about evaluation depending on the background of the stakeholder group. Involving key stakeholders in the development of an agreed program theory and/or program logic builds clarity about program intent. Alternatively, stakeholders may be involved in review and updating of an existing document. The subsequent development of the evaluation questions would follow. This involves participants considering the predeveloped draft set of evaluation questions that are then further developed to the point of optimal consensus and ownership. The involvement of key stakeholders in the different stages of the development and implementation of the Monitoring and Evaluation Framework is depicted in Figure 5.5.

**Figure 5.5** Entry Points for Stakeholder Engagement in Development of the Monitoring and Evaluation Framework

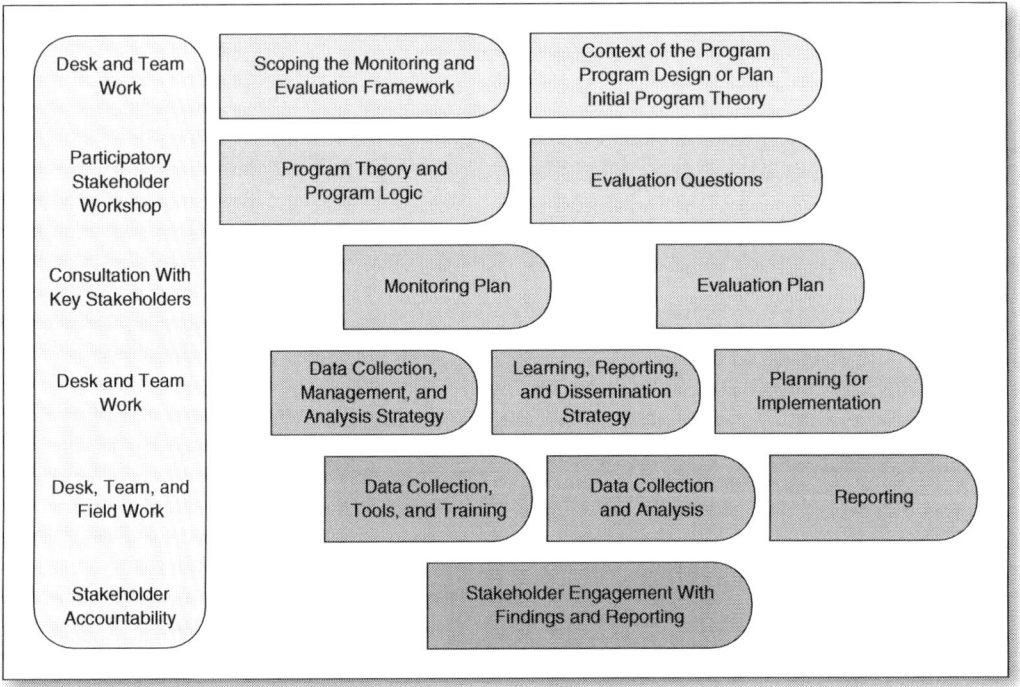

**Chapter 5** Evaluation Questions—Determining What We Want to Know

If holding a workshop for stakeholders is not feasible or practical, a range of other forums or meetings could be substituted. The main consideration is to develop opportunities for eliciting input from key stakeholders in a participatory way. Evaluation questions should be formulated through discussion, debate, negotiation, and forming consensus.

## *Step 3: Scope Number and Range of Questions Against Data and Resources Available*

Once a level of stakeholder consensus has been achieved in relation to the evaluation questions, the next step is to check the availability of data and the feasibility of its collection. Checking data availability assists in determining whether a question can be reasonably answered and is therefore valid and viable for inclusion in the Monitoring and Evaluation Framework. It is possible that this issue will also be partially addressed in the stakeholder workshop. Early investigations should be made into issues such as data reliability and completeness, the extent to which available data can support answers to the evaluation questions, the need for additional data, and the highest priorities for data collection (McDavid et al., 2013). For example, there is little value in including an evaluation question that tracks progress or trends over time from point X if there is no baseline data available for point X. This is a common flaw within evaluation question setting. As a result of these investigations, some evaluation questions will be modified or removed. To use a more agricultural metaphor, this process may be termed as *winnowing* (Fitzpatrick et al., 2011).

Choice of evaluation methodology will impact on the type and range of data to be sought and in particular contexts, may lead to issues with data availability and feasibility. For example, in using the Most Significant Change technique, the availability and willingness of stakeholders to generate the required stories would be an important consideration. When using surveys, scoping logistical arrangements, and the availability and cooperation of respondents is important.

Under ideal circumstances, performance data would be identified and collected following the completion of the Monitoring and Evaluation Framework, with the Framework serving as a guide as to what data are to be collected. In reality, this is not always the case. In many instances the Monitoring and Evaluation Framework is developed after the performance monitoring system and related performance indicators have already been selected, developed, and made operational. This then requires some "retrofitting" of existing performance monitoring data sources and indicators against the developed evaluation questions and their subsequent incorporation into the Monitoring and Evaluation Framework for the program.

Following assessment of data availability, the evaluation questions should then be reviewed to ensure that the number and range of questions developed are realistic in terms of available resources. Resource issues include the budget for monitoring and evaluation functions; available staff for data collection, analysis, and reporting; and levels of staff knowledge, skills, and experience in monitoring and evaluation. Further adjustments may occur at this stage to reduce or otherwise rationalize the list of evaluation questions.

> **Practice Example**
>
> **Streamlining Evaluation Questions**
>
> Stakeholders concerned with the delivery of a large national preventative health program worked with the evaluator to develop a set of guiding evaluation questions for their Monitoring and Evaluation Framework. Initially, an ambitious number of questions was identified. The questions were then classified into the five domains, which provided greater clarity as to the areas of program performance requiring examination. Once the questions were grouped, consideration was given to the level of resources available to support monitoring and evaluation activities. As a result, the number of questions was reduced. Use of headline and subsidiary evaluation questions assisted the process of streamlining undertaken. After further discussion and iterations, a final list of evaluation questions to guide monitoring and evaluation of the health program was agreed upon. Some subsequent cutting back of the evaluation questions occurred during the process of developing the Monitoring Plan and the Evaluation Plan and further scoping of data availability. Heightened understanding and appreciation of data gaps and limitations in capacity to collect and manage data influenced these decisions.

## Step 4: Present Questions to Stakeholders for Final Endorsement

As the list of evaluation questions is progressively refined, various iterations may be shared with a small representative working group or even the broader

**Chapter 5** Evaluation Questions—Determining What We Want to Know

stakeholder group. The ability to do this depends on the context and stakeholder characteristics. Presentation and finalization of the evaluation questions with the stakeholder group may occur in a special meeting or other forum. In this context, the evaluator may need to adopt an educative approach to assist stakeholders to understand why and how evaluation questions are being prioritized and rationalized.

### *Step 5: Finalize Evaluation Questions*

The process used for finalizing the selection of evaluation questions to be included in the Monitoring and Evaluation Framework should ideally be based on the achievement of consensus wherever this is possible. For the evaluator, this entails both being inclusive to the degree possible and also exercising a degree of pragmatism. In addition to accommodating the interests of a broader stakeholder group, the evaluator is necessarily sensitive to the priorities of the client or funder. This critical stakeholder group needs to be assured that the evaluation questions will provide the data, analysis, and findings that its members need to make the necessary decisions about the program, its design, and its future. The evaluators need to feel confident that the range and quality of available data and that resources are sufficient to answer the evaluation questions. Concerns with identifying a realistic and accepted set of evaluation questions should also motivate the inclusion of broader stakeholder views and interests.

Balancing of different interests is inherent to the setting of evaluation questions. This is consistent with what Fitzpatrick et al. (2011) identify as the operation of both a divergent and a convergent stage in setting evaluation questions. Divergent, broader stakeholder consultation typically generates a range of questions that then becomes subject to a more convergent process of weighing and selecting. Fitzpatrick et al. (2011) observe that "no evaluation can answer responsibly all the questions generated during a thorough, divergent planning phase" (p. 328). As a response, they propose use of a matrix for ranking or selecting the evaluation questions based on criteria such as the level of continuing interest in the question, the capacity of the question to reduce uncertainty and provide important information, the level of importance of the question to the scope and impact of the evaluation, and the level of its answerability given resource constraints, data methods, and technology. In a contrasting and somewhat cautionary observation, Bamberger et al. (2012) argue that truncating the number of evaluation questions can potentially limit the range of interests of different stakeholder audiences and that by arbitrarily limiting the number of questions, the interests of some stakeholders may be ignored. As identified in this text, both compromise and pragmatism need to be exercised to appropriately balance stakeholder interests while maintaining the feasibility of monitoring and evaluation.

Where possible, agreement should also be reached between the evaluator and key stakeholders on the criteria and standards that will be used for assessing the data gathered to answer the agreed set of evaluation questions. This aspect is discussed in greater detail in both Chapter 7, "The Evaluation Plan" and in Chapter 8, "Collecting, Managing, Analyzing, and Synthesizing Data to Reach Evaluative Conclusions."

## SUMMARY CHECKLIST

- Has the program logic been used to inform the development of clear and concise evaluation questions?
- Have the questions been organized under domains such as appropriateness, effectiveness, efficiency, impact, and sustainability?
- Does the scope of the questions appear to cover the main areas of program performance that will require assessment?
- Has there been an adequate level of stakeholder engagement and ownership in the process of developing evaluation questions?
- Are the questions that have been developed cohesive and logical?
- Is the number and scope of the questions appropriate when assessed against available resources to support monitoring and evaluation and the implementation of the Framework specifically?
- Are the questions asked in an evaluative manner, that is, using phrasing such as "To what extent?" or "To what degree?"
- Are the questions clear, dealing with one concept at a time, and not "double-barreled"?
- For each question, are there available data to support an answer?
- Are sufficient data available in the context of both monitoring and evaluation functions?
- Will the answers to the questions contribute to an understanding of the program's success, limitations, and areas of required improvement?
- Has the final set of evaluation questions been presented to and endorsed by key stakeholders?
- Overall, can the evaluation questions be regarded as agreed, practical, and useful?

## CHAPTER REVIEW QUESTIONS

1. How would you approach the development of a set of evaluation questions for a program using program theory and program logic to guide the development of these questions?

2. What are the advantages of developing the questions under domains such as appropriateness, effectiveness, efficiency, impact, and sustainability?

3. How would you promote a participatory process and stakeholder ownership in developing the evaluation questions?

4. What are the advantages of using headline evaluation questions and subsidiary evaluation questions?

5. How would you review the wording of the questions to ensure they are phrased evaluatively and are not "double-barreled"?

6. How would you review the overall set of evaluation questions, removing any superfluous questions, and simplifying any overly complex questions?

7. How would you ensure that the final number and range of evaluation questions are realistic against available resources, practical to implement, and useful?

# CHAPTER 6

# The Monitoring Plan

# Chapter 6  The Monitoring Plan

*The Monitoring Plan determines how monitoring will contribute to answering the evaluation questions. The evaluation questions represent a common reference point incorporated in both the Monitoring Plan and the Evaluation Plan, these being key subsections of the Monitoring and Evaluation Framework. With the evaluation questions as a focus, the Monitoring Plan provides a guide to the ongoing and systematic collection of routine performance information. Monitoring particularly highlights the progress of implementation and identifies early results being produced.*

## 1. INTRODUCTION

Program monitoring is integral to, and fully aligned with, program evaluation. Evaluation questions that are organized under the five domains of appropriateness, effectiveness, efficiency, impact, and sustainability, and linked to program theory and program logic, guide the collection and analysis of monitoring data as they do evaluation data. This chapter identifies the areas within a program and its operations that are commonly monitored and discusses the development and use of performance indicators and targets. It presents the Monitoring Plan format that is used to detail monitoring arrangements. The Monitoring Plan fully articulates with the Evaluation Plan format presented in Chapter 7. The complementary relationship between monitoring and evaluation functions and their mutual focus on answering the evaluation questions was discussed in the introductory chapter. The relationship is illustrated in Figure 6.1.

## 2. INTRODUCTION TO PROGRAM MONITORING

The word *monitoring*, when traced to its Latin roots, means "to warn." In practice, it warns managers of deviations from the original design and intent of the program as highlighted during its implementation (Kettner et al., 2013, p. 230). This orientation underlines the reality that program implementation can be challenging and involve unexpected developments and constraints. These could include, for example, activities only being partially implemented, staff turnover, and withdrawal of support from a program partner. In such circumstances, monitoring has an essential role to play in tracking implementation and prompting corrective action. While monitoring incorporates a cautionary notion of being "ever watchful," under most circumstances it can also be expected to highlight positive attributes and the early achievements of a program. Effective monitoring therefore can provide to program management a balanced view of the status and results of implementation.

**Figure 6.1** Monitoring and its Role in Answering Evaluation Questions

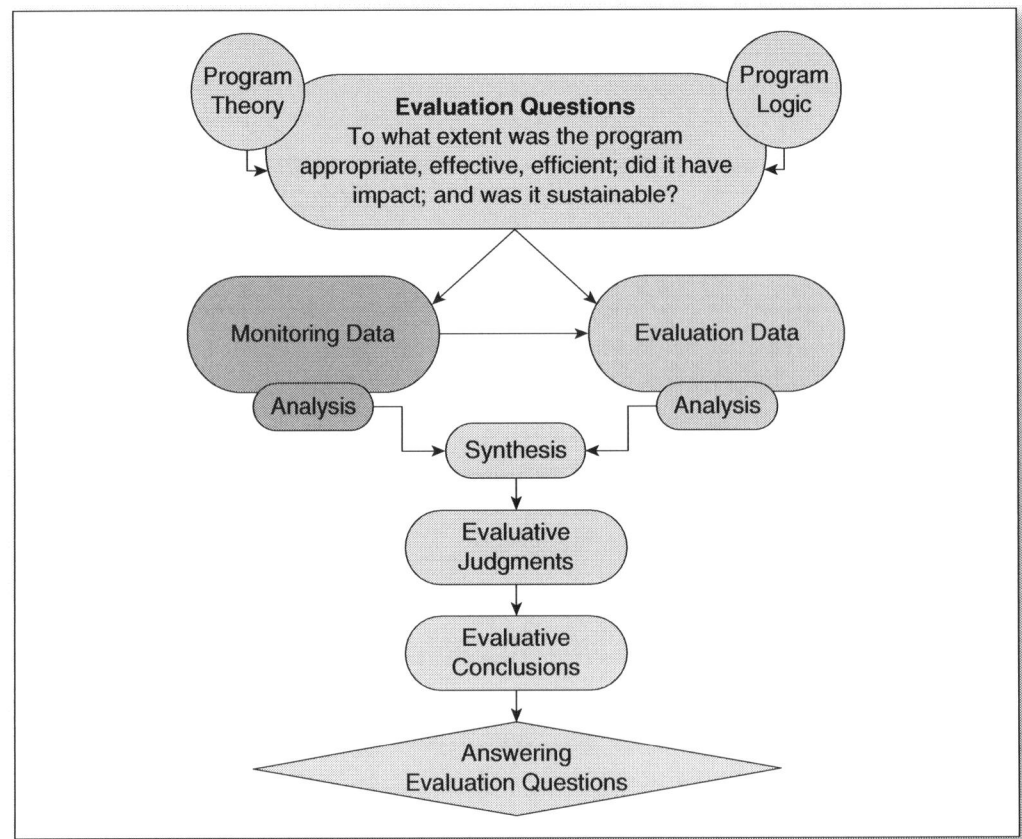

Monitoring systematically tracks progress against a range of predetermined areas, often against performance indicators and targets. Areas monitored include staffing and administrative arrangements, activities and outputs produced, initial outcomes, reactions of key stakeholders, financial and budgetary factors, and any implementation issues experienced. Monitoring is therefore well placed to support organizational management and accountability functions. Data collected may include, for example, activity records, observations, assessments made during field visits (often recorded on a checklist), and feedback provided by stakeholders following activities. Some or all of this information may be entered into an appropriate computer database that allows for data entry, storage, management, and retrieval and may also support data analysis. The data system may consist of a central information unit coordinating with an organization's local units using a web-based interface (Chen, 2005). The data are subject to analysis, and usually the results are periodically collated into a report for management. Such reports, and in some cases the primary data involved, will provide important reference points for evaluation. Evaluation uses the results of monitoring, complemented by other forms of data gathering, to undertake further and deeper investigations, and through a logical pattern of reasoning, arrives at evaluative conclusions.

Of course, the effectiveness of monitoring is dependent upon certain preconditions. These include the existence of adequate staff or capable partners to undertake monitoring; development and use of appropriate performance indicators; availability of reliable data; the existence of a viable database; the commitment, interest, and time availability of management and leaders to use monitoring results; and ultimately whether monitoring results are actually used in decision-making processes. Additionally, some programs may be more intrinsically difficult to monitor due to, for example, their geographic remoteness and security issues and problems with accessing certain client groups. Organizations may also be conflicted or face pressures from governments or funders as to program monitoring priorities and therefore be unclear concerning which areas to actually monitor (Poister, 2010). These issues are discussed further in Chapter 8, "Collecting, Managing, Analyzing and Synthesizing Data to Reach Evaluative Conclusions."

The key differences between monitoring and evaluation functions have been presented in Table 1.1 in the Chapter 1. An issue for debate is the extent to which the concept of monitoring crosses over with that of *formative evaluation* or *process evaluation*. Formative and process evaluations are concerned with program implementation and contrast with summative or outcome evaluations that focus on identifying and assessing results. In this regard, there are areas of overlap between the focus of program monitoring and formative or process evaluation. The points of distinction lie predominantly in the regularity of the process and the depth of analysis, with monitoring being routine in nature and undertaken in real time, while evaluation is periodic with a deeper level of analysis. A possible future trend may see the functions of monitoring and evaluation converge through the provision of "streams of information," rather than classifying data as either monitoring or evaluation (Rist, 2006). For the purposes of this text, monitoring and evaluation are identified as separate but inextricably linked processes that operate in tandem to support management and accountability functions and to facilitate learning and program improvement.

## *Performance Management and Program Monitoring*

In the corporate organizational context, monitoring and evaluation functions operate at different levels. While this text is focused on *program monitoring* at the level of an individual program, the use of monitoring at the broader organizational level highlights a range of lessons for program-level monitoring. Both program and organizational monitoring provide performance information used to assess the achievement of corporate objectives. Additionally, in any one organizational context, a range of separate programs may operate that have subsidiary arrangements for monitoring and evaluation. This also applies to the range of projects that usually underpin the operation of programs. The connection between organizational-, program-, and project-level arrangements is depicted in the notion of cascading Monitoring and Evaluation Frameworks as outlined in Chapter 1 and further presented in Figure 6.2.

Reflecting the challenges involved, considerable discussion has occurred in relation to how to more closely link monitoring and evaluation functions with organizational planning functions. The term *performance management* is used to refer to this organizational management context, within which the complementary components of monitoring and evaluation are embedded (Hunter & Nielsen, 2013). The Results-Based Management approach, introduced in Chapter 2, is one type of performance management approach. It is iterative and commences with strategy development and planning, which are then followed by implementation monitoring. Monitoring processes particularly support organizational needs for effective management and accountability. Importantly, monitoring results also inform and provide a basis for evaluation. Evaluation processes are strongly linked to the purposes of learning and improvement. The results of both monitoring and evaluation are used together to guide subsequent revision of plans.

**Figure 6.2** Cascading Monitoring and Evaluation Frameworks at Organizational, Program, and Project Levels

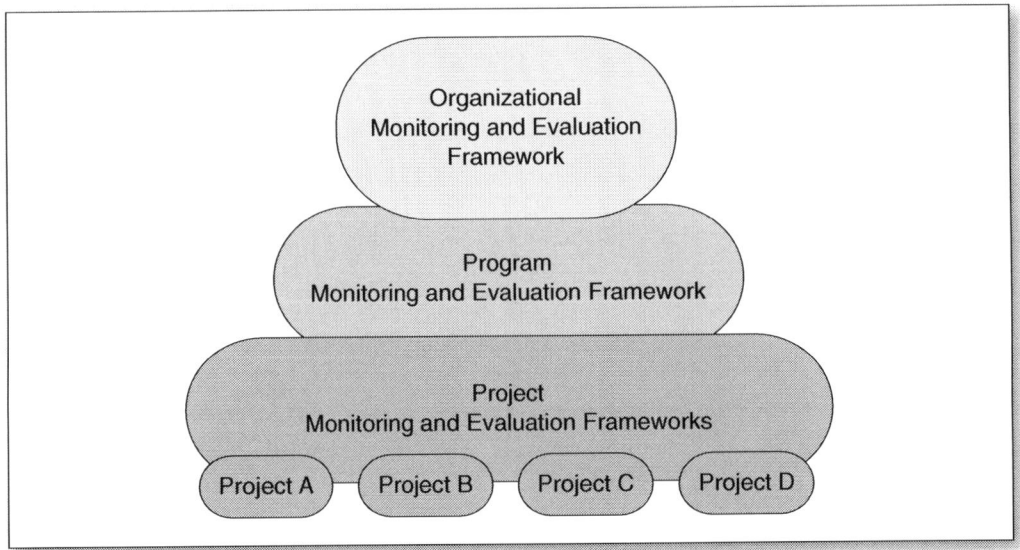

To support such a performance management approach, organizational leaders need to appreciate how monitoring and evaluation processes and products assist an organization to achieve results. Vital ingredients are a significant use of data in management processes and decision making and an open and reflective organizational culture enabling refinement in direction and approach. A performance management system requires "leaders, managers, accountability systems, performance budgeting, measuring and monitoring, and evaluation" (Hunter & Nielsen, 2013, p. 7). In order to highlight and reinforce these attributes as a defining feature of performance management, the following figure from Chapter 1 is represented here.

**Figure 6.3** Components of Performance Management

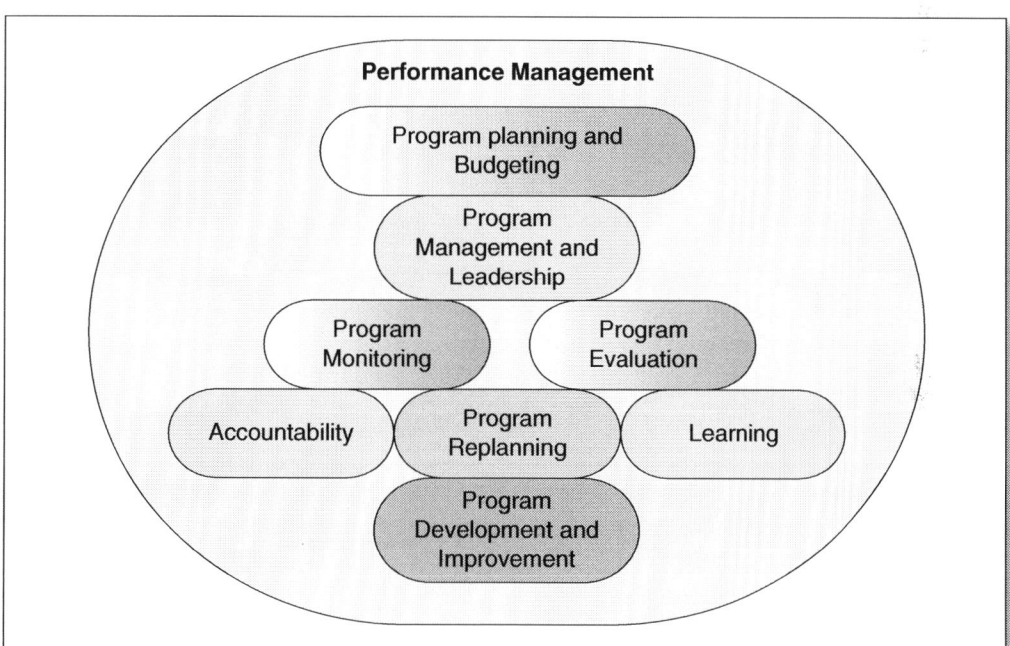

Principles that guide effective performance management systems, particularly the emphasis on coordination and integration, also apply to program monitoring. In this integrated context, the use of program monitoring is lifted beyond merely servicing needs to report on program implementation and support accountability through progress reports.

## 3. THE MONITORING PLAN

The use of the one set of evaluation questions unifies the Monitoring and Evaluation Framework and also its two subsidiary plans. The Monitoring Plan and the

Evaluation Plan are ideally developed concurrently by the same people but are then used to individually guide distinct areas of practice, with the Monitoring Plan used internally to guide ongoing monitoring processes and the Evaluation Plan used to guide periodic internal or external evaluation processes. Both plans use a matrix layout, which organizes the evaluation questions and subquestions within rows and identifies associated measures and data sources within respective columns. A structure of this kind represents an easy-to-follow guide that allows stakeholders to readily identify how respective questions will be addressed (McDavid et al., 2013). The format of the Monitoring Plan is provided in Table 6.1. The respective sections that are included are as follows:

- Evaluation Questions—organized under domains, with questions and subquestions
- Focus of Monitoring—providing a succinct statement of what will be monitored to assist in answering the evaluation questions
- Indicators—demonstrating the type of change, event, or condition expected from the area being investigated (see Section 4 below)
- Targets—showing the level of the result toward which efforts are being directed (see Section 4 below)
- Monitoring Data Sources—identifying where monitoring data will be obtained
- Who Is Responsible and When—detailing personnel and timing factors

**Table 6.1** Monitoring Plan Format

| Evaluation Questions | Focus of Monitoring | Indicators | Targets | Monitoring Data Sources | Who Is Responsible and When |
|---|---|---|---|---|---|
| Appropriateness | | | | | |
| Effectiveness | | | | | |
| Efficiency | | | | | |
| Impact | | | | | |
| Sustainability | | | | | |

The use of the Monitoring Plan format is demonstrated in Table 6.2 using an example of a community education program targeted to families in a disadvantaged community where rates of school attendance of children are low. The program specifically aims to positively influence the attitudes and behavior of

**Table 6.2** The Monitoring Plan With Example Provided

| Evaluation Questions | Focus of Monitoring | Indicators | Targets | Monitoring Data Sources | Who Is Responsible and When |
|---|---|---|---|---|---|
| **Appropriateness** To what extent did the target group participate in the program? | Participant characteristics | Number of participants from target group Gender balance of participants | 75% participation by target group Minimum 40% male participants | Attendance records | Staff member X Monthly |
| **Effectiveness** To what extent did participants increase their knowledge of the benefits of regular school attendance? | Changes in knowledge following participation in sessions | Difference between participant knowledge of the benefits of regular school attendance before and after sessions attended | 75% of participants report increased knowledge of the benefits of regular school attendance | Pre-post survey | Staff member Y Following completion of series of sessions |
| **Efficiency** Was the cost of delivering the program within budget? | Costs against budget and areas where overruns or underspends occurred | Performance against budget | Less than 10% variation between actual costs and budget | Financial records | Staff member X Monthly |
| **Impact** To what extent was there an increase in regular school attendance in the community? | Trends in school attendance in local schools | Changes in school attendance patterns from the baseline | No target | Administrative data from schools | Staff member Y Six monthly |
| **Sustainability** Was there evidence of ongoing benefits beyond the program? | Development of partnership agreements for continued initiatives | Number and type of partnership agreements developed | No target | Records of partnership meetings Partnership documentation | Staff member X Annually |

family members regarding supporting regular school attendance for their children. Only one evaluation question per domain is shown in this example. See Chapter 7 for the Evaluation Plan that is associated with this Monitoring Plan.

Guidance on developing the respective parts of the Monitoring Plan is provided in the following sections.

A variation to the above format noted in other types of monitoring plans, is to additionally include details on the program's program theory or program logic. In that case, for specific questions the relevant area of the program theory or program logic is identified. This approach is most commonly used for questions pertaining to the impact and effectiveness domains. For simplicity, this approach has not been adopted in the earlier format. It is rather assumed that the relevant questions were generated with reference to the program theory and the program logic.

In completing the monitoring plan, consideration should be given to those questions that may require, and would benefit from, the development of performance indicators with or without associated targets. Some questions may require a very narrow area of investigation. An example of such a question would be, "Was the community education program implemented by provincial health authorities?" Despite possibly representing a critical aspiration of the program, for this type of closed question, the answer would be self-evident, and the use of a target would thus not be required or appropriate. An answer to a question may also be largely derived from evaluation processes rather than monitoring, making specification of an indicator or an associated target inappropriate. For some evaluation questions, more than one indicator may be required, and in other circumstances, the one indicator developed may be employed in relation to a range of different questions. These issues are discussed in the next section.

## 4. STEPS IN DEVELOPING THE MONITORING PLAN

Table 6.3 presents the major steps involved in developing a Monitoring Plan.

**Table 6.3** Steps Involved in Developing a Monitoring Plan

| *Monitoring and Evaluation Plans* | | |
|---|---|---|
| *Stage 6 Develop Monitoring Plan* | | |
| Steps | | |
| 1 | Identify focus | • Identify the focus of monitoring in order to provide answers for evaluation questions. |

| 2 | Develop performance indicators and targets | • Develop performance indicators and targets where these are appropriate to the questions.<br>• Identify relevant baselines, as appropriate, for conditions to which indicators refer. |
|---|---|---|
| 3 | Identify data collection processes and tools | • Identify data collection processes and tools that will require development. |
| 4 | Determine responsibilities and time frames | • Determine responsibilities and time frames for the implementation of monitoring activities. |

Details on how each respective step is undertaken are provided next.

## Step 1: Identify Focus

The first major step in developing the Monitoring Plan is to determine what will need to be monitored to assist in answering each evaluation question. The appropriateness question identified in the first column of Table 6.2 above serves as an example. This question is, "To what extent did the target group participate in the program?" To address this question, the focus of monitoring is on identifying the characteristics of participants (2nd column). This focus is further specified by the choice of indicators and involves examining characteristics such as number and gender (3rd column).

Monitoring in this case only provides a partial answer to the question, and we will need to gather additional information such as what motivated target group members to participate, how target group members responded to the program, and reasons for nonparticipation. This complementary information will be provided through evaluation processes. Monitoring is best placed to illuminate facts and trends, but evaluation highlights reasons for trends and what should be done as a consequence (Hatry, 2006).

A similar pattern of determining the focus of monitoring is used for all evaluation questions. In each case, this involves considering what type of investigations the answer requires, the nature of monitoring, and how it can contribute to the answer. Such deliberations involve consideration of the interrelationship and demarcation between investigations through monitoring and evaluation.

While each evaluation question and its context are unique, it is possible to generalize about different areas of investigation that are undertaken through monitoring to provide an answer. Typical areas of monitoring are identified in Table 6.4, together with the evaluation domain with which they are commonly associated.

**Table 6.4** Common Areas of Focus for Monitoring

| Monitoring Area (example) | Focus of Monitoring (example) |
|---|---|
| The Context [Related domain: Appropriateness] | Changes to the incidence, prevalence, and nature of the issue or problem being addressed |
| | Changes in understandings about the issue or problem that have emerged over time |
| | New policies, initiatives, strategies, programs, or projects that may have an effect on the program being monitored |
| Implementation [Related domain: Effectiveness] | Delivery of activities and outputs as per the program plan |
| | Any variations taking place with reasons for these occurring |
| Management and Governance [Related domain: Efficiency] | Management and administrative arrangements (processes used during program implementation) |
| | Staffing levels and skills (available personnel with sufficient training and experience to deliver the required services) |
| | Availability and use of resources (financial and human) |
| | Stakeholder relationships (formation and maintenance of relationships needed for program results) |
| | Delivery of intended program outputs in key areas (program deliverables on time and budget) |
| Initial Program Results [Related domain: Impact] | Tracking progress toward the program's stated goal and objectives (progress in achieving what the program intended) |
| | Identifying short- to medium-term outcomes (what the program has started to achieve in key result areas) |
| | Stakeholder views as to the progress of the program |
| | Changes against the baseline (changes that have occurred over time since the program commenced) |
| Initial Program Benefits [Related domains: Impact and Sustainability] | Stakeholder feedback on program benefits achieved |
| | Evidence of increased capacity to respond to the issue or problem being addressed |

## Step 2: Develop Performance Indicators and Targets

Specification of indicators in the Monitoring Plan allows us to detail what will show or indicate progress in a specific area of program performance. Indicators demonstrate a type of change, event, or condition. In this case, the focus is on the performance area highlighted in the evaluation question. An example is the effectiveness question contained in Table 6.2, "To what extent did participants increase their knowledge of the benefits of regular school attendance?" The indicator which shows the degree to which this occurs is "Difference between participant knowledge of the benefits of regular school attendance before and after sessions attended." The indicator is not to be confused with the tool that measures levels of knowledge, which in this instance is a pre-post training survey. The target specified in relation to this area is "75% of participants report increased knowledge of the benefits of regular school attendance." Targets specify factors such as number, timing, and location of results toward which program efforts are directed. When indicators are tracked over time, they highlight progress (or not) toward a specific target. In this context, targets may therefore be regarded as the quantifiable levels of the indicators that the program wants to achieve over a given time.

Determination of indicators and targets in relation to an evaluation question will need to consider the immediate program context and also any guidance or expectations deriving from higher level organizational contexts beyond the program. The latter may include, for example, possible guidance from a funder, government department, coordinating body, or the program's own host organization regarding collection of certain kinds of information. There may be expectations that monitoring and evaluation activities will be integrated vertically and/or horizontally to provide more comprehensive data in certain results areas.

Other expectations may include use of common indicators such as those pertaining to a certain sector including recognized international indicators. Indicators commonly used in the justice sector represent one example (Vera Institute of Justice, 2003). The challenge for the program manager in this context is to accommodate requirements for coordination in data collection, while ensuring that information collection is, as much as possible, consistent with internal planning and management requirements. Methodological issues can arise where higher level indicators are taken as a given and "retrofitted" into a Monitoring and Evaluation Framework developed for a program. This contrasts with the tailored approach where indicators are generated to match specific evaluation questions and are also consistent with the program theory and the program logic.

Use of common indicators across different levels and spheres of activity are aimed at overcoming fractured uncoordinated datasets. This aspiration, however, is often controversial, which is most evident in the case of ambitious efforts to promote the use of 60 common indicators to track the Millennium Development Goals (MDGs) across developing countries (United Nations, 2013). Associated critiques identify inappropriate, top-down planning approaches and limitations with consistency and comparability of data between different contexts (Martens & Debiel, 2008).

> **Practice Example**
>
> ### Careful Selection of Performance Indicators
>
> A Monitoring and Evaluation Framework was in place for an international development program concerned with family violence prevention. The Framework, however, was used very little, with monitoring and evaluation generally regarded as weak areas of program performance. The original Framework had been designed by an outside specialist with limited involvement by program staff. At the time, staff had felt uncomfortable but not in a position to critique the Framework. It was easier to ignore its existence than to tackle it. In an attempt to reinvigorate the monitoring and evaluation area and provide a workable Framework, an evaluator was engaged. Initial examination of the Framework showed that it included over 100 performance indicators, with substantial expectations of collecting associated performance data. Both primary and secondary data were required. Primary data were to be collected through large-scale surveys, while a range of government agencies was expected to provide secondary data. It was apparent that when the Framework was designed, little attention had been given to checking the availability of secondary data or ensuring that the program had the resources to undertake large-scale surveys with subsequent data analysis. Additionally, a substantial proportion of the indicators included were geared to tracking changes in the program context, specifically in relation to demographic conditions expected to influence family violence such as local employment levels. Tracking these indicators required research data that were largely unavailable. The program had very limited capacity to undertake research of this kind.
>
> To address these issues, the evaluator worked with program staff and representatives from several partner agencies to identify the key result areas of the program and scale back performance assessment to these areas. Program

> theory and logic were developed, together with associated evaluation questions. New plans for associated monitoring and evaluation functions emphasized what was realistic and achievable. These did extend the focus of the previous Framework, which had been largely monitoring orientated. However, in contrast to the previous Framework, the overall scope of what was to be undertaken was more modest. Use of indicators was scaled back to include only those considered critical to identifying program performance. The evaluator provided advice about engaging a staff member with a specific focus on monitoring and evaluation functions and building the capacity of the program to collect and analyze data and produce required reports. The evaluator suggested reviewing the Monitoring and Evaluation Framework 12 months after implementation to establish whether its contents were realistic and achievable. An implementation plan was developed that focused on putting the Framework into operation incrementally, adding more detailed data collection and analysis over time. Starting small and building up over time, rather than creating an "overengineered" Framework in the first instance, appeared to be the best solution for this program.

## Baselines

A baseline study may be required to support assessment of specific conditions for which performance indicators have been developed. The baseline provides a means to assess change relative to the situation before program commencement. A baseline study provides an analysis using either primary or secondary data, of the situation that existed prior to the intervention, against which future progress can be assessed or comparisons can be made (Kusek & Rist, 2004). It is important that specification of performance indicators with targets based on expected changes over time are in fact developed with reference to a baseline. Despite their potential value for assessing change, baseline data may not be present or may require undertaking special studies. Such special studies may not, however, be supported due to resource constraints or there may be resistance to openly mapping preexisting situations due to their political sensitivity (Bamberger et al., 2012).

Where a baseline does not exist, there are a range of techniques that can be used to attempt to reconstruct baseline data in order to re-create the situation as it was prior to program commencement (Bamberger, 2010). These include accessing retrospective population-level data, analyzing administrative records, drawing on past project reports, undertaking retrospective studies, or conducting interviews or surveys (Bamberger et al., 2012; UNDP, 2009). If retrospectively developing a baseline, it is important to test the accuracy of the data being collected and to eliminate any possible bias that may occur in collecting information after the fact. This bias may particularly apply to retrospective surveys or stakeholder interviews where recall may be prone to inaccuracies.

Ideally, baseline studies should occur concurrently with the development of performance indicators. These studies should align directly with the indicators developed to ensure that the data are available to identify the situation as it existed prior to the program and to support the tracking of progress from the baseline at regular intervals through program monitoring.

**Debates on Use of Indicators**

While commonly applied, controversy regarding the use of performance indicators extends across a range of areas. Developing performance indicators can absorb considerable time and resources that are sometimes disproportionate to their benefits for program management. Concerns have been raised that indicators are approximations of the complete performance area they are intended to highlight. Information they generate may be inaccurate and unreliable (Perrin, 1998; Whitehouse, n.d.). For example, in the case of the community education program discussed earlier, assessment of the level of participation of the target group may be inaccurate in some contexts if it solely relies on use of an indicator relating to numbers attending. It may be critical in some contexts for community leaders to attend to provide support for an initiative and subsequent behavior change. Adding a quantitative indicator focusing on "participation levels of leaders" and on a qualitative indicator such as "views of community leaders regarding activity success and follow-on activities" would be warranted in this case.

Another area of critique is that indicators and associated targets are often selected without existing baselines to establish the level of change expected in relation to the base. This can contribute to inaccurate "guesstimates" about levels of change achieved. Additionally, there are arguments that use of performance indicators can inappropriately skew program design and implementation toward certain forms of achievement. This concern is exemplified, for example, in programs selecting participants who are more likely to contribute to the achievement of performance targets and lead to the underparticipation of more challenging and disadvantaged target group members. Finally, use of indicators has been dismissed more categorically by those who do not agree with the linear, cause-and-effect model of change upon which they are based. Rather, from a systems perspective, change is seen as dependent on multiple factors working synergistically. From this view, attributing change to a single intervention appears mistaken.

Despite the preceding critiques, considerable support remains for the use of performance indicators within evaluations and Monitoring and Evaluation

Frameworks in particular. Advocates argue that indicators are not inherently flawed but rather limited by the approaches adopted for their construction, that insufficient resources are dedicated to their development and testing, and that data collection and processing capabilities are underdeveloped. More effective use of performance indicators relies on their careful development in a spirit of consensus with key stakeholders (Poister, 2010). They should be carefully selected, tested over time, and regularly reviewed and revised (Kusek & Rist, 2004; Poister, 2010). Capabilities for processing of data generated need to be in place or otherwise developed (Hatry, 2006).

**Judicious Use of Indicators**

The approach advocated in this text is for indicators to be used carefully and judiciously. In every case, indicators should be meaningful and well-aligned to the area to be measured. It is important to define the performance area prior to the indicator and to be aware that the indicator's purpose is solely to show this area. Such an approach reduces risks of creating an "indicator-driven" performance management system where indicators appear to have an independent status, as performance areas on their own. The primary concern of monitoring is to determine what needs to be assessed to understand progress, rather than to monitor according to what data are readily available. When developing a Monitoring and Evaluation Framework, it is advisable to initially include a limited number of indicators and build them up over time, if required. Otherwise, the likelihood increases of creating an "overengineered" monitoring system that is bound to fail through being unrealistic and unachievable.

Consideration of which combination of indicators and targets is appropriate for different evaluation questions also reinforces a judicious approach. This could involve using indicators together with targets, indicators on their own with no targets, or no indicators or targets at all. There may be some evaluation questions, for instance, that are better answered through assessment of results against performance indicators and others that will be better answered through evaluation data collection and analysis. Assessing the performance of programs attempting to address complex social or cultural problems ("wicked problems") is often difficult and challenging. Change in areas such as "valuing school attendance and completion" may be subtle and long term in nature and possibly involve stepwise improvements or intergenerational dimensions. In such contexts, assessment of change may be most effectively addressed through the use of qualitative evaluation approaches. Evaluation may involve use of what are termed "indicator-free" methods, such as case studies and the Most Significant Change technique (see Chapter 7, "The Evaluation Plan"). Table 6.5 illustrates circumstances in which an indicator and target may or may not be appropriate.

**Table 6.5** Application of Performance Indicators and Targets

| Performance Indicators | Examples of Application |
|---|---|
| Indicator and target | • When a change, condition, or trend can be identified (using percentages, proportions, numbers, rates of change, ratios, levels of satisfaction, etc.) and a baseline exists to establish the situation at program commencement<br>• When there are agreed benchmarks in place for identifying optimal performance in practices, operations, compliance, and so on |
| Indicator no target | • When a change, condition, or trend can be identified but does not lend itself to quantification or identification of a particular level<br>• When the program is not expected to be sufficiently mature to show distinct changes, conditions, or trends<br>• When no baseline exists to indicate the situation prior to the program or at program commencement |
| No indicator no target | • When a learning focus is being adopted<br>• When changes, conditions, or trends are likely to be best determined through evaluative assessment based on use of multiple methods and the collection of different types of data<br>• When concepts embedded in evaluation questions require clarification and are best understood through the process of developing agreed evaluative criteria and standards (see Chapter 7, "The Evaluation Plan") |

Overall, the use of indicators can be regarded as important, but it is only one way of identifying program progress and particularly applicable in assessing implementation and initial program outcomes. In a Monitoring and Evaluation Framework, a suite of different ways of measuring performance will usually be identified. This is consistent with the view of Perrin (1998) who suggests that performance indicators should be used selectively as one aspect of a broader, more comprehensive evaluation strategy. The following provides further guidance on the judicious and effective use of indicators, with consideration of how they are selected and applied (Castro, 2011; Hatry, 2006; Kusek & Rist, 2004; McDavid et al., 2013; Perrin, 1998; Poister, 2010):

### Criteria for Selection

- Indicators have been developed and agreed upon in a participatory manner involving those affected by them and likely to use them.
- Those whose performance will be judged through use of the selected indicators are satisfied that they are appropriate measures.
- Indicators selected are meaningful, fit for purpose, and easy to understand.
- Indicators selected have a track record, have been successfully field tested, and will be regularly reviewed over time.

- Indicators selected are initially limited in number so that the monitoring plan is realistic and can be implemented, building on these over time.
- Data in relation to the indicator can be collected and quantified in a meaningful way.
- If use of the indicator involves measurement of relative change, relevant baseline data should be available.

## Application of Indicators

- Indicators should be applied when there is a need to check progress in program implementation against program plans, milestones, and targets
- Indicators should be used for planning and monitoring rather than for evaluation functions.
- A standard measure is needed that can compare changes over time or place (trend data).
- Balanced use of both quantitative and qualitative indicators is involved.

## Other Attributes

- Financial and human resources are available to allow the indicator to be applied for measurement, and the benefits of measuring using the indicator are worth the costs.
- Use of indicators is supported by a variety of different ways of measuring progress and change.

## SMART and CREAM

The acronyms *SMART* and *CREAM* represent schemas detailing the preferred qualities of performance indicators and thereby provide additional guidance to good practice. Both acronyms contain some similar criteria, although differently expressed. CREAM includes the distinctive criteria of economic (available at reasonable cost) and monitorable (amenable to independent validation). The acronym SMARTER extends SMART with the concepts of evaluate and reevaluate.

**SMART** (Castro, 2011; Department for International Development [DFID], 2006; Department of Planning and Community Development, 2013)

| | |
|---|---|
| Specific | Specific to the area of performance being assessed |
| Measurable | Based on measurable factors that can be observed, documented, and verified |

| | | |
|---|---|---|
| Achievable | Required data can be collected and capacity is available to do this | |
| Relevant | Relevant to the area of performance being assessed | |
| Time-bound | Has a clear and appropriate timeframe for assessing performance | |

**CREAM** (Kusek & Rist, 2004)

| | |
|---|---|
| Clear | Precise and unambiguous |
| Relevant | Appropriate to the subject at hand |
| Economic | Available at reasonable cost |
| Adequate | Provides a sufficient basis to assess performance |
| Monitorable | Amenable to independent validation |

### Types and Features of Indicators

Pragmatically, the selection of indicators is guided by the purpose and context in which they will be used. A basic typology of indicators highlights the different purposes and contexts to which they are applied. This involves three pairs of contrasting categories. A further distinction is specified in relation to whether the indicator is stated separately to the target (as in the approach used in this text) or together. The typology, including examples, is depicted in Table 6.6.

**Table 6.6** Indicator Types

| *Indicator Types* | *Explanation* | *Examples* |
|---|---|---|
| • Quantitative<br>• Qualitative | • Percentages, proportions, numbers, units, rates of change, ratios, and so on<br>• Satisfaction, quality, perceptions, compliance, standards, practices, and behaviors | • Proportion of intended target group members participating in the program<br>• Participant satisfaction with the program |

| Indicator Types | Explanation | Examples |
|---|---|---|
| • Process<br>• Impact | • Process indicators focus on the status of implementation and the delivery of outputs.<br>• Impact indicators focus on the achievement of outcomes and impacts. | • Process indicator: Number of community education sessions delivered<br>• Impact indicator (short-term change): Evidence of attitudinal changes following participation in sessions<br>• Impact indicator (medium-term change): Changes in behavior following participation in sessions |
| • Direct<br>• Indirect/proxy | • Direct indicators relate to the changes, conditions, or trends that are being identified.<br>• Proxy indicators are used where direct indicators are not available.<br>• Use of proxy indicators can result in inaccuracies as they attempt to measure one change as a proxy for another. | • Direct indicator: number of people from the intended target group participating (indicator for effective program targeting)<br>• Proxy indicator: number of people from the intended target group participating (indicator for motivation to change attitudes and behavior) |
| • Indicator and target separated<br>• Targets included with the indicator<br>• Note: indicators often appear separately without targets | • Indicators and targets are not included in the same statement but are presented separately.<br>• Indicators and targets incorporated into same statement | • Indicator: Percentage of people attending the community education sessions drawn from the intended target group<br>• Target: 75%<br>• Indicator with target: 75% of program participants drawn from the intended target group |

## Examples of Indicators

A selection of indicators is detailed in Table 6.7 and focuses on various levels of achievement against a results chain (program logic). Possible indicators at output, outcome, and impact levels are identified for a community education program targeted to families with children who do not attend school regularly. Indicators are not usually used for the input or activity levels. Note that for some areas being assessed, both numbers and percentages have been used as indicators. The specification of both kinds of indicators is good practice in many situations to provide information on the significance of a change or condition. Such use provides information on both raw numbers and the rate of success (or lack of success; Kusek & Rist, 2004).

**Table 6.7** Sample Indicators for a Community Education Program

| Indicator Level | Examples |
|---|---|
| Output | **Community Education**<br>• Number of community education sessions held<br>• Frequency of community education sessions delivered<br>• Number of parents from target group attending sessions<br>• Percentage of parents from target group attending sessions<br>• Gender balance of participants attending sessions<br><br>**Participating Schools**<br>• Number of schools participating in the community education program<br>• Percentage of schools participating in the community education program<br><br>**Partnership Development**<br>• Number of memorandums of understanding (MOU) or agreements (MOA) developed with partner organizations<br>• Percentage of partner organizations that have entered into MOUs or MOAs with the program |
| Outcome | **Children From Target Group**<br>• Percentage of school-age children enrolled in the first year of school<br>• Percentage of students who, during the compulsory years of schooling, have maintained at least a 70% attendance rate<br><br>**Families From Target Group**<br>• Satisfaction of parents with the knowledge gained through community education sessions delivered<br>• Percentage of parents who report greater willingness to enroll their children in school<br>• Percentage of parents who report provision of greater support for regular school attendance<br><br>**Participating Schools**<br>• Number of schools participating in the program where at least 80% of staff report increased understanding of the needs of students from the target group |

| Indicator Level | Examples |
|---|---|
| | • Number of schools participating in the program that provide additional support for students in the target group<br>**Partnerships**<br>• Numbers of partner organizations that have entered into agreements with the program that now provide supplementary support to the target group where this is required<br>**Program**<br>• Quality of community education program against agreed standards |
| Impact | • Percentage of children from target group able to complete a functional literacy/numeracy test<br>• Percentage of children from target group who complete their compulsory years of education |

## Setting of Targets

Useful targets rely on the availability of appropriate baselines to support measurement of change, as well as being realistic and acceptable to major stakeholders. Table 6.8 provides an illustration in relation to an education program targeted to children with low school attendance and completion rates and poor academic results.

Actual targets set need to be commensurate with program scope and duration and organizational capacity. Target setting requires careful consideration of the level of results to be expected from particular activities and outputs. The outcome targets specified in the Table 6.8 are all matched to the program end point, but other targets may involve shorter periods. This particularly relates to output targets, which are likely to be achieved closer to program commencement and involve shorter time frames. Targets need to be periodically reviewed and revised in line with changing circumstances, which can occur as part of a more general review and update process for the Monitoring and Evaluation Framework.

As a point of reminder, and as detailed above in Table 6.5, not all areas of performance require targets. They should be applied with discretion, and for some program areas, such those that are learning focused, they may be inappropriate. Consistent with the principles of SMART and CREAM, an indicator should be stated as precisely as possible. In some cases, however, there may be justification to set an indicator more generally. An example is that there will

**Table 6.8** Sample Indicators, Baseline, and Targets for Community Education Program

| Change, Condition, or Trend for Target Group | Indicator | Baseline (at program commencement) | Target (by end program) |
|---|---|---|---|
| Increased enrollment from children in target group in the first school year | Eligible students from target group enrolled in first year of school | 70% of eligible students from target group enrolled | 95% of eligible students from target group enrolled |
| Increased completion by students from target group of the compulsory years of education | Students from target group complete their compulsory education | 50% of students from target group complete their compulsory education | 75% of students from target group complete their compulsory education |
| Students from target group completing their compulsory education have increased numeracy and literacy | Students from target group completing their compulsory education perform at average or above-average levels for numeracy and literacy | 25% of students from target group who complete their compulsory education achieve average or above-average results in literacy and numeracy | 50% of students from target group who complete their compulsory education achieve average or above-average results in literacy and numeracy |

simply be an "increase" or "decrease" in expected results. As Van Dooren, Bouckaert, and Haligan (2010) assert, in circumstances such as these where the exact level of performance cannot be anticipated "it is better to be roughly accurate than precisely wrong" (p. 171).

A further influence on target setting is the political dimension. In organizational contexts, programs may come under pressure from funders and stakeholders to raise targets to appear to meet broader goals or commitments. Alternatively, targets may be lowered so that an organization does not appear to underperform. Targets are most appropriately set when they are achievable and realistic. Determining such targets involves program managers and evaluators in not only assessing what is practically achievable and realistic but at times negotiating between contrasting stakeholder expectations to achieve agreement as well.

### *Step 3: Identify Data Collection Processes and Tools*

As part of the process of determining the focus of monitoring and accompanying indicators and targets, attention is given to identification of sources of data. This involves consideration of whether the anticipated data are actually available to allow assessment against any possible performance indicator and whether it is feasible to collect it. The source of monitoring data is specified in the fifth column of the Monitoring Plan as identified in Table 6.2. Depending on the specific data source, this will include information on the type of data, its location, and possibly specifying tools to be used to collect it. The collection of monitoring data is often relatively straightforward and may involve accessing project records or administrative data or undertaking observations in the field. More complicated data collection tools are sometimes also used in monitoring as in the pre-post survey used in conjunction with community education sessions in the earlier example. Although in general, data collection methods are more complex and time consuming in the context of evaluation, this is not always the case. The key determinant is what is required and what is reasonable and feasible for the program to collect. A range of different data collection methods and tools is discussed in Chapter 8.

In general, when planning data collection arrangements for a program, personnel will consider what is already in place in the program and agency context, what data can be accessed from other agencies or affiliated sources, and what further processes need to be developed. As in the example in Table 6.2, some monitoring data sources are primary and others secondary to the program. Primary data collection is within the remit of the program and under its direct control. An example of primary data collection would be the design and use of attendance records. Analysis of completed records would identify actual against expected participation rates. These data would in turn allow the extent of program utilization to be determined and inform the answer to a question on the appropriateness of the program's design.

Secondary data collection, by contrast, relies on data collection systems operated by other agencies or obtained through other sources. One example of this would be analysis of school records to determine actual against expected enrollment rates in order to determine effectiveness in meeting objectives. Another example would be use of data sets, such as those provided by the OECD Program for International Student Assessment (PISA), based on a triennial survey of 15-year-old students in over 70 countries.

In the case of primary monitoring data, consideration will need to be given to database design, data storage, data management, and subsequent data analysis. What is developed needs to be commensurate with the size and scale of the program (Calley, 2011; Kettner et al., 2013). Data collection and entry is increasingly occurring through mobile technology such as use of apps on smartphones and tablets. With links to web interfaces and sophisticated software, processes for data collection, entry, and analysis can be significantly streamlined. These trends reinforce increased data collection and use of primary data, trends notable in developing and developed countries. In many contexts, pen and paper techniques persist, particularly where data collection capacity limitations are evident.

Program beneficiaries may also have varying responses to requests for data and data use depending on their background and prior experience. Beneficiaries are most likely to agree to data disclosure if the purpose is purely for monitoring and evaluation, and the data are de-identified or distinguished by a numerator rather than a person's name. Issues may arise where beneficiaries do not fully understand an informed consent process and provide a perfunctory or negative response. They may be resistant based on concerns about how the data will be used, despite assurances made. The most disadvantaged or vulnerable may be the most likely to refuse consent. If this occurs, resultant unbalanced participation will skew results. Data limitations can also apply with the use of longitudinal data sets, although recent advances in the number, capabilities, and quality of large-scale databases have increased their trustworthiness (Penuel & Means, 2011). These issues are discussed further in Chapter 8.

With secondary data, constraints may be experienced in relation to access and with the overall quality and reliability of the data. Programs may face constraints where data collection systems of other agencies are limited or where agencies are reluctant to share their data. Many government agencies are prohibited by legislation from sharing data beyond that which are normally publically available. Use of secondary data can pose a challenge in view of privacy provisions that may apply.

### *Step 4: Determine Responsibilities and Time Frames*

The final step in developing the monitoring plan is to identify responsibilities and specify timing factors for different stages of data collection and analysis. In Table 6.2, the program team is identified as responsible for the collection of primary monitoring data in areas such as participant attendance records, pre-post survey results, financial records, and partnership documentation. Similarly, program team members are responsible for secondary data collection from sources such as schools. The program team would ensure the collection and entry of data from the various sources, check data accuracy and identify data gaps, and then analyse the collected data, presenting it in tables, charts, graphs, and so on. The intervals of data collection and analysis can vary. Intervals frequently used by programs include monthly, quarterly, half yearly, annually, and at the completion of a sequence of program activities.

> **Practice Example**
>
> **Dealing With Data Gaps in Monitoring**
>
> A Monitoring and Evaluation Framework was to be developed for an established education program in a developing country context. It became clear during the scoping of the Framework that there were significant data gaps in the monitoring data available to the program. Much of the required monitoring data were either not collected or were incomplete. The evaluator worked with the program to identify key areas where accurate monitoring data could be collected. This involved development and application of a Monitoring Plan with initially limited areas of data collection. Over time, the program staff members were able to extend the areas of monitoring data collected. The program staff became clearer through involvement in the development of the Framework that they required greater levels of internal resourcing for monitoring functions and also needed to develop data management capabilities, including a program-specific database. These areas became priorities for the program going forward as staff progressively increased resources available for monitoring.

## 5. THE FUTURE OF PROGRAM MONITORING

While monitoring serves the needs of management with real-time data generated regarding a program's implementation, performance, and early results, it is limited in its utility without its accompanying partner, program evaluation, to provide a deeper analysis and give meaning to a program's performance and results over time. Monitoring and evaluation are interlinked but remain conceptually distinct and treated within separate dedicated plans in the Monitoring and Evaluation Framework. It is also essential, as advanced in this text, that there is close coordination and integration forged between the two functions in order for monitoring and evaluation to be effective.

It is possible that in future the interrelationship between monitoring and evaluation could go further with the two functions merging. Rist (2006) has suggested that in the future, evaluations could use continuous "streams of information" rather than involving stand-alone, episodic events. The functions of monitoring and evaluation certainly do connect and overlap, especially when tracking program implementation and measuring the more immediate program outcomes. The demarcation between the two functions can thus be somewhat blurred in practice. Distinguishing between the two is partially dependent on how often evaluation occurs within a program cycle and thus the extent to which it can provide the real-time data that monitoring can and the extent that routine monitoring is able to undertake some of the deeper levels of analysis of a program's results over time, including its quality and value, as provided by evaluation.

The future of monitoring is to position it within an approach that more seamlessly links planning, monitoring, and evaluation functions. In this way, both monitoring and evaluation support the use of results for program review and replanning. Over time, as this approach matures, it may result in the development of a new concept that does not use the terms *monitoring* and *evaluation* separately but rather encapsulates both in one process. It is possible that such a term could be *Planning and Monitoring Informed Evaluation* or *P&E* rather than *M&E*.

## SUMMARY CHECKLIST

- Have the evaluation questions been incorporated into the Monitoring Plan?
- Have performance indicators and targets been identified against appropriate evaluation questions?
- Has the selection of indicators and targets included in the Monitoring Plan been undertaken carefully and judiciously?
- Has the availability of information to support the performance indicators been confirmed?
- Where targets have been included, were these determined with reference to prior performance and baseline benchmarks?
- Are the targets selected realistic and achievable?
- Does monitoring draw on a range of data, not just data in relation to indicators and targets?
- Have data availability and data collection and analysis capabilities required to support the Monitoring Plan been appropriately scoped?
- Has the Monitoring Plan identified time frames and responsibilities for data collection?
- Is there a process in place to review the Monitoring Plan and its implementation?
- Overall, does the Monitoring Plan appear well designed, providing a coherent focus for the organization of monitoring activities?

## CHAPTER REVIEW QUESTIONS

1. How does a Monitoring Plan assist in answering evaluation questions?

2. What qualities would be required of indicators and targets for their effective use within a Monitoring Plan?

3. How would you assess whether the indicators and targets that you have selected are realistic and appropriate?

4. What other ways of measuring program performance would you want to include in a Monitoring Plan?

5. What kinds of monitoring data would be required to assess performance areas identified in relation to different evaluation questions?

6. What methods would you need to use in order to collect the required monitoring data?

7. What issues might arise in relation to the potential validity or reliability of these data?

8. How would you ensure that the Monitoring Plan was regularly reviewed to ensure its effective implementation?

# CHAPTER 7

# The Evaluation Plan

**Chapter 7** The Evaluation Plan

*The Evaluation Plan determines how evaluative processes will add to and complement information collected through monitoring to provide answers to evaluation questions. Evaluation is particularly focused on assessing whether the program is achieving its intended results, what works well or not and why, the program's quality and value, and the extent to which it meets the expectations of key stakeholders. Evaluation questions represent a common reference point incorporated in both the Monitoring Plan and the Evaluation Plan, these being key subsections of the Monitoring and Evaluation Framework.*

## 1. INTRODUCTION

This chapter is focused on developing the Evaluation Plan which is the format used to identify and organize evaluative processes. The Evaluation Plan summarizes and complements information collected through monitoring and then adds to this through planning for evaluation to provide answers to the evaluation questions. To aid planning for evaluation, this chapter provides background on the nature of evaluation and on key evaluation approaches and methods, building on that presented in Chapter 3. This background is intended to inform choices made regarding the specific contents of an Evaluation Plan.

The foundations for the development of the Evaluation Plan, as detailed in preceding chapters, are assumed to be in place. These include clarification of the focus of the Monitoring and Evaluation Framework and scoping its parameters, especially against stakeholder expectations, and considering budgetary factors and data availability. The following stages involve developing and gaining consensus from stakeholders regarding the program theory, program logic, and evaluation questions and preparation of a Monitoring Plan.

Both monitoring and evaluation processes, which are detailed in their respective plans, are intended to be fully articulated with each other. This connection is shown in Figure 7.1, which identifies how both monitoring and evaluation data are subject to analysis, and through a process of assessment, findings are reached that provide answers to evaluation questions. The evaluator exercises judgment in weighing the available data in order to develop a set of individual findings leading to an overall finding. Evaluation processes are highlighted as our immediate concern in this chapter.

This chapter details the different steps involved in the preparation of the Evaluation Plan, including considering the evaluation approach to be adopted and deciding on the focus of evaluation. Subsequent steps include selection of evaluation methods to collect and analyze data and determining responsibilities and timing factors.

**Figure 7.1** Evaluation and Its Role in Answering Evaluation Questions

```
      Program                                           Program
      Theory          Evaluation Questions              Logic
                   To what extent was the program
                   appropriate, effective, efficient; did it have
                   impact; and was it sustainable?

         Monitoring Data         →        Evaluation Data
              Analysis                        Analysis
                        → Synthesis ←
                             ↓
                        Evaluative
                        Judgments
                             ↓
                        Evaluative
                        Conclusions
                             ↓
                         Answering
                      Evaluation Questions
```

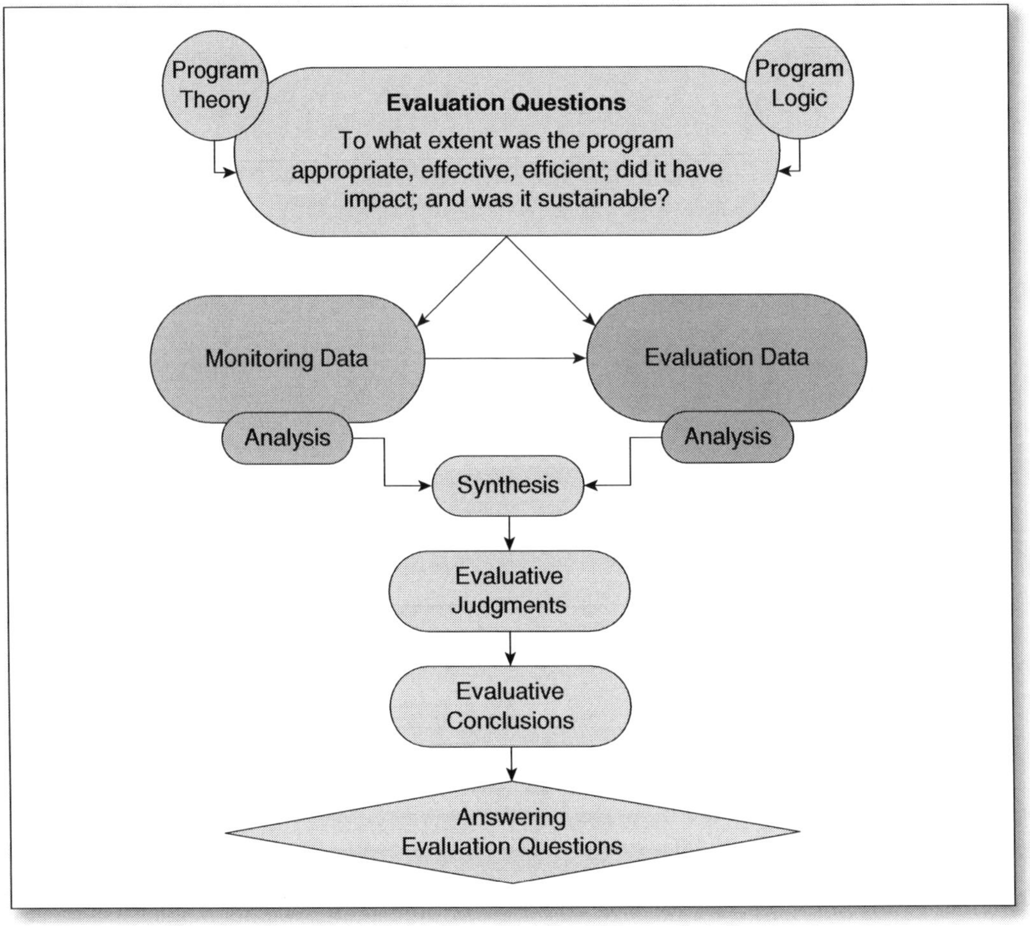

## 2. FOCUSING ON EVALUATION

The definition of evaluation as introduced in Chapter 1 is as follows:

> The planned, periodic, and systematic determination of the quality and value of a program, with summative judgment as to the achievement of a program's goals and objectives.

The process of evaluation builds on monitoring information to identify the degree to which outcomes and longer term impacts have resulted and objectives have been achieved. Evaluation identifies approaches that worked well and those that did not and reasons for success or failure and learning from both. Evaluation also undertakes broad inquiry into the processes of program implementation. The evaluation process provides a level of judgment in relation to the program overall.

In this text, five evaluation domains were introduced as areas of investigation for both monitoring and evaluation, with actual assessments made against evaluation questions under each domain as appropriate (Chapter 5). While the generic focus of monitoring and evaluation are reflected in their definitions, their precise focus will be nuanced in the context of a specific program and its Monitoring and Evaluation Framework. This will in turn be influenced by a range of guiding documentation and the views of the evaluation team and different stakeholders. Such influences will affect the relative weight given to different domains, the choice of individual questions, and the specific approach and methods used (Chapter 5). An additional influence on choice of evaluation questions and the manner in which evaluation is conducted is the understanding and preferences of stakeholders and the evaluation team in relation to different evaluation approaches. In this regard, eight broad evaluation themes and the types of thinking which they entail were introduced in Chapter 3. This chapter further expands on these themes and provides examples of specific approaches under each. The purpose here is to expand the range of options available to those selecting evaluation approaches for inclusion within a Monitoring and Evaluation Framework.

## *Quality and Value*

The above definition of evaluation includes a focus on exercising judgment in relation to a program. This judgment includes assessment of a program's quality and its value. This is consistent with the importance attributed to these areas in the many definitions of evaluation. Scriven (1991) identifies evaluation as "the process of determining the merit, worth or value of something, or the product of that process" (p. 139). There are a range of similar definitions, some of which employ related terms such as *significance*. Davidson (2005), drawing on Scriven's work, has defined evaluation as "the determination of something's quality, value or importance or the product of such a determination (e.g. a report)" (p. 240). Fitzpatrick et al. (2011) emphasize the importance of using criteria in the process of value determination. They state that evaluation is "the identification, clarification and application of defensible criteria to determine an evaluation object's value (worth or merit) in relation to those criteria" (Fitzpatrick et al., 2011, p. 7).

The key terms *quality* and *value* have been incorporated in this text, and their determination has been included as part of assessments undertaken within the effectiveness domain. In Chapter 5 ("Evaluation Questions"), effectiveness was defined as "the extent to which the program and broader stakeholder objectives were achieved, or are expected to be achieved, taking into account their relative importance. This includes an overall assessment of the quality and value of the program and the fidelity of its implementation." Headline evaluation questions are set in relation to both quality and value and require investigation and responses.

Clarification of terms is an important starting point. The use of equivalent terms provides some assistance in discerning meaning, noting that in the literature the terms *value* and *worth* and *quality* and *merit* are often used interchangeably. Further distinction and reference to the use of the terms is provided in Patton's (2008) definition of *merit* as "intrinsic" to a program and *worth* as "extrinsic" to those outside the program (p. 113). Stake and Schwandt (2006) illuminate the manner in which judgments are made of concepts such as *quality* and *value*, stating that these can be based on a combination of measurement ("quality-as-measured") or perceptions ("quality-as-experienced") (pp. 407–408). For the purposes of this text, quality and value are therefore defined as follows:

| Term | Definition |
|---|---|
| Quality | The intrinsic merit of a program in relation to meeting a stated or implied need, as determined by measurement and/or based on experience |
| Value | The extrinsic worth, significance, usefulness, or benefit of a program to its key stakeholders including funders, program partners, and intended beneficiaries |

Based on the preceding table, the following examples illustrate how the concepts of quality and value apply within a program.

### *Example of Quality*

A community education program could be said to be of high quality if its practice is evidence based, it meets related national standards, and is perceived by beneficiaries to be highly professional in orientation.

### *Example of Value*

A community education program could be said to have value if its stakeholders and beneficiaries believe it has provided benefits such as filling a service gap and producing positive outcomes and that it has been well managed and delivered.

Section 4 illustrates how criteria and standards are employed to provide a frame of reference for the determination of a program's quality and value. The use of criteria and standards allows for an informed judgment to be made. They may also be employed in relation to other questions that incorporate concepts the require determination as to what characterizes *good* so that program performance can be assessed.

## *Types of Evaluation: Formative and Summative*

Evaluation may have different roles, according to the context and need. One important distinction in roles is between formative and summative evaluation. As Scriven (1996), the originator of these terms, has emphasized, they are not necessarily mutually exclusive but assist in classifying the orientation and purpose of evaluation in a particular context. In this way, the terms may also be usefully applied within a Monitoring and Evaluation Framework. Formative evaluation is undertaken during the development or implementation of a program with the aim of providing feedback to program staff so that they are able to make any necessary adjustments. In contrast, summative evaluation is more retrospective and orientated toward making judgments about a program's performance over a significant period. Summative evaluation usually has a major concern with program results and is commonly conducted at a program's completion or at other significant junctures. This kind of evaluation is likely to support more profound decisions such as program refunding or replication of a program model.

In some contexts, formative and summative evaluation may be clearly differentiated. For example, a program team may annually conduct a formative internal evaluation (sometimes called a review) of the program with a principal purpose of informing the development of a plan for the following year. At the end of the program, a summative evaluation is also conducted by external consultants. In another context, formative and summative elements may combine. For example, a major part of a program's evaluation activity may involve six monthly stakeholder workshops that both assess progress over the prior 6-month period and also contribute to forward planning.

In general, formative and summative evaluations are complementary approaches that combine to provide a complete picture of a program. Summative evaluations build on the results of formative evaluation. As above, program personnel are more likely to be involved in formative evaluation so that they can review and change the program's direction when needed. If conducted internally, formative evaluation may also provide a context where staff and stakeholders are more ready to provide comment as to why a program is working or not and identify improvements.

The overlap between formative evaluation and program monitoring was discussed in Chapter 6 where it was noted that the differences between the two concepts lie predominantly in the regularity of the process, with monitoring being routine in nature and undertaken in real time, while evaluation is periodic with a deeper level of analysis. In addition, program evaluation, whether formative or summative, will generally produce more significant data than can be produced by performance measurement systems alone. Evaluations are able to make deeper investigations, adopt greater rigor in their inquiry, and identify unintended as well as intended positive and negative consequences (Hatry, 2013).

The summative stage of the evaluation aims to determine if the program is of quality and value in the broadest sense of the term and will often be used to inform major reports and decision as to whether and how the program should continue (Davidson, 2005). This type of evaluation is most likely to be conducted externally to ensure its objectivity and independence. The key differences between formative and summative evaluation are identified in Table 7.1.

**Table 7.1** Key Differences Between Formative and Summative Evaluation

|  | *Formative Evaluation* | *Summative Evaluation* |
| --- | --- | --- |
| Audience | Program managers and personnel | Program funders and decision makers, external stakeholders, and beneficiaries |
| Timing | At predetermined stages during a program's life | End of a program; may also occur midterm |
| Focus | Prospective, forward-thinking | Retrospective, looking back |
| Approach | Guidance provided for program improvement | Assessment of program quality, value, and results |
| Intended Outcome | Improvement in program implementation | Judgment of program quality, value, and results for decision making |

### Practice Example

#### Formative and Summative Evaluations

An evaluator worked with a national-level government department to develop a Monitoring and Evaluation Framework for a newly introduced program aimed at providing increased access to specialist mental health services

> through decentralized service delivery. The department had decided that a major focus was to be a formative evaluation conducted at a midterm point (after 18 months) and an end-of-project summative evaluation (after 3 years). Working with a team of internal stakeholders, the evaluator suggested that the evaluation questions be divided according to whether they had a formative or a summative focus. This resulted in two subsections in the Monitoring and Evaluation Plans. The formative focus was on program implementation and the identification of achievements, barriers, and challenges in launching the new initiative. Monitoring data were to be collected and analyzed to indicate the degree to which the intended program outputs had been delivered and the extent to which the program model had been implemented as envisaged, with reasons for any variations. During this initial phase, the formative focus also involved examining the governance and management of the initiative, considering how well it had been integrated within everyday departmental business. The summative evaluation was to incorporate the formative evaluation findings and build on these to focus on the results achieved with an overall judgment made as to the program's value. The department found the process of clarifying the purpose of the two scheduled evaluations to be very useful and viewed them as complementary and interconnected initiatives. The formative evaluation was undertaken internally using staff resources, while the summative evaluation involved an externally commissioned consultancy.

## 3. THE EVALUATION PLAN

This section presents and discusses the preparation of the Evaluation Plan. The format for the Evaluation Plan is different from, but also related to, that used in the Monitoring Plan. The latter was introduced in Chapter 6 and is represented in Table 7.2. The Evaluation Plan format that is shown in Table 7.3 draws on the Monitoring Plan by summarizing the approach to monitoring in relation to each evaluation question. This appears in the second column adjacent to the evaluation question. The specific focus of evaluation in relation to the evaluation question is then detailed in the third column. This shows how investigations are extended beyond that of monitoring. In the next column, the Evaluation Plan specifies the methods to be used for data collection and what type of data is to be collected. A following column provides information on how the method is implemented, which is likely to include information on the location and frequency on the use of the method. A final column identifies responsibilities and timing factors for implementation of evaluation activities.

**Table 7.2** Monitoring Plan Format

| Evaluation Questions | Focus of Monitoring | Indicators | Targets | Monitoring Data Sources | Who Is Responsible and When |
|---|---|---|---|---|---|
| Appropriateness | | | | | |
| Effectiveness | | | | | |
| Efficiency | | | | | |
| Impact | | | | | |
| Sustainability | | | | | |

**Table 7.3** Evaluation Plan Format

| Evaluation Questions | Summary of Monitoring | Focus of Evaluation | Evaluation Method | Method Implementation | Who Is Responsible and When |
|---|---|---|---|---|---|
| Appropriateness | | | | | |
| Effectiveness | | | | | |
| Efficiency | | | | | |
| Impact | | | | | |
| Sustainability | | | | | |

To further appreciate the complementarity between the two plans, the Monitoring Plan developed for the community education case study, as discussed in Chapter 6 is re-presented in Table 7.4. This is followed by the Evaluation Plan for the case study (Table 7.5). The examples illustrate one question per domain only. The hypothetical case study used here, which appears throughout the text, is of a community education program targeted to families where children are unable to maintain a regular regime of school attendance.

**Table 7.4** Monitoring Plan for Community Education Program

| Evaluation Questions | Focus of Monitoring | Indicators | Targets | Monitoring Data Sources | Who Is Responsible and When |
|---|---|---|---|---|---|
| **Appropriateness** To what extent did the target group participate in the program? | Participant characteristics | Number of participants from target group Gender balance of participants | 75% participation by target group Minimum 40% male participants | Attendance records | Staff member X Monthly |
| **Effectiveness** To what extent did participants increase their knowledge of the benefits of regular school attendance? | Changes in knowledge following participation in sessions | Difference between participant knowledge of the benefits of regular school attendance before and after sessions attended | 75% of participants report increased knowledge of the benefits of regular school attendance | Pre-post survey | Staff member Y Following completion of series of sessions |
| **Efficiency** Was the cost of delivering the program within budget? | Costs against budget and areas where overruns or underspends occurred | Performance against budget | Less than 10% variation between actual costs and budget | Financial records | Staff member X Monthly |
| **Impact** To what extent was there an increase in regular school attendance in the community? | Trends in school attendance in local schools | Changes in school attendance patterns from the baseline | No target | Administrative data from schools | Staff member Y Six monthly |
| **Sustainability** Was there evidence of ongoing benefits beyond the program? | Development of partnership agreements for continued initiatives | Number and type of partnership agreements developed | No target | Records of partnership meetings Partnership documentation | Staff member X Annually |

**Table 7.5** Evaluation Plan for Community Education Program

| Evaluation Questions | Summary of Monitoring | Focus of Evaluation | Evaluation Method | Method Implementation | Who Is Responsible | When |
|---|---|---|---|---|---|---|
| **Appropriateness** To what extent did the target group participate in the program? | Participant characteristics:<br>• Number coming from target group<br>• Gender balance | Motivation for participation by target group | Case studies | Five case studies per region | Program team | Following completion of series of sessions |
| | | Response to program by target group | Case studies | Five case studies per region | Program team | Following completion of series of sessions |
| | | | Participant interviews | Twelve interviews per region | Evaluation team | Mid- and end program |
| | | Reasons for nonparticipation by target group members | Community forums | Two community forums per region | Evaluation team | Mid- and end program |
| **Effectiveness** To what extent did participants increase their knowledge of the benefits of regular school attendance? | Changes in knowledge from participation in sessions:<br>• Results of pre-post testing | Areas of success and lack of success and reasons for both | Case studies | Five case studies per region | Program team | Following completion of series of session |
| | | | Participant interviews | Twelve interviews per region | Evaluation team | Mid- and end program |
| | | | Community forums | Two community forums per region | Evaluation team | Mid- and end program |

| Evaluation Questions | Summary of Monitoring | Focus of Evaluation | Evaluation Method | Method Implementation | Who Is Responsible | When |
|---|---|---|---|---|---|---|
| | | | Interviews with session facilitators | All facilitators | Program team | Following completion of series of sessions |
| **Efficiency** Was the cost of delivering the program within budget? | Costs against budget and areas where overruns or underspends occurred | Identification of reasons for budget variations | Interviews with program funders and managers | Three stakeholder interviews | Program team | Six monthly |
| | | Adequacy of budget in meeting program requirements | Staff forum | Staff meeting | Evaluation team | Mid- and end program |
| **Impact** To what extent was there an increase in regular school attendance in the community? | Changes in school attendance patterns from baseline | Identification of changes attributable to program as well as any unintended results | Contribution analysis workshop | Special workshop | Evaluation team | End program |
| **Sustainability** Was there evidence of ongoing benefits beyond the program? | Development of partnership agreements for continued initiatives | Viability of partnerships developed | Partnership workshop | Key partner workshop | Evaluation team | End program |
| | | Commitment of community stakeholders to ongoing participation | Key stakeholder interviews | Twelve stakeholder interviews per region | Evaluation team | End program |

## 4. STEPS INVOLVED IN DEVELOPING THE EVALUATION PLAN

Development of the Evaluation Plan involves determining which evaluation data will be collected and the methodology that will be employed to do so. The focus is on answering the evaluation questions, with data collection complementing that gained through monitoring. The completion of the Monitoring Plan and the Evaluation Plan provides a foundation in that all data to be collected are specified. Subsequent arrangements for data collection, management, and analysis are considered in Chapter 8.

Table 7.6 details the steps to be undertaken in developing the Evaluation Plan.

**Table 7.6** Steps Involved in Developing an Evaluation Plan

*Stage 3: Develop Monitoring and Evaluation Plans*
*The Evaluation Plan*

| *Steps* | | |
|---|---|---|
| 1 | Determine overall evaluation approach | • Select the most suitable approach and methods to be adopted from the range of options available.<br>• Consider evaluation principles and standards for guidance.<br>• Identify ethical issues that may emerge during the implementation of the Monitoring and Evaluation Framework. |
| 2 | Identify evaluation questions requiring criteria and standards | • Identify evaluation questions that require criteria and standards.<br>• Identify the headline evaluation questions that relate to determining a program's quality and value.<br>• Develop criteria for determining quality and value.<br>• Develop standards against the criteria.<br>• Develop an evaluation rubric that includes the criteria and standards. |
| 3 | Identify focus of evaluation and methods for each question | • Consider types of evaluative processes that will augment monitoring conducted in order to answer the evaluation question.<br>• With reference to each evaluation question, identify the focus of evaluation and the types of evaluation methods to be used.<br>• Identify the parameters of selected methods, specifying the breadth and depth of the inquiry to be conducted. |

| | Steps | |
|---|---|---|
| 4 | Determine responsibilities and time frames | • Determine responsibilities for undertaking evaluation activities and whether they will be internally or externally conducted.<br>• Identify agreed intervals and time frames for implementation of the Evaluation Plan. |
| 5 | Review the monitoring and evaluation plans | • Reassess capacity for data collection across the Framework in its entirety including routine monitoring and periodic evaluation. |

## Step 1: Determine Overall Evaluation Approach

The field of evaluation is characterized by a range of approaches. As outlined in Chapter 3, these reflect an array of different worldviews, values, and different orientations to evaluation and social research that are held by theorists and practitioners. Whether articulated or not, the types of choices made in constructing a particular Monitoring and Evaluation Framework or design for an evaluation typically reflect an underlying commitment to a certain approach or possibly several approaches.

This text has already incorporated and reflects a commitment to one major approach, which is the program theory–driven approach that can be applied to a program to identify the links and connections between a program's actions and its intended results. While program theory and program logic are now widely accepted constructs for use in evaluation, this is not universally the case. Some of the hesitations expressed by theorists in the use of theory-based approaches in evaluation were outlined in Chapter 2. The use of program theory and program logic in this text is consistent with an approach that seeks to link and integrate monitoring and evaluation with planning. This involves a commitment to ongoing refinement of planning and management through reflecting on the results of monitoring and evaluation.

Beyond the suggested use of program theory and program logic, those involved in developing a Monitoring and Evaluation Framework are advised to consider the range of broad evaluation approaches and also the specific theories and methods available in order to identify those which may be applicable and useful for the Evaluation Plan. Any efforts made to classify these evaluation approaches and theories will inevitably be subject to debate. Alkin (2013) has classified evaluation theorists, using the analogy of a tree, assigning them variously to the branches of *use, methods,* and *valuing. Use* brings together a set of pragmatic approaches that emphasize stakeholder engagement to optimize the use by these stakeholders of evaluation results. *Methods* theories are those which emphasize maximizing program effectiveness through measurement of results and commonly use quantitative methods. In contrast, *valuing* theories have a focus on interpreting multiple values and perspectives and commonly use qualitative methods. Mertens and Wilson (2012) have extended Alkin's classification system by adding an extra branch within the tree metaphor. They posit the addition of a fourth paradigm, that being social justice, which incorporates transformative approaches that promote human rights, social justice, and inclusion.

Incorporating and extending on the preceding classification system, this text has elaborated on the range of approaches and theories that are commonly found in the evaluation field. Eight broad headings for different kinds of evaluation approaches were introduced in Chapter 3. These are reproduced in Table 7.7 with examples of specific, defined theories that are grouped under the headings. The list is not intended to be comprehensive or definitive but rather to illustrate considerations involved in selecting an evaluation approach or approaches to guide a Monitoring and Evaluation Framework.

Efforts to group or categorize evaluation approaches and theories represent a contested area with a history of significant debate. In recent times, debates have shifted away from arguing the technical merits of one approach or theory over another and rather have looked for middle ground and accommodation between approaches. From this perspective, Mertens and Wilson (2012) have suggested that the various approaches in evaluation should be regarded as intermingling rather than discretely classified. In practice, it is likely that a program evaluation design will draw elements from the different evaluation approaches detailed earlier rather than adhering to one approach in its entirety. Adopting a mixed-methods approach to designing an evaluation is thus becoming a more prominent and accepted practice (Creswell & Plano Clark, 2007; Mertens & Wilson, 2012).

While some of the theories adopt specific methodologies that involve sequential steps to be followed, these theories are still often applied to only some aspects of evaluation activities. Additionally, the specific approach adopted is likely to be affected by the professional orientation of the evaluators or clients, who may derive their perspectives from a range of different professional and disciplinary backgrounds and apply their foundation theories, philosophies, and values to program evaluation.

While it cannot be expected that the different epistemological and philosophical bases of different evaluation approaches can be reconciled, pragmatism represents an appropriate orientation in the selection of an evaluation approach

**Table 7.7** Broad Approaches and Specific Theories in Evaluation

| Approach | Theories | Summary | Reference (example) |
|---|---|---|---|
| Participation | Participatory Evaluation | Where evaluations are required to forge a working partnership and collaboration between evaluators, stakeholders, and program beneficiaries in order to increase evaluation ownership and use | Cousins and Earl, 1995 |
| | Empowerment Evaluation | Where evaluation supports stakeholders and program beneficiaries, through evaluation capacity-building efforts, to evaluate their own programs in order for them to achieve self-determination and empowerment | Fetterman and Wandersman, 2005 |
| Stakeholder | Contribution Analysis | Where assessment of causality and the contribution of a program to change is required; achieved by engaging stakeholders in the development of a contribution story | Mayne, 2001 |
| | Outcome Mapping | Where evaluation needs to focus on the role that program partners play in the achievement of collective results, to support plausible assessments of a program's contribution to the results achieved | Earl, Carden, and Smutylo, 2001 |
| | Most Significant Change | Recognition of the value of personal stories of change selected on the basis of their significance; can illustrate program effects in areas that are otherwise difficult to measure by quantitative means | Dart and Davies, 2003 |
| Social Justice | Transformative Evaluation | Where an emphasis on diversity and inclusion is required in a social justice/human rights approach and where evaluation needs to make a contribution to social justice and social transformation by informing social policies and guiding program development | Mertens, 2009 |
| | Reflective Evaluation | Where the evaluation fosters transformational learning processes in order to facilitate organizational change | Preskill and Torres, 1999 |
| Program Theory Driven | Program Theory | Identification of the causal processes required to achieve desired program outcomes and the underlying assumptions or key conditions under which they are believed to operate | Chen, 2005; Donaldson, 2007 |

*(Continued)*

**Table 7.7** (Continued)

| Approach | Theories | Summary | Reference (example) |
|---|---|---|---|
| Learning | Realist Evaluation | Where evaluation needs to consider what works, for whom, in what circumstances; this is done by uncovering the interaction between the three variables of context, mechanisms, and outcomes | Pawson and Tilley, 1997 |
| | Appreciative Inquiry | Focus on an organization, program, and/or its beneficiaries and their strengths rather than weaknesses; useful when the approach required is to learn from peak experiences and past successes in order to design and implement future actions | Preskill and Catsambas, 2006 |
| | Case Study Research | In-depth focus adopted on a person, community, context, or project to explore and illustrate program implementation and its effects | Simons, 2009 |
| Use | Utilization Focused Evaluation | Where the evaluation develops strategies to increase the use of evaluation knowledge generated by the primary intended users | Patton, 2012 |
| Systems | Developmental Evaluation | Development of innovative, adaptive approaches for evaluation for use in complex and dynamic contexts where the evaluator adds value by becoming part of the program team, fully participating in decisions as to how to evaluate | Patton, 2011 |
| Experimental | Controlled Experiment | An experimental or quasi-experimental approach using randomized or nonrandomized selection of the program or context that receives the treatment, and the program or context that does not, comparing the effects | Shandish, Cook, and Campbell, 2002 |
| Cost Benefit | Social Return on Investment | Where the evaluation needs to attempt to reveal the economic value generated by social and environmental program outcomes | SROI Network http://www.thesroinetwork.org/ |

for a Monitoring and Evaluation Framework. From this perspective, an approach and specific methods are selected on the basis of what will work in providing information to answer identified evaluation questions. This view is consistent with that of Donaldson (2007), who has argued that a focus on program theory and evaluation questions provides a higher focus for evaluation and enables a "method neutral" orientation. The evaluator is thereby freed from the dictates of method choice and will select an approach and exercise discretion on the basis of feasibility and whether specific methods provide credible evidence in answering a particular evaluation question.

**Selection of Methods**

Methods for data collection may be either qualitative or quantitative in orientation and extend to the use of mixed methods where methods are combined (Creswell, 2015; Creswell & Plano Clark, 2007; Mertens & Wilson, 2012). Mixed-methods approaches use both quantitative and qualitative data sets, integrating the two and forming interpretations based on their combined strengths (Creswell, 2015). The quantitative and qualitative options available in evaluation mirror those of classic social science research, with quantitative data being depicted as "closed-ended" and qualitative data as "open-ended" (Creswell, 2015, p. 2). In mixed-method approaches, the rationale for combining quantitative and qualitative perspectives and associated data is explicit and not accidental. Commonly, it draws on the advantages of combining the breadth that quantitative data provide in relation to a situation or issue, with qualitative data offering depth. Any method can be operationalized through the development of specific data collection tools, sometimes also referred to as data collection instruments. For example, conducting a survey would be the identified method, while the tool would entail development of a questionnaire instrument that includes a range of structured questions laid out in a questionnaire format.

Examples drawn from the range of qualitative and quantitative methods available to evaluation are summarized in Table 7.8.

The use of mixed-methods approaches, also known as methodological pluralism (Asif, 2013), is a means to overcome limitations in the use of qualitative or quantitative methods alone. The use of mixed-methods approaches also represents a means to transcend the long-standing paradigm war operating between these two contrasting orientations. Quantitative methods have been classified as positivist or postpositivist as they rely on developing understandings through scientific methods. Qualitative methods have been termed constructionist as they develop understandings through interpreting the meanings that people

**Table 7.8** Data Collection Methods for Evaluation

|  | Qualitative Methods | Quantitative Methods |
|---|---|---|
| **Methods for Individuals** | • Semistructured interviews<br>• Case studies<br>• Stories of change<br>• Narrative studies<br>• Phenomenological studies | • Pre-post or before-after rankings<br>• Longitudinal tracking<br>• Testing<br>• Observation (with checklists) |
| **Methods for Groups** | • Social and economic assessments<br>• Case studies<br>• Focus groups<br>• Observation<br>• Collection of visual records<br>• Workshops<br>• Community meetings<br>• Stakeholder analysis<br>• Ethnographic studies<br>• Narrative studies<br>• Network analysis<br>• Community scorecards<br>• Participatory Rapid Appraisal (PRA)<br>• Participatory Learning and Action (PLA) | • Social and economic assessments<br>• Onetime questionnaires<br>• Interval or panel questionnaires<br>• Experimental designs<br>• Quasi-experimental designs<br>• Cost-benefit analysis |
| **Other Methods** | • Document reviews<br>• Literature reviews | |

generate of their realities. Where possible, the use of both quantitative and qualitative methods for evaluation data collection and analysis will provide a more holistic view of a specific context and offset the limitations of using either data set on its own. The validity and reliability of data are further reinforced through use of data triangulation, which involves drawing on different methods, sources, and stakeholder perspectives. The use of mixed methods may involve the collection of qualitative and quantitative data in sequence or concurrently. Where the predominant paradigm used is quantitative, qualitative data can add value in identifying how program implementation and outcomes were affected by contextual socioeconomic, political, environmental, or cultural factors. Conversely, where the predominant paradigm used is qualitative, quantitative data enable a sample or specific situation to be compared against the wider population or setting (Bamberger et al., 2012).

> **Practice Example**
>
> **Building Capacity for Use of Evaluation Methodologies**
>
> A Monitoring and Evaluation Framework was developed for a program providing services to families experiencing poverty and social isolation in a rural community. During the scoping of the Framework, program personnel expressed an interest in using an Appreciative Inquiry approach that would promote a strengths-based rather than a deficits-based orientation. They also expressed an interest in the construction of in-depth case studies as a way of further examining the types of changes experienced by families involved with the program. Program personnel, however, had limited training in these approaches and methods or in their application. The program personnel thus contracted external evaluators to provide in-house training in these two areas so that they would feel confident in applying them to their internal evaluation activities. Following the training, some personnel went on to undertake more advanced training in these areas. Over time, program personnel were able to build up their expertise in the use of Appreciative Inquiry and case-study methods and regularly applied them to their internal evaluations. The program subsequently developed a positive reputation among partner organizations for their work in this area, sharing their experiences with their professional networks.

## Evaluation Principles and Standards

Within a field characterized by a multiplicity of evaluation approaches and different contexts for evaluation practice, efforts to promote common high standards of professional practice are notable. A range of principles and standards identified by professional evaluation associations and organizations that commission or coordinate evaluations provide guidance to common features of an acceptable, professional approach to be included in a Monitoring and Evaluation Framework.

The American Evaluation Association's (2004) *Guiding Principles for Evaluators* are a key source of reference and identify five guiding principles:

**Systematic inquiry:** Evaluators conduct systematic, data-based inquiries with high technical standards and with approaches and methods that are well discussed and communicated.

**Competence:** Evaluators provide competent performance to stakeholders through holding and updating their knowledge and skills, operating within their area of training and competence, and demonstrating cultural competence.

**Integrity/honesty:** Evaluators display honesty and integrity in their own behavior and attempt to ensure the honesty and integrity of the entire evaluation process.

**Respect for people:** Evaluators respect the security, dignity, and self-worth of respondents, program participants, clients, and other evaluation stakeholders.

**Responsibility for general and public welfare:** Evaluators articulate and take into account the diversity of general and public interests and values that may be related to the evaluation.

The Program Evaluation Standards (Yarbrough, Shulha, Hopson, & Caruthers, 2011) were developed in the United States under the guidance of the Joint Committee on Standards for Educational Evaluation. A total of 30 standards appear under five main headings:

**Utility:** Standards intended to increase the usefulness of evaluation processes and products in ways that meet the needs of program stakeholders

**Feasibility:** Standards intended to increase the effectiveness and efficiency of evaluation

**Propriety:** Standards that promote proper, fair, legal, right, and just evaluative practice

**Accuracy:** Standards intended to promote truthful and dependable evaluation findings and products, especially those that provide interpretations and judgments about quality

**Evaluation Accountability:** Standards that encourage appropriate documentation and examination of evaluation quality through meta-evaluation.

While some variation exists between different guidelines on evaluation principles and standards, these typically cover both the process and products of evaluation, with most also covering ethical dimensions. Some guidelines represent more generic guides to practice (e.g., AES, 2013; Canadian Evaluation Society, 1996), while others pertain to specific contexts, particularly international development (e.g., African Evaluation Association, 2006; OECD DAC, 1991, 2010).

The importance of independence and objectivity is frequently emphasized in practice guidelines for evaluation, a concern amplified in the often politicized environments in which evaluation operates. Similarly, the need for *credibility* of evaluation is often accentuated, a term which is used to encompass a range of different concepts such as accuracy, fairness, believability, honesty, balance, defensibility, validity, reliability, justifiability, impartiality, and lack of bias (Markiewicz, 2008).

The terms *independence* and *objectivity* are often used interchangeably to depict the process of adopting an autonomous and impartial position in the conduct of an evaluation. They are distinct but inextricably linked concepts. Independence generally refers to the evaluator being awarded the freedom to conduct the evaluation without undue control being exerted by the commissioners of the evaluation, the organization delivering the program, or program delivery personnel. Objectivity refers to the evaluator's capacity to undertake unbiased and objective assessments and form conclusions during the evaluation (Markiewicz, 2008). These concepts have relevance to the development of Monitoring and Evaluation Frameworks where credibility is important and achieved in part by ensuring the Framework operates without pressure to determine particular outcomes and allows for unbiased evaluative conclusions to be drawn. Another important ethical consideration is protecting privacy, including maintenance of confidentiality and use of informed consent processes.

## *Step 2: Identify Evaluation Questions Requiring Criteria and Standards*

The use of criteria and standards provides a means to compare evaluation findings against a pre-identified reference point. This reference point allows for an informed judgment to be made about the relative degree to which a particular situation or condition can be deemed to have merit or otherwise. Criteria and standards need to be employed to assist in answering some but not all evaluation questions. Questions that require judgments about relative degree of success (Fitzpatrick et al., 2011) and that also involve aspects of performance requiring definition, interpretation, or specification, will benefit from use of criteria and standards.

Criteria can be regarded as "aspects of an evaluand [the object being evaluated] that define whether it is good or bad and whether it is valuable or not valuable" (Davidson, 2005, p. 239). A question requiring criteria would be, "To what extent could the community education program be regarded as being of good quality?" Examples of criteria of success include that the program is evidence based, that the program is culturally appropriate, and that it conforms to relevant practice standards such as those that come from a professional association. Standards would be set for each criteria and are "the level of performance expected on each criterion" (Fitzpatrick et al., 2011, p. 332). For the program being evidence based, a relevant standard would be that it is based on a good practice literature. Similarly, for it being culturally appropriate, a standard might be that it is designed and operating according to culturally appropriate principles. Standards may typically be identified for different levels of performance against the criteria such as *excellent*, *good*, *acceptable*, and *poor*. Scales with different numbers of categories, either even or odd in number, may be used.

In what Scriven (1980, 1981, 2007) identifies as the "logic of evaluation," criteria and standards have a prominent role in determining a program's quality and value. This logic is summarized by Fournier (1995) as involving four steps where criteria of merit are initially developed, followed by the construction of standards (p. 16). Performance is then measured for each criteria compared to the agreed set standards. Finally, results are integrated into judgments to determine the merit or worth of the evaluand. Davidson (2005), in expanding on this formulation, identifies how criteria and standards, when formulated and agreed to, are placed in a matrix called an "evaluation rubric." A rubric is used when there are two or more standards and supports assessment against these standards.

Criteria and standards may be derived from a range of sources, including interaction with stakeholders, literature reviews and research, professional standards, expert opinion, and the evaluator's own judgment (Fitzpatrick et al., 2011). Drawing from different sources can serve to overcome challenges traditionally faced by evaluators in answering questions that involve interpreting and defining concepts such as *quality*. What is meant by quality can be regarded in an arbitrary manner, is often contested, and is never fully representable (Stake & Schwandt, 2006). Making a determination of a program's quality can be based on a combination of measurement (quality-as-measured) or perceptions (quality-as-experienced). Identifying criteria and standards for specific questions should be undertaken as part of the development of the Monitoring and Evaluation Framework and preferably in a participatory manner with stakeholders so that there is early agreement as to what constitutes different levels of program performance.

To illustrate the development of criteria and standards and the use of a rubric, two evaluation questions involving the determination of quality and value respectively have been identified and drawn from the community education case study. The questions are based on the notion used in this text that quality is an intrinsic attribute of a program and that value is an extrinsic attribute as discerned by program stakeholders.

| Quality | To what extent could the community education program be regarded as being of good quality? |
|---|---|
| Value | To what degree can the community education program be assessed as being of value to its key stakeholders and beneficiaries? |

A rubric for quality is presented in Table 7.9 and for value in Table 7.10.

**Table 7.9** Criteria and Standards for Assessing Program Quality

| *Evaluation Question:* To what extent could the community education program be regarded as being of good quality? | | | |
|---|---|---|---|
| *Evaluation Rubric* | | | |
| *Standards* | | | |
| *Excellent Performance* | *Good Performance* | *Adequate Performance* | *Poor Performance* |
| *Criterion 1: Community Education Program is Evidence Based* | | | |
| Program significantly developed based on good practice literature | Program mostly developed based on good practice literature | Program adequately developed based on good practice literature | Program is not based on good practice literature |
| *Criterion 2: Community Education Program is Culturally Appropriate* | | | |
| Program extremely well designed and operating according to culturally appropriate principles | Program well designed and operating according to culturally appropriate principles | Program adequately designed and operating according to culturally appropriate principles | Program not adequately designed or operating according to culturally appropriate principles |
| *Criterion 3: Community Education Program Meets Professional Association Standards* | | | |
| Program exceeds professional association standards for community education | Program largely meets professional association standards for community education | Program just meets professional association standards for community education | Program does not meet professional association standards for community education |

For identifying criteria for evaluation questions pertaining to a program's value, the concept of "value-for-whom" may be usefully applied. Perceptions of what represents value are likely to vary between stakeholder groups. For some stakeholders, an assessment of the worth of the results achieved by the program may provide an agreed criterion for assessing value. For other stakeholders, value may include examination of whether the program met a need and filled a service gap. Other stakeholders may be interested in defining value through processes used rather than results generated. The latter may be represented by notions such as whether the program was successfully implemented, partnerships and alliances were formed, and community engagement was undertaken. An example of the different definitions of value that may be established for different stakeholder groups is represented in Figure 7.2. The example involves the notional use of three stakeholder groups, which are beneficiaries, funders, and program personnel. Only one possible criterion is presented for each group.

**Figure 7.2** Criteria for Assessing Program Value to Beneficiaries, Funders, and Program Personnel

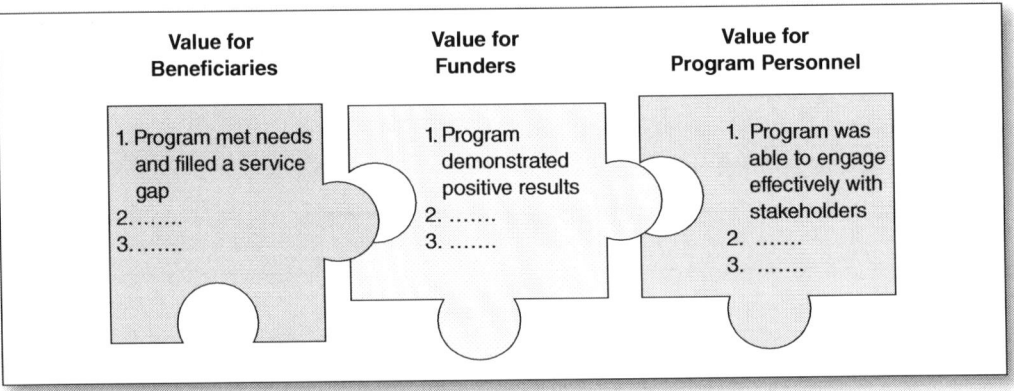

In practice, different perceptions of value held by different stakeholder groups are identified, debated, and moderated during the process of developing criteria and standards with the aim of reaching consensus. The process of developing a rubric can assist with the definition and subsequent assessment of agreed criteria and standards of value. Table 7.10 presents examples of criteria relating to aspects of value pertaining to the community education case study. These criteria are indicative of those which may be identified by different stakeholder groups.

Subsequent stages in design and implementation of the evaluative activities will make use of rubrics, where developed. The preparation of data collection tools will need to refer to any related rubric to ensure that necessary information is available, while in the process of data analysis the same rubric will serve as a reference point to guide assessments (King, McKegg, Oakden, & Wehipeihana, 2013). Chapter 8 considers further how data are collected, managed, and analyzed in order identify the answers to the evaluation questions.

**Table 7.10** Criteria and Standards for Assessing Program Value to Beneficiaries, Funders, and Program Personnel

| Evaluation question: To what degree can the community education program be assessed as being of value to its key stakeholders and beneficiaries? | | | |
|---|---|---|---|
| *Evaluation Rubric* | | | |
| *Standards* | | | |
| *Excellent Performance* | *Good Performance* | *Adequate Performance* | *Poor Performance* |
| *Criterion 1: Program Met Needs and Filled a Service Gap* | | | |
| Program significantly developed on the basis of needs assessment and identification of service gaps | Program mostly developed on the basis of needs assessment and identification of service gaps | Program adequately developed on the basis of needs assessment and identification of service gaps | Program not based on needs assessment or identification of service gaps |
| *Criterion 2: Program Demonstrated Positive Results* | | | |
| Evidence of significant positive outcomes achieved in priority areas | Evidence of mostly positive outcomes achieved in priority areas | Evidence of adequate outcomes achieved in priority areas | Program has not produced positive outcomes in priority areas |
| *Criterion 3: Program Design was Able to Engage Effectively With Stakeholders* | | | |
| Key stakeholders significantly engaged in program design, implementation, and evaluation | Key stakeholders mostly engaged in program design, implementation, and evaluation | Key stakeholders adequately engaged in some program functions including design, implementation, and evaluation | Key stakeholders not successfully engaged in program functions |

## Step 3: Identify Focus of Evaluation and Methods for Each Question

Following the preparatory steps, our attention turns to the manner in which evaluation will contribute to answering the evaluation questions and specifically to completion of the Evaluation Plan (Table 7.3). In the Evaluation Plan, a summary is first made of the focus of monitoring, followed by identification of the related focus of the evaluation. In general, while monitoring will let us know *what* is happening, evaluation will provide a more complete understanding, illuminating the dimensions of *why* and *how*. To illustrate this point, the community education case study has been used together with an example of an appropriateness question: "To what extent did the target group participate in the program?" Table 7.11 presents the relevant parts of the Evaluation Plan and shows how for this specific evaluation question, the focus of monitoring is summarized and reproduced from the Monitoring Plan followed by identification of the focus of evaluation, specification of evaluation methods to be used, and their implementation. In the example presented next, the column "Summary of Monitoring," highlights the *what* of participant characteristics (who actually participated), while the following column, "Focus of Evaluation" emphasizes factors relating to *why* people responded or did not respond to the program and *how* they reacted to the program.

**Table 7.11** Section of Evaluation Plan

| Evaluation Question | Summary of Monitoring | Focus of Evaluation | Evaluation Methods | Method Implementation |
|---|---|---|---|---|
| **Appropriateness** To what extent did the target group participate in the program? | Participant characteristics:<br>• Number participating from target group<br>• Gender balance | • Motivation for participation by target group<br>• Response to program by target group<br>• Reasons for nonparticipation by target group members | • Case studies<br>• Participant interviews<br>• Community forums | For each region<br>• Five case studies<br>• Twelve interviews<br>• Two community forums |

Once the focus of the evaluation has been clarified, the next step is to identify which evaluation methods are best suited to provide appropriate and robust data. As discussed in Step 1, a wide range of methodological options are available in the field of evaluation, including quantitative and qualitative methods, mixed methods, and method-specific approaches. The approach adopted in this text is pragmatic in using methods selectively to best suit the approach required for establishing the answer to the particular evaluation question being posed.

The notion of "causal inference," as detailed by Davidson (2005, p. 72) can also usefully inform the selection of evaluation methods. Methods need to provide data that allow the evaluator to draw conclusions, based on what is identified as a reasonable causal connection between the program actions and its results. For example, mixed methods are likely to be appropriate to apply to an evaluation question such as "To what extent did the program motivate people to change their behavior?" In this case, program participants can be directly asked about the extent that the community education program motivated them to change their behavior. Other stakeholders, including program deliverers, program facilitators, and school teachers, can also be asked to comment on the degree of causality that they perceive between the program and assumed effects. This involves qualitative methods for data collection such as focus groups, interviews, workshops, case studies, community forums, and simple quantification of responses. These methods range in their level of intensity and scope of contact with people. Case studies are an example of a method that usually involves relatively more intense contact with a relatively smaller number of people. Participant interviews exemplify medium intensity qualitative methods, while community forums usually involve less intense contact with larger numbers of target group members.

For the evaluation question "Were outcomes for those schools operating the community education program better compared to those that did not?" quantitative methodologies may be better suited for establishing causality. These could include comparison and analysis of the enrollment, participation, and completion rates between schools. The methodology would involve comparisons being made across schools in similar contexts, schools with similar sociodemographic characteristics, and involving similar time frames or with adjustments made for differences.

Evaluation methods may also be selected on the basis of pragmatic considerations such as resources available to the evaluation activities, access to data, time constraints, and political influences (Bamberger et al., 2012). A balance should be maintained in accommodating such factors but without compromising the credibility and defensibility of the evaluation. Ethical factors also need to be considered.

Once the evaluation method has been identified, a further column in the Evaluation Plan requires details on method implementation. This involves itemizing the range and respective numbers of different data collection processes that will take place (e.g., two case studies in each of four districts). Details of representativeness are also included. This involves identifying stakeholder groups such as parents, teachers, and community members and sampling approaches for each method. The latter involves determining how many stakeholders should be included in the use of different methods in order to gain a strong enough picture of trends. Affirmative sampling may be used to ensure sufficient participation from small and possibly marginalized stakeholder groups. Issues of representativeness and sampling are discussed in greater detail in Chapter 8.

Consideration of method implementation is an important step for work planning and use of resources in terms of timing, costs, and required staffing. This process includes scoping the proposed evaluation methodology against the available budget to ensure that it is realistic and achievable.

## Step 4: Determine Responsibilities and Time Frame

In this step, consideration is given to who is responsible for implementing the Evaluation Plan and at what stages data collection should ideally occur. A key demarcation and decision point relates to the use of internal versus external personnel for evaluation functions. In Table 7.5, there is a division of responsibilities depicted between the program team and the external evaluation team with both groups collecting different kinds of evaluation data at different times. Whether evaluation data are best collected through internal evaluation activities or through an externally commissioned evaluation, or a combination of both, is a point of contention (Conley-Tyler, 2005; Le Menestrel, Walahoski, & Mielke, 2014). Some of the strengths and limitations of internal and external evaluation approaches are summarized in Table 7.12.

**Table 7.12** Internal Versus External Evaluation

| Role | Strengths | Limitations |
|---|---|---|
| **Internal Evaluator** | • Familiar with program and context<br>• May be more economical if able to undertake tasks in a reasonable time frame considering other work commitments<br>• Available in real time<br>• More likely to link findings to program development and decision making<br>• May be in a better position to disseminate results<br>• Being involved in evaluation builds evaluation capacity in the organization | • Not as objective or independent, may be "captured" by the program<br>• May not have sufficient skills and experience to undertake evaluative roles<br>• May have conflicting work priorities and find it difficult to make time for evaluation<br>• Stakeholders may be guarded in what they say to program staff<br>• May be hesitant to "rock the boat" with challenging findings and recommendations |
| **External Evaluator** | • More objective and independent<br>• Specialist evaluation skills and experience<br>• Can devote concentrated time to evaluation activities<br>• May elicit more honest information from stakeholders<br>• May be more prepared to make bold or challenging recommendations | • Not as familiar with the program or its context<br>• More costly per hour, overall costs dependent on efficiency with which tasks are completed<br>• Not as available on a day-to-day basis<br>• Not as able to drive the use of evaluation findings for decision making<br>• Limited control over how results are disseminated<br>• May not build evaluation capacity |

Personnel considering whether to undertake internal or external evaluations should be cognizant of the strengths and limitations of each approach. For an evaluation that requires a higher level of skill and experience and where objectivity and independence are paramount, an externally commissioned evaluation may be more suitable. Conversely, where the evaluation requires real-time data to derive lessons that inform program development, internal evaluation may be more suited. Where the intention is to build evaluation capacity within the organization, a partnership arrangement between internal and external evaluators may be most appropriate. This model addresses the internal-external dichotomy by using external evaluators for their independence and objectivity and internal evaluators and stakeholders for their content knowledge and ownership of the program and its results (Le Menestrel et al., 2014).

If using an internal evaluation approach, it is important that the roles, responsibilities, and tasks of different personnel involved within the program or organization are specified and understood. Many plans fall short when staff members are not clear of their roles in implementing a Monitoring and Evaluation Framework. Roles may include taking responsibility for collection of different sets of data, its analysis, and the reporting of findings. If staff members involved with collecting and analyzing data have been involved in the development of the Monitoring and Evaluation Framework, they will be better prepared for, and engaged with, its implementation.

The intervals at which evaluation data collection and analysis occur vary, with common intervals being monthly, quarterly, half yearly, annually, mid-program, and the end of program. The determination of data collection and analysis intervals will be influenced by the nature of evaluation activities involved and by related reporting requirements. The latter may extend from more limited progress and activity reports, through to mid-program formative evaluation reports and end-of-program summative evaluation reports.

Data collection and management strategies are discussed further in the following chapter. As discussed in Chapter 3, an available option is to implement the Monitoring Plan and Evaluation Plan incrementally, in a staged manner. If this style of implementation is used, the relevant timing arrangements should be incorporated in the final column of the Evaluation Plan.

## *Step 5: Review the Monitoring and Evaluation Plans*

As a final step, both the Monitoring Plan and the Evaluation Plan should be reviewed together in terms of scope and resource requirements and checks made against staff and funding availability, as well as demands on key stakeholders involved in the process. With both plans developed, this step follows up

**Table 7.13** Integrated Monitoring and Evaluation Plan Format

| Evaluation Questions | Focus of Monitoring | Indicators and Targets | Monitoring Data Sources | Who and When | Focus of Evaluation | Evaluation Methods | Method Implementation | Who and When |
|---|---|---|---|---|---|---|---|---|
| Appropriateness | | | | | | | | |
| Effectiveness | | | | | | | | |
| Efficiency | | | | | | | | |
| Impact | | | | | | | | |
| Sustainability | | | | | | | | |

on the initial scoping of the Monitoring and Evaluation Framework that was undertaken, as discussed in Chapter 3. In general, it can be expected that a number of iterations of the Monitoring Plan and the Evaluation Plan will be required before there is general agreement by all involved stakeholders that the plans are realistic in view of the available data, timing issues, budget, and other resources at hand.

It is possible to integrate the Monitoring Plan and the Evaluation Plan into one combined format. This is demonstrated in Table 7.13. Such a format has advantages in terms of drawing together details of monitoring and evaluation processes for respective questions. However, it may also be difficult to depict the level of detail required across one page resulting in an unwieldy document.

## SUMMARY CHECKLIST

- Have the evaluation questions been incorporated into the Evaluation Plan?
- For each evaluation question, is it clear how evaluation will be used as a complement to monitoring to provide an answer?
- Have an overall evaluation approach and specific methodologies been selected that will best answer the evaluation questions?
- Have evaluation questions requiring criteria and standards been identified? If so, has a process for the development of criteria and standards been established?
- Have the planned evaluation activities been scoped in relation to available funds, staffing, and timelines?
- Are the focus and scope of evaluative activities in accord with stakeholder expectations?
- Are evaluative activities planned to occur at both the formative and summative stages and possibly at other intervals during program implementation?
- Has data availability for the conduct of evaluative activities been adequately scoped?
- Have the different kinds of data collection tools that will need to be developed been clearly identified (questionnaires, interview guides, etc.)?
- Have capacity requirements been clearly considered in relation to the use of the range of methods and tools specified?
- Have appropriate approaches to sampling in data collection been considered?
- Have any risks or ethical issues that may arise in implementing evaluation activities been identified together with potential responses?

- Has the mode of evaluation activities been considered in relation to whether they are conducted internally, externally, or possibly a mixture of both?
- Is the Evaluation Plan well articulated with the Monitoring Plan?
- Overall, does the Evaluation Plan appear well designed, providing a coherent focus for the organization of evaluation activities?

## CHAPTER REVIEW QUESTIONS

1. How does an Evaluation Plan assist in answering evaluation questions?
2. How would you scope the Evaluation Plan against available resources?
3. Are there particular evaluation approaches and methodologies that you consider may be appropriate for the envisaged evaluation activities?
4. Is capacity available to apply these approaches and methodologies, or would it need to be developed or externally sourced?
5. How would you ensure these approaches and methods fit the context and interests of stakeholders?
6. How would you go about developing criteria and standards for specific evaluation questions, and who would you involve in the process?
7. Would the overall orientation in evaluation data collection be qualitative, quantitative, or mixed methods? Why?
8. What kinds of data collection tools would need to be developed, and how would you ensure there was capacity to use these tools?
9. Would you need to use sampling during data collection, and if so, how would you approach this task?
10. What ethical issues may arise during data collection? How would these be managed?
11. How would you decide at what intervals during a program's life cycle to undertake evaluation activities?
12. Would you undertake evaluation activities internally using program or other personnel, externally using consultants, or use a mix between the two approaches? What do you see as the relative advantages and disadvantages of each approach?

# CHAPTER 8

# Collecting, Managing, Analyzing, and Synthesizing Data to Reach Evaluative Conclusions

*Significant* products of the monitoring and evaluation process are sound evaluative judgments and subsequently identified evaluative conclusions. Their development relies, in the first instance, on the establishment of the building blocks of program theory and logic and evaluation questions, followed by the development of effective plans for monitoring and evaluation. Once developed, a further set of preconditions comes to attention, which is the focus of this chapter. These are planning for the collection of quality data, arrangements to promote the effective management and storage of these data, and their subsequent analysis and synthesis using an appropriate approach.

Specifically, this chapter covers the development of a Data Collection Plan to guide the collection of monitoring and evaluation data, incorporating an appropriate approach to sampling as required. It also covers the development of a Data Management Plan to guide arrangements for entering, storing, managing, and analyzing collected data, with particular reference to monitoring data stored in a program's database. Finally, the chapter provides guidance on integrating and synthesizing monitoring and evaluation data to form evaluative judgments and reaching evaluative conclusions against each question and for the program as a whole

## 1. INTRODUCTION TO DATA PROCESSES THAT SUPPORT SOUND CONCLUSIONS

While considerable effort may be undertaken in determining evaluation questions and identifying an approach to monitoring and evaluation processes, this will have little benefit without a sound approach to data collection, management, and analysis (Kettner et al., 2013). For this reason, further consideration and planning are required to build on aspects related to data included in the Monitoring Plan and the Evaluation Plan. These two plans, discussed in Chapters 6 and 7 respectively, identify the different data sources and methods that will be employed for data collection in order to answer the evaluation questions. Consideration is now given to determining how this initial planning for data collection is put into operation while also addressing important technical concerns.

The purpose of this section of the Monitoring and Evaluation Framework is to ensure that high quality data are first obtained (data collection), appropriately managed and stored (data management and analysis), and appropriately integrated (data synthesis) to support sound evaluative judgments and conclusions. Subsequent steps including identifying learning and recommendations and undertaking reporting and communications functions are considered in Chapter 9, "Learning, Reporting and Dissemination Strategies."

## Chapter 8 Collecting, Managing, Analyzing, and Synthesizing Data

This chapter provides guidance on the development of two plans, one for data collection and the other for data management. It also presents associated guidance for data analysis, synthesis, forming evaluative judgments, and the identification of evaluative conclusions. The relationship of these functions to other aspects of the Monitoring and Evaluation Framework is illustrated in Figure 8.1.

Prior to discussing the development of specific plans and guidance for data collection and management, it is important to consider the broader organizational context that will influence arrangements made for handling data and their effectiveness. It is assumed that in most cases a program is not operating in isolation and will either use or be influenced by the manner in which data are handled in its host organization. A second broader issue considered here derives from our concern with ensuring that data are of high quality. Any

**Figure 8.1** Planning for Data Collection, Management, Analysis, and Synthesis to Reach Conclusions

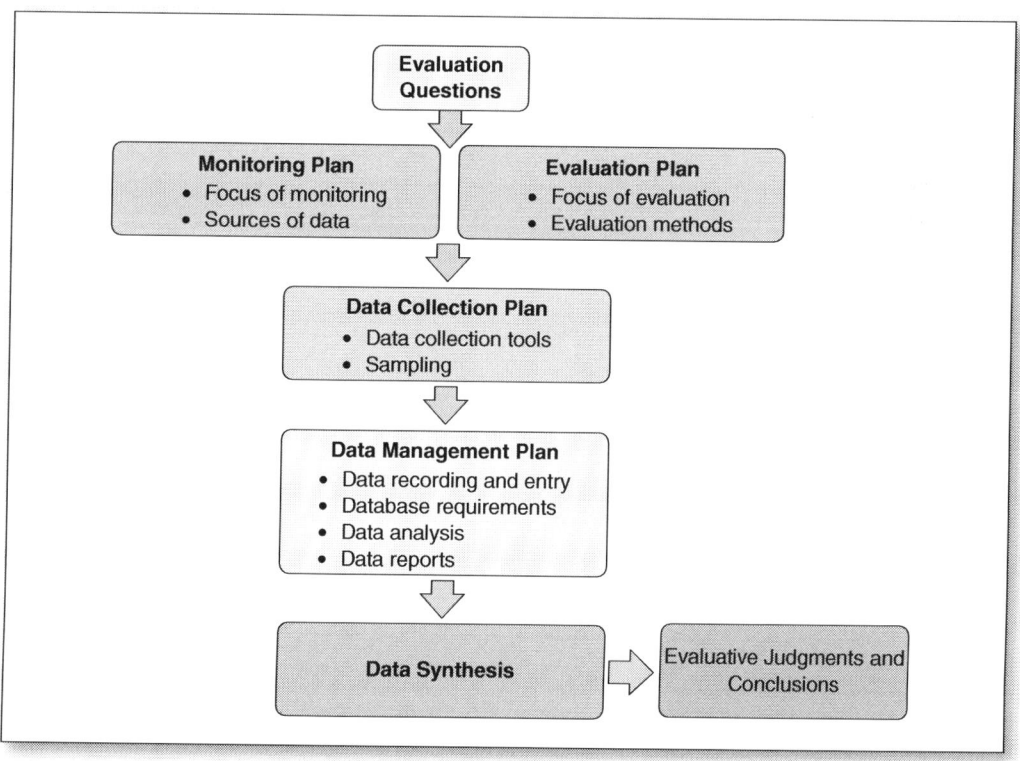

arrangements for data collection, management, and analysis need to be based on an understanding of the distinguishing features of quality data and how such quality can be promoted.

## 2. ORGANIZATIONAL CONTEXT FOR DATA COLLECTION, MANAGEMENT, AND ANALYSIS

Organizations vary considerably in terms of their level of need and capacity for data collection, management, and analysis functions. Some organizations have a range of needs to handle and process data in relation to clients, customers, employees, and so on and may have an established management information system (MIS). Handling of data for monitoring and evaluation functions may already be integrated within these systems or represent a dedicated subsystem and be supported by information technology (IT) professionals.

The preceding can represent an ideal situation from which there is considerable variance. Where there is a degree of integration with organizational MIS functions, this may only relate to monitoring functions. Evaluation functions and their products, such as lessons learned and evaluative conclusions, are often poorly integrated. Frequently, monitoring and evaluation of a specific program and associated data systems operate in isolation from other organizational MIS functions. This may reflect a disjuncture between monitoring and evaluation and management decision making in the organization (Van Dooren et al., 2010) and possibly other related issues. The latter can include a lack of mainstreaming of the program, limits in capacity, geographical isolation, and differences in data type and use compared to that with which the organization is accustomed. Many organizations have inadequate information systems or lack the ability to extract required data from those systems. Information systems may be underused due to factors such as lack of staff awareness and capacity and lack of system maintenance (Laudon & Laudon, 2012; Preskill & Torres, 1999).

For those developing a Monitoring and Evaluation Framework, and providing associated guidance for handling data generated through monitoring and evaluation, planning and negotiating access to organizational MIS and IT resources can be challenging. Such challenges may be managerial and technical in nature. While it is not expected that staff responsible for evaluation will have high-level skills in the technical aspects of data management, familiarity with systems and approaches will be an asset in this context. Engagement of specialist services to design databases and integrate with other information systems is often warranted, especially for programs operating in relative isolation.

An important principle in designing approaches to handling data associated with monitoring and evaluation is to commence planning and implementation at an early stage. This avoids a common mistake of addressing arrangements for data as an afterthought once a program and other monitoring and evaluation processes have begun. In this context, the quality and availability of data are likely to be negatively affected (Kettner et al., 2013).

Building support from organizational leadership and ownership by managers and data users are other means to promote effective data systems (Chen, 2005; Morra Imas, & Rist, 2009). Ownership of data systems is facilitated when leaders or champions prioritize data collection, management, and analysis as vital elements of management practice. Such a perspective affirms the role of data and their products in supporting organizational accountability, facilitating learning, and contributing to program improvement. As a consequence, emphasis is placed on performance data that are entered in a timely and accurate manner, analyzed appropriately, and the results then shared and reported (Kusek & Rist, 2004; McDavid et al., 2013). A further strategy to increase commitment from leadership and program personnel is to use a participatory approach (as outlined in Chapter 3) and advocate for their involvement in the development of the Monitoring and Evaluation Framework (Chen, 2005).

Building the capacity of staff for handling data, regular review of how data are handled, and promoting use of data will further reinforce the development of effective data systems. Specific strategies in this area include the following:

## Staff Capacity

- Provide personnel with training and support to develop data collection tools and assist in identifying database requirements.
- Ensure that the personnel who use data collection tools fully understand related procedures and protocols, including any factors likely to impact on data validity or reliability or cause potential harm to respondents.
- Ensure that a database is in place and sufficiently well developed to facilitate ready data entry and analysis with capacity to generate the requisite data reports.
- Train and support personnel to enter the data correctly and encourage them to do this in a timely way to increase data accuracy.
- Train and support personnel to read and understand data reports, to integrate and synthesize monitoring and evaluation data, and, where appropriate and applicable to the context, to translate such data into judgments of program performance and progress.

### Review

- Regularly review data collection and management processes and the functionality of the database to ensure that they are operating effectively and efficiently, and implement any modification required to enhance their operation.

### Promoting Data Use

- Ensure that data generated and synthesized are captured in regular reporting processes that identify and disseminate conclusions reached and recommendations made. Reporting should be augmented with opportunities for team meetings and stakeholder discussions to reflect on implications for program design and operations (as discussed further in Chapter 9).

---

**Practice Example**

#### Building Capacity for Data Collection

An evaluator worked with a national program to develop a Monitoring and Evaluation Framework for a program working with Indigenous communities. Only limited performance data had previously been collected, and there was similarly limited prior assessment of the program's implementation or its results. During initial scoping of the Framework, it was apparent that the program's field officers who were involved in the delivery of the program to urban, regional, and remote communities would be indispensable to data collection. They worked directly in the program target areas and had a close connection with local Indigenous communities. Previously, the field officers had received little training in data collection and data entry systems. Several field officers were subsequently involved in determining the scope of the Framework, identifying the evaluation questions, and generating the Monitoring Plan and Evaluation Plan. New arrangements for data collection were then rolled out. This involved collection of quantitative and qualitative data on field work activities, processes, and immediate results. Field officers were trained in data collection, associated formats, and the use of a customized database. In addition to a range of activity and process related data, field

> officers were trained to complete a journal to enter their practice experience. The journal entries enabled the scope of monitoring to be considerably broadened and also to introduce evaluative elements in relation to what was working, or not, and why. The input of field officers into the design of the Framework provided a reality test as to what data were practical and achievable to collect. Field officers were committed to the timely collection of valid and reliable data and keen to demonstrate the program's contributions and achievements but needed the skills and tools to do so. As a result of the program developing its data collection capability, it was better positioned to produce useful reports that could be disseminated within the department and more widely to program partners and interested stakeholders. This also potentially increased the degree of work satisfaction of field officers who felt that their perspectives on program performance were valued and listened to. In many cases, they were also able to demonstrate, and have verified, that they were contributing to positive results for their communities.

## 3. DATA QUALITY

It may appear self-evident that instruments used for data collection, such as surveys, should focus on the area of planned assessment, and that data collected should be correct and reasonable. Actually advancing these ends is complex and the subject of considerable discussion, particularly in literature on research methodology and also in the evaluation literature (Mertens & Wilson, 2012). Concerns with validity and reliability are particularly prominent in discussions of the quality of monitoring and evaluation data

The notion of validity is connected with that of measurement and is particularly associated with quantitative methods. A data collection instrument is considered to be valid when it actually measures what it intends to. Qualitative researchers may substitute the related term *credibility* instead of *validity*, reflecting their concern with the nature of engagement between the evaluator and the subject and how data are interpreted. Data *reliability* refers to whether the data collected are consistent over time and the results are repeatable. Qualitative researchers are less concerned with consistency of measurement as they have an expectation of adapting methods to changing circumstances. Instead, they tend to refer to the related notion of *dependability* and are particularly concerned with whether qualitative data are recorded accurately and appropriately (McDavid et al., 2013; Mertens & Wilson, 2012). Reliability is considered as a precondition for data validity (McDavid et al., 2013).

A range of approaches are available and well established in disciplines such as education and psychology to test validity in quantitative approaches to data collection. These include testing constructs involved in data collection instruments for alignment with what the program actually covers and with the expected behaviors of subjects. The credibility of data collection using qualitative approaches may be reinforced using methods such as ensuring that sufficient trust and insight are developed into a particular context, observations are made at different times of day, and debriefing is undertaken with a fellow researcher. Such methods are well documented in disciplines such as anthropology and sociology.

Planning for data collection, management, and analysis as part of a Monitoring and Evaluation Framework can promote data validity and reliability. Data validity is increased through data triangulation involving the use of different sources and types of data. In this manner, inconsistencies found in one data source may be offset by the other. In the same manner, undertaking repeated data collection over time is likely to balance out one-off aberrations. Data triangulation is supported through use of a mixed-methods approach and may involve, for example, speaking to a range of different people to gain different perspectives (Bamberger et al., 2012). The validity and reliability of data collection are also enhanced through attention to sampling, with sampling approaches carefully selected and justified.

To increase data validity within the data management process, quality controls and checks should be in place to detect data inaccuracies or missing data. Checks can be undertaken with respondents, either individually or in a group, in relation to accuracy as well as the credibility of interpretations drawn from the data. Internal and peer review processes may also be used (Bamberger et al., 2012). Furthermore, strategies should be in place to ensure that those who interpret the data do so with independence and objectivity. This involves checking that generalizations and evaluative judgments are clearly and explicitly supported by available data (Bamberger et al., 2012; Markiewicz, 2008). The term *objectivity* needs to be treated with care and is used here to refer to the impartial use of various forms of data. In a broader sense, the term has become contested as it can be used in a value-laden manner indicating a preference for scientific-based evaluation approaches over other approaches.

In cases where inaccurate or incomplete data are encountered, it is important to make appropriate disclosures to avoid misinterpretations and incorrect judgments. All evaluative judgments drawn need to be corroborated by sufficient supporting evidence. Additional constraints sometimes encountered that diminish capacity for drawing credible judgments include limited budgets and restricted time frames for evaluation and political, organizational, and administrative influences (Bamberger et al., 2012). Issues of credible evaluation reporting are discussed further in Chapter 9.

Data quality in collection, management, and analysis functions can be enhanced through acknowledgment and adherence to standards set by evaluation societies. Ethical codes, practice guidelines, and practice standards can provide a form of quality assurance for the Monitoring and Evaluation Framework (Markiewicz, 2008). Guidance is available on interpretation and promotion of important principles including accuracy and credibility; honesty, integrity, and fairness; validity and reliability; and avoidance of conflicts of interest (McDavid et al., 2013).

## 4. STEPS INVOLVED IN DATA COLLECTION, MANAGEMENT, ANALYSIS, AND SYNTHESIS

This section details the key steps involved in the preparation of a Data Collection Plan and a Data Management Plan. The two plans are followed by guidance on data synthesis and an approach to making evaluative judgments in order to reach evaluative conclusions. The areas of guidance provided in Steps 3 and 4, however, are more likely to be applicable to programs intending to undertake internal program evaluations, where program team members will become responsible for data synthesis that leads to the formulation of evaluative judgments and conclusions. If it is intended that the evaluation component is undertaken through external consultancy, then it is more likely that the program will follow Steps 1 and 2 and develop Data Collection and Data Management Plans and undertake a preliminary level of data analysis, but that the external evaluation team will be responsible for overall data synthesis and the progression to evaluative judgments, conclusions, and recommendations. In taking account of how many of the following steps identified are incorporated into the Monitoring and Evaluation Framework, the program needs to determine how far it intends to proceed with evaluation activities internally versus commissioning external evaluation projects.

**Table 8.1** Steps Involved in Data Collection, Management, Analysis, and Synthesis

| *Stage 4: Data Collection, Management, Analysis, and Synthesis* | | |
|---|---|---|
| *Steps* | | |
| 1 | Develop Data Collection Plan | • Confirm data needs for implementation of the Monitoring Plan and the Evaluation Plan.<br>• Determine which data are already collected by the program.<br>• Identify additional types of data collection methods to be used.<br>• Identify the focus of each method, sampling approaches, implementation requirements, and any potential ethical issues.<br>• Determine specifications for the development of data collection tools. |
| 2 | Develop Data Management Plan | • Identify the range of data to be managed.<br>• Identify requirements for database systems.<br>• Determine how data analysis will be undertaken.<br>• Consider required data reports and their contents.<br>• Consider and plan for the development of staff capacity for data management.<br>• Plan for regular reviews of the data system. |
| 3 | Consider approach to data synthesis | • Consider how monitoring and evaluation data will be integrated and who will be responsible for undertaking data synthesis.<br>• Consider how synthesized data will be used to assess performance against indicators and targets, and against criteria and standards, and determine who will be responsible for undertaking such synthesis. |
| 4 | Consider approach to making evaluative judgments and reaching evaluative conclusions | • Consider how synthesized data can be used to form evaluative judgments and who will be responsible for undertaking this.<br>• Consider how evaluative judgments made translate to the identification of evaluative conclusions.<br>• Ensure that the range of evaluative conclusions developed can lead to an overall conclusion in relation to the program. |

### *Step 1: Develop Data Collection Plan*

The first step in developing a Data Collection Plan involves confirming data requirements and processes for data collection related to the Monitoring Plan and the Evaluation Plan. Both the Monitoring Plan and the Evaluation Plan will have identified the different data requirements and collection methods to be used for monitoring and evaluation functions, respectively. Confirmation of data requirements is followed by a review of existing data available to the organization or program, with identification of additional data to be collected that is not already available.

The quantity and quality of available existing data will be in part dependent on the state of development of the program and its host organization. New programs located in new organizational contexts may need to start the process of data collection from first principles and build their data capability. New programs located in mature organizations may be able to leverage some existing data from the organization but may also need to build data capability that is specifically related to the program. Mature programs located in mature organizations may have a wealth of existing data to draw from but may still require it to be adapted to the program context or to be further developed.

In the Data Collection Plan, details of the design and use of different data collection methods are elaborated. This covers the purpose and focus of the method; sampling arrangements for selection of respondents; guidance to implementation of the method, including timing factors; potential ethical issues that may arise in relation to use of the method; and other arrangements required to put the method into operation, such as development of data collection tools and instruments with their associated documentation.

Chapters 6 and 7 have outlined a range of methods that could be selected and subsequently included in the Monitoring Plan and the Evaluation Plan. These selected methods are further elaborated in the Data Collection Plan. For ease of reference, some of the most frequently used qualitative and quantitative methods are summarized in Figure 8.2.

At a minimum, a Data Collection Plan will provide guidance as to the development of methods and sampling approaches to be incorporated. Beyond this, completed data collection tools (e.g., survey instruments, workshop plans, semi-structured interview guides, focus group guides) and further details of the sampling process (including sampling frames and sampling method) are often attached as appendices to the Monitoring and Evaluation Framework. Whether fully developed tools are included as part of the Monitoring and Evaluation Framework will depend on the specific nature of the program and its requirements. The need for early development of complete tools and details of sampling may be reinforced where ethics approval is required for implementation of evaluation activities. An ethics committee may request their submission to ensure that there are no potential risks or harms associated with their application. Development of a complete set of data collection tools as part of Monitoring and Evaluation Framework can also reduce the risks of delays in implementation due to lack of continuity, turnover of program personnel, and other organizational factors.

**Figure 8.2** Types of Data Collection Methods

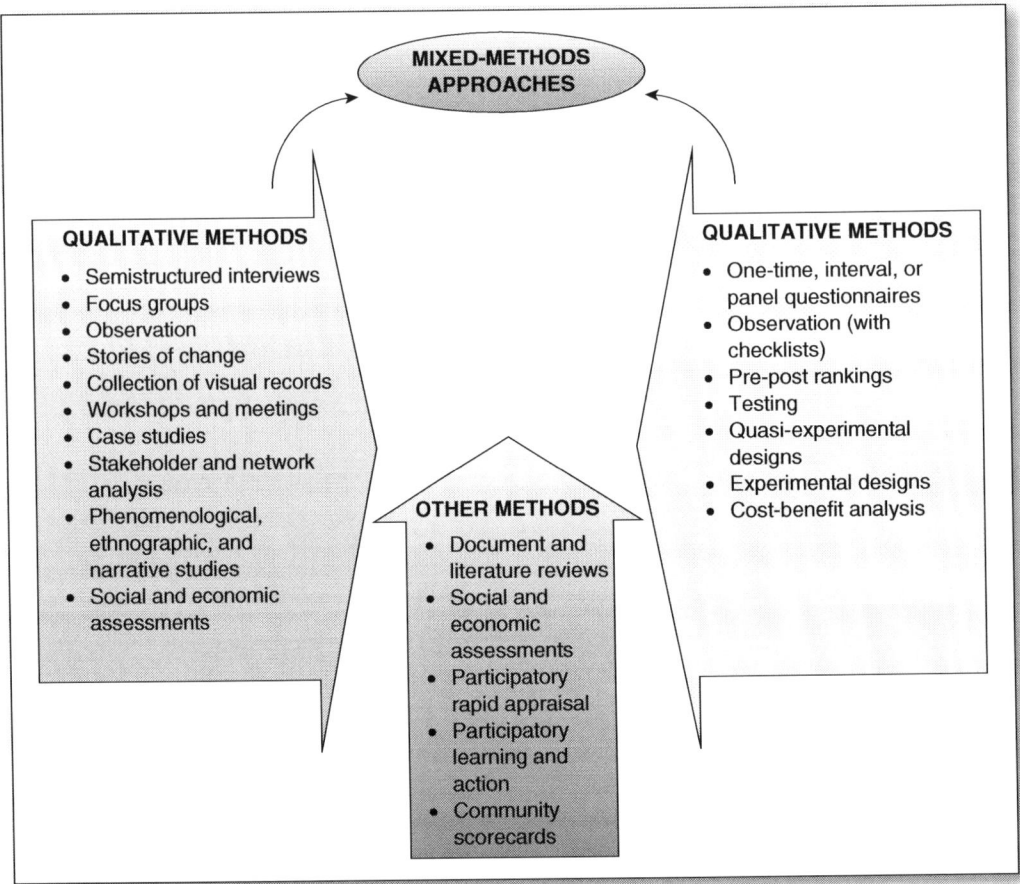

The Data Collection Plan illustrated in Table 8.2 presents three selected examples of data collection methods involved with the community education case study used in this text. These are pre-post surveys, case studies, and semistructured stakeholder interviews. The Data Collection Plan format can be extended to include each individual method specified in the Monitoring and Evaluation Framework.

As stated earlier, appendices relevant to specific methods identified in the Data Collection Plan may include the following items:

- Fully developed data collection tools (e.g., survey instrument)
- Further details of sampling approaches adopted for the different types of data collection tools including sampling frames and sampling method

**Table 8.2** Data Collection Plan: Example

| | Pre-Post Survey | Case Studies | Semistructured Stakeholder Interviews |
|---|---|---|---|
| Purpose | • To identify the extent to which program participants increased their knowledge of the benefits of regular school attendance | • To illustrate and explore program participant experiences of participating in program | • To identify perspectives of allied services in relation to collaborative relationships and service partnerships |
| Focus | • New knowledge acquired regarding<br>  ○ Benefits of regular school attendance<br>  ○ Consequences of nonattendance<br>  ○ Strategies to support school attendance and overcome barriers | • Motivation for participation<br>• Response to program<br>• Areas of success/lack of success in increasing knowledge, changing attitudes, and motivating behavior change<br>• Reasons for success/lack of success | • Strength of stakeholder relationships<br>• Areas where collaboration could be improved |
| Sampling | • Aim to include as many participants as possible in pre-post survey<br>• Participants will self-select whether to participate or not | • Purposive sampling stratified to ensure a cross section of participants with overrepresentation of the most disadvantaged families<br>• Aim to include 5% of total participants | • Purposive sampling stratified to ensure a cross section of services with overrepresentation of those located in remote regions<br>• Aim to include 25% of services |
| Implementation | • Administer to participants just before and immediately after their participation in sessions | • Case studies to take place within 3 months of participants completing program | • Semistructured interviews to take place at 6 month intervals |

*(Continued)*

**Table 8.2** (Continued)

| | Pre-Post Survey | Case Studies | Semistructured Stakeholder Interviews |
|---|---|---|---|
| Potential Ethical Issues | <ul><li>Privacy and confidentiality of data collected</li><li>Informed consent so respondents know how data will be used and how their identities will be protected</li><li>Implications if respondents are not literate</li><li>Implications if respondents have limited English language proficiency</li><li>Implications if respondents have limited education</li><li>Implications if respondents have a disability</li></ul> | <ul><li>Privacy and confidentiality of data collected</li><li>Informed consent so respondents know how data will be used and how their identities will be protected</li><li>Process used to offer financial or other forms of appreciation for participation and time spent in data collection</li><li>Potential issues with disclosures that reveal either illegal behavior or emotional concerns that may require professional follow-up or referral</li></ul> | <ul><li>Privacy and confidentiality of data collected</li><li>Informed consent (where applicable) so respondents know how data will be used and how their identities will be protected</li></ul> |
| Requiring Development | <ul><li>Survey instrument</li><li>Introductory letters</li><li>Informed consent forms</li><li>Database for entry of results</li><li>Processes for generating data reports</li></ul> | <ul><li>Case study guides</li><li>Introductory letters</li><li>Informed consent forms</li><li>Sampling approach</li><li>Format for writing up case studies</li></ul> | <ul><li>Semistructured interview guides</li><li>Introductory letters</li><li>Informed consent forms (where required)</li><li>Sampling approach</li><li>Format for writing up interviews</li></ul> |

- Introductory letters required to explain the purpose of the data collection and how the data collected will be used and confidentiality and privacy protected
- Informed consent forms for use with program beneficiaries and other stakeholders, as relevant
- Protocols for managing any risks associated with data collection
- Ethical approval for implementation of evaluation activities where this is required and has been obtained

Unless a data collection method covers all members of the relevant population group, a sampling approach will need to be specified in the Data Collection Plan. Sampling is based on knowledge of a particular population, representing all the people or items with the characteristics that an evaluation wishes to explore or understand. From the population, a subset is specified with consideration of a range of factors. The rationale and precision with which this subset is determined is important to the accuracy of results. Sample populations, including their size and other characteristics, can be determined through either probability sampling involving random selection or nonprobability sampling where subsets are selected according to specific assumptions. Within these two categories, there are a number of different types of sampling methods. These are detailed in Table 8.3. Nonprobability sampling may be informed by the views of evaluation stakeholders as to what size sample would be credible given the type of evaluation activity being conducted and the nature of the respondents who are likely to be involved (Fitzpatrick et al., 2011).

Purposive sampling is frequently employed in evaluation practice, particularly where the population to be sampled is very small, and random sampling is therefore not considered appropriate (Bamberger et al., 2012). Many qualitative methods, such as case studies, will involve only a small number of respondents with cases typically being selected through purposive sampling. Purposive sampling offers "information rich cases" that can generate lessons for the program (Patton, 2008, p. 458). Purposive stratified sampling ensures that groups with low representation, such as disadvantaged or marginalized groups, are included in data collection. Such groups may not otherwise be adequately represented through use of random approaches.

Determination of an appropriate sample size needs to consider the available budget, while ensuring that the sample size selected is sufficient to provide an evidence base for required forms of analysis. Data collection processes typically comprise one of the largest items of an evaluation budget, but significantly reducing sample sizes to stay within budget can compromise the evaluation process (Bamberger et al., 2012).

**Table 8.3** Sampling Methods and their Potential Application

| Sampling Method | Sampling Description | Potential Application |
|---|---|---|
| Probability Sampling: Each subject has equal probability of selection in a population, or subjects are organized into strata and then sampled randomly ||| 
| Simple random sampling | Respondents drawn randomly from a population | • Large scale surveys |
| Stratified random sampling | Random selection occurs from population subgroups, usually groups not likely to be adequately represented through the use of random sampling alone | • Surveys |
| Nonprobability Sampling: Potential respondents are selected by the evaluator |||
| Purposive sampling | Deliberate selection of respondents according to the value of the perspectives they will provide by participating. This can also include use of stratified sampling to ensure that certain groups are included or overrepresented | • Interviews<br>• Case studies<br>• Focus groups<br>• Workshops<br>• Forums<br>• Stakeholder meetings |
| Convenience sampling | Opportunistic sampling through data collection that involves speaking with respondents who are available at the time | • Community events<br>• Meetings<br>• Community or street polls |
| Snowball sampling | Building a sample by asking one respondent to refer or recommend another potential respondent for participation | • For accessing hard to reach groups in the community |
| Self-selection sampling | Forming a sample through volunteers who self-nominate to participate | • Recruiting participants from an identified community of interest |

Foreshadowing potential ethical issues is important in planning for data collection. Most data collection tools will require the development of protocols for protecting respondent privacy and confidentiality. In more sensitive contexts, it will be necessary to identify potential issues and procedures for any necessary follow-up in the case of disclosures made. Particular care needs to be taken during data collection with vulnerable populations where the principle of avoidance of harm is paramount. Examples of ethical issues that may arise in use of a selection of data collection tools are identified in Table 8.4. The community education case study is used to illustrate these points.

**Table 8.4** Possible Ethical Issues Arising in Use of a Selection of Tools for Data Collection

| Data Collection Tools | Potential Ethical Issues |
|---|---|
| Participant attendance records | • Implications of asking sensitive information, such as school attending status<br>• Privacy and confidentiality of data collected |
| Participant pre-post survey | • Implications if respondents are not literate or do not feel they have been able to grasp concepts<br>• Privacy and confidentiality of data collected |
| School administrative data | • Privacy and confidentiality of data collected |
| Stakeholder meetings and interviews | • Dealing with sensitive issues that may be raised by stakeholders<br>• Privacy and confidentiality of data collected |
| Participant Interviews, Focus Groups, Case Studies, Community Forums | • Attaining informed consent from participants with limited language proficiency, literacy, or other limitations to their comprehension<br>• Implications of offering financial or other forms of appreciation for participation in recognition of participant time spent in data collection<br>• Potential issues with disclosures that reveal either illegal behavior or emotional concerns that require professional follow up or referral<br>• Privacy and confidentiality of data collected |

## Step 2: Develop Data Management Plan

The Data Management Plan provides guidance for management processes required to enter, store, arrange, and analyze data following its collection. In most cases, this involves use of a system that houses a collection of data in a computer using dedicated software for its organization and analysis. This is referred to in this text as a computer database. The factors considered in developing the Data Management Plan include the handling and storing of data and the types of analysis and reports that will be generated, such as descriptive statistics and cross-tabulations. The Data Management Plan will typically also provide guidance as to the design requirements of program databases including hardware and software arrangements.

The Data Management Plan can be adjusted according to the size and complexity of the data involved and the resources available in the program's host organization. Typically, most planning for data management concerns monitoring functions that involve relatively large amounts of quantitative data relating to program processes and outputs. Quantitative data generally requires statistical analysis, and thus computer software is usually required to support its analysis. Evaluation activities may involve further demands on both data management and analysis through detailed arrangement and examination of available data and conduct of special studies. In some cases, these data may be entered into a program's database dependent on the type of data involved and whether evaluation functions are undertaken internally or otherwise handled externally, possibly by consultants. The different aspects of data management and their relationship to monitoring and evaluation functions are illustrated in Figure 8.3.

In an organization, arrangements for functions such as developing databases and data entry may be the responsibility of areas outside the immediate remit of those involved with monitoring and evaluation. In such cases, liaison and negotiation with such areas will be critical for putting monitoring and evaluation arrangements into place and determining the guidance included in the Data Management Plan.

The development of plans for managing data are likely to involve an iterative process that considers the interrelationship between the characteristics of the data to be managed and the data reports required and the nature of the

**Figure 8.3** Aspects of Data Management and Relationship to Monitoring and Evaluation Functions

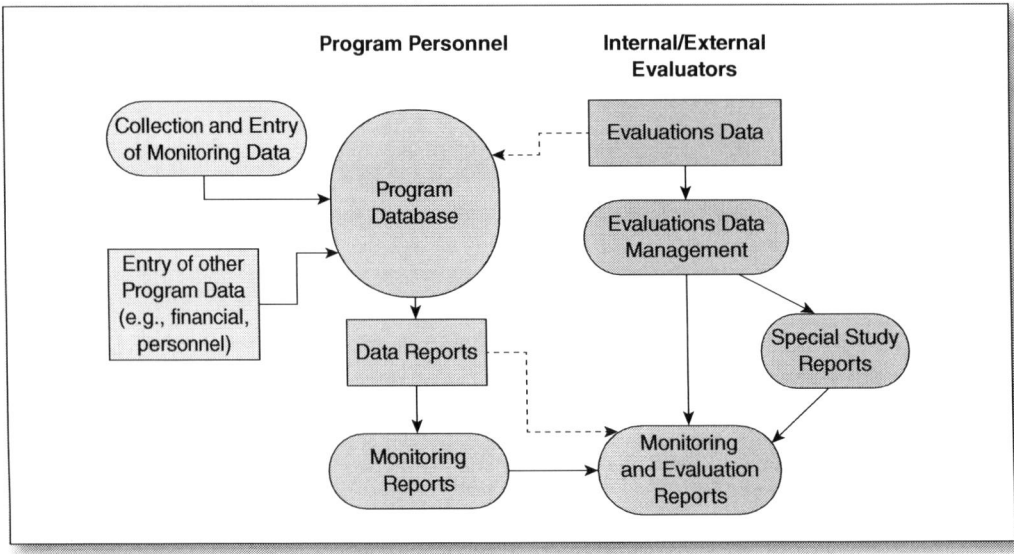

database or broader data system that will handle the data involved. The design, development, and implementation of a database or data system of a type, size, and cost suitable for the program will thus vary from program to program.

In many instances, program personnel may choose to use or refine a system that is already in place. In larger organizations, monitoring and evaluation functions may be integrated within an electronic information system together with functions such as accounting and budgeting, human resource management, and client information management (Calley, 2011). In contrast, many small organizations and programs operate multiple data systems in order to address different functions. This partly reflects more limited budgets and a smaller scope of operations. An overall lack of capacity in such systems can be a barrier to implementation of a Monitoring and Evaluation Framework. Differing data and reporting requirements of different funders can work to place additional pressure on the design and performance of data management systems.

The following are the main activities to be completed, leading to the development of a Data Management Plan:

- Database requirements are identified to guide the specification of computer hardware and software capabilities and arrangements.
- Different areas of collected data that require entry into the database are identified, such as participant numbers, gender, age, geographic location, and so on. Included data areas are particularly informed by the Monitoring Plan and to a lesser extent by the Evaluation Plan, as discussed earlier.
- Any necessary data collection forms or spreadsheets for data entry are designed with reference to available computer software.
- Data entry procedures, roles and responsibilities, and timing of expected data entry are outlined. Data entry is potentially undertaken by specialized personnel or by those who also collect the data.
- Data analyses is undertaken, which may include a range of cross-tabulations. These summarize categorical data used to create a contingency table, which then allow the relationship between variables to be identified. An example is a cross-comparison of location data of families with school attendance data to identify whether parents located in some areas send their children to school with greater frequency than other areas. Statistical analyses that are required should also be specified and may be undertaken using specialized software.
- Required database reports are identified, including details of their focus and timing. Most software applications do contain built-in reporting tools that respond to specific database queries. For instance, a database report may be produced following a query as to how many participants had traveled for 1 hour or more to attend the program. Requirements for specific data reports are usually not able to be fully anticipated. It is important, however,

that the more critical reports are identified in the Data Management Plan to reinforce the collection and entry of specific data (e.g., travel time).
- Training and support requirements for personnel responsible for data entry are identified in order to promote the input of accurate and timely data. Additional aspects include the development of procedures and support for staff to undertake data quality checks and organize and manage data for the production of data reports.

The suggested format for a Data Management Plan is presented in Table 8.5, which uses examples of data collected in the community education case study. Details are provided for only two categories of data, although in practice a more extended range of data categories would be expected.

**Table 8.5** Data Management Plan: Example

*Database Requirements*
- Hardware and software requirements
- Access arrangements (including possible web portal)
- Formats for data entry (e.g., spreadsheets)
- Required technical capabilities (e.g., level of statistical analysis, cross-tabulations)

| Data collected | Data entry | Data analysis | Database reports | Staff training/ orientation |
|---|---|---|---|---|
| Participant numbers and characteristics, such as<br>• Gender<br>• Age<br>• Location<br>• Language<br>• School attending status | **Responsible:** Administrative officer<br>**Tasks:** Enter participant details from attendance records onto spreadsheet<br>**Timing:** Quarterly | Participant numbers per course<br>• Mean (average)<br>• Mode (most frequent)<br>Cross tabulations<br>• Location × school attendance status<br>• Language × school attendance status | Quarterly reports on participant numbers and characteristics by location | • Data entry<br>• Generating required data reports |
| Pre/post survey results per course<br>• Result Course 1<br>• Result Course 2 | **Responsible:** Facilitator<br>**Tasks:** Enter results from completed surveys onto spreadsheet<br>**Timing:** End of each course | Cross-tabulations:<br>• Pre/post results × location<br>• Pre/post results × language | Quarterly reports on results from each course | • Administration of survey<br>• Managing ethical issues<br>• Data entry<br>• Generating data reports |

## Data Analysis

Data analysis involves identifying, organizing, and assessing the constituent elements of each set of collected information and also considering the interrelationships between data sets (Stufflebeam & Shinkfield, 2007). The purpose is firstly to identify whether the data are dependable and will support the drawing of reasonable conclusions. Subsequently, the meaning of the analyzed data in relation to answering specific evaluation questions is identified and often presented in data reports. As Stufflebeam and Shinkfield (2007) emphasize, data analysis precedes data synthesis, but the two functions are interdependent. Data synthesis, as considered in the following section, is concerned with combining analysis findings from different data sets to reveal an aggregate meaning in relationship to answering evaluation questions.

For both quantitative and qualitative data, decisions as to which approach to take in undertaking data analysis will be influenced by factors such as the type of analysis required; the quantity and complexity of data involved; the amount of time available; and available skills, equipment, and resources (Mertens & Wilson, 2012).

Approaches used to analyze data vary between quantitative and qualitative data sets. For quantitative data, emerging themes and trends are usually presented graphically in tables, charts, and graphs using predetermined categories. Such categories may include, for example, frequencies of occurrence, percentages, ratios, and other trends. Data may be analyzed for meaning through use of measures of central tendency (means, medians, and modes). Determining statistical significance may be undertaken for quantitative data, particularly when collecting large data sets. Commonly available computer software applications are frequently used to organize the data and provide graphic representations. Complex quantitative analysis may be handled outside the program's database, sometimes using specialist statistical software with an associated database and analytic capabilities. It is also possible that Internet-based surveys will be used in a standalone manner by drawing on their in-built capacity for data analysis and report generation.

Qualitative data may be sorted, coded, and analyzed manually using word processing or spreadsheet programs or entered into a computer system that supports qualitative data analysis (Bernard & Ryan, 2010). The aim of qualitative data analysis is to identify common themes emerging across the different data sources such as interviews, focus groups, case studies, meetings, consultations, and workshops. Increasingly, specialized software packages are being used:

> Qualitative data analysis has been transformed by the use of computer-based software packages that have been developed explicitly for that purpose. . . . The advantages of using computer-based software are that

you only have to enter the data once, and you can go through many different types of sorting activities as your understanding of the phenomenon changes. (Mertens & Wilson, 2012, pp. 443–444)

It is the entry of qualitative data into various categorizations and the coding of data that poses the challenge for data management. Categories can be selected according to the themes outlined in the evaluation questions. For example, if the theme highlighted in an evaluation question was participant satisfaction, then all data drawn from a range of different sources related to that theme would be assembled and aggregated in a particular category. If an initial scan of data, such as transcripts of interviews, highlighted that intended program participants spoke of difficulties in accessing the program, then the term *access* could become a code and used to classify further data. This approach to data management assists with the data analysis process against each evaluation question.

### Review of Data Management System

Once a database is up and running, a review of the system will be required to ensure that it is producing quality information. The status, as well as staff and stakeholder perceptions of the data system, are critical to ensure that the results of monitoring and evaluation are well-regarded and used. Quality assessment needs to cover the areas of reliability, validity, and timeliness. A reliable data system will be stable over time, a valid system will provide data that correctly tracks a program's performance, and a timely system will provide current data with appropriate frequency and availability (Kusek & Rist, 2004; Morra Imas & Rist, 2009).

Additionally, the database should be reviewed for its legitimacy in ensuring there is no data manipulation. This could be motivated by factors such as staff wishing to appear to meet targets, win bonuses, bid for increased resources, avoid scrutiny, or otherwise experiencing frustration with data reliability and inaccuracy. Manipulation can include instances of selective presentation and data gaming (taking advantage of the loopholes in rules and systems such as changing starting times or periods of data measurement). Such patterns are less likely to occur when staff ownership of the data system is high (Van Dooren et al., 2010). The review should also check that the data collected are actually being used and how they are being used (Calley, 2011). Guidance as to the timing and process for this review can be included as part of the Data Management Plan.

# Chapter 8   Collecting, Managing, Analyzing, and Synthesizing Data

## Step 3: Consider Approach to Data Synthesis

In order to identify its broader, aggregate meaning and significance in relation to the different evaluation questions, the range of data derived from both monitoring and evaluation processes requires synthesis. Data synthesis, also known as data interpretation, refers to the process of integrating and deriving meaning from various forms of data. In the approach taken within this text, monitoring and evaluation data are synthesized in relation to each evaluation question as organized under the five domains.

The process of data synthesis is assisted by reference to two types of constructs already developed as part of the Monitoring and Evaluation Framework. These are performance indicators and targets that highlight key areas and expected levels of program performance and criteria and standards that are developed to apply to assessment of evaluation questions that pertain to issues of quality and value. As detailed in Chapter 7, criteria and standards are usefully arrayed within a rubric that provides a structure to guide assessment. The use of evaluation rubrics therefore becomes part of the process of data synthesis. In addition to explicit criteria identified at the outset, criteria may also be developed implicitly by the evaluator with or without the involvement of key stakeholders. These implicit criteria may not become explicit until the data synthesis stage is reached.

Synthesis of data provides the basis for the process of reaching evaluative judgments against evaluation questions, which involves reference to the program theory and logic and underlying program assumptions. Following this, evaluative conclusions are identified. The process of forming evaluative conclusions is discussed in the following section. Figure 8.4 illustrates the connection between data synthesis and these subsequent steps in the evaluation process.

The process of data synthesis, which brings together a range of different types of data collected at different times and with different means, can be a "highly challenging activity" (Stufflebeam & Shinkfield, 2007, p. 605). The use of the format as illustrated in Table 8.6 is intended to assist in ordering and streamlining this process. The contents of Table 8.6 relate to the case study example of a community education program targeted to families where rates of school attendance of children are low. The material is not intended to be complete but rather is indicative of the approach used for data synthesis. Adjacent to each evaluation question, performance indicators and targets (as applicable) are arrayed. While indicators and targets are mostly quantitative in orientation, they may also be qualitative. Additionally, the range of monitoring and evaluation data that is presented in the subsequent columns is both quantitative and qualitative in nature. An important point regarding the monitoring data assembled and considered is that it is not limited to data directly relating to indicators and targets but includes other dimensions of performance identified through monitoring. The final column illustrates the synthesis of these data, which represents the aggregate, broader meaning derived from the data in relation to the evaluation question.

Effectiveness questions that pertain to quality and value will be potentially answered with reference to an evaluation rubric. Chapter 7, "The Evaluation Plan," included an evaluation rubric in Table 7.9. In this rubric, three criteria were identified for establishing program quality. These were that the program was based on evidence, was culturally appropriate, and met association standards. There were also three criteria identified for establishing value: that the program met needs and filled a service gap, demonstrated positive results, and was able to engage effectively with key stakeholders. Taking these six criteria, available data from routine monitoring and periodic evaluation can be assembled and synthesized to establish whether the performance can be considered to meet a particular standard. Standards used in this case are excellent, good, adequate, and poor. In order gain a range of perspectives, the process of data interpretation is often best undertaken in conjunction with key stakeholders. Synthesizing data in relation to quality and value

**Figure 8.4** Data Synthesis Leading to Evaluative Judgments and Conclusions

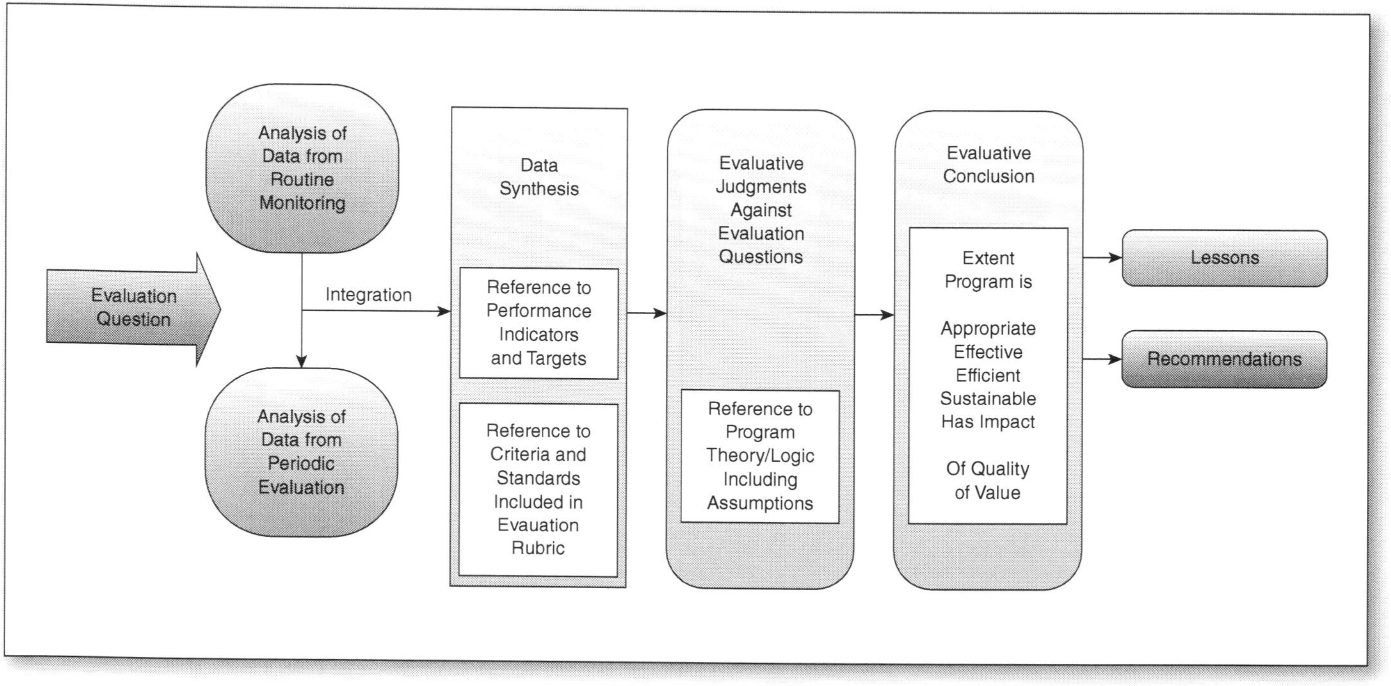

**Table 8.6** Data Synthesis Against Evaluation Questions

| Evaluation Questions | Performance Indicators and Targets | Monitoring Data | Evaluation Data | Data Synthesis |
|---|---|---|---|---|
| **Appropriateness** To what extent did the target group participate in the program? | **Indicator:** Number of participants from target group **Target:** 75% participation from intended target group **Indicator:** Gender balance of participants **Target:** Minimum 40% male participants | • 45% participation from target group • 55% female, 45% male participants • Facilitator reports indicate gender balance achieved but underrepresentation of some target group members | Case studies, interviews, and community forums: • Low motivation to participate by some target group members due to identified language barriers • Males who did participate were generally happy to attend and perceived the content as relevant | • Considerably less participation from target group than intended • Gender balance achieved |
| **Effectiveness** To what extent did participants increase their knowledge of the benefits of regular school attendance? | **Indicator:** Knowledge of the benefits of regular school attendance **Target:** 75% of participants report increased knowledge | • 85% of participants reported increased knowledge • Facilitator reports indicate that emphasis on provision of factual information strengthened knowledge acquisition | Case studies, interviews, and community forums: • For those who participated, content found to be very valuable and significantly increased participant knowledge | • Increased knowledge reported across all methods of data collection |
| **Efficiency** Was the cost of delivering the program within budget? | **Indicator:** Performance against budget | • Financial reports indicate 30% variation between budgeted and actual costs | Interviews and forums: • Extent of unanticipated remote travel resulted in budget overruns | • Budget overruns attributed to unanticipated level of remote travel |

| Evaluation Questions | Performance Indicators and Targets | Monitoring Data | Evaluation Data | Data Synthesis |
|---|---|---|---|---|
| | **Target:** Less than 10% variation between actual costs and budget | • Facilitator reports indicate program overspent due to not sufficiently budgeting for required remote travel | • Remotely based agencies were not sufficiently engaged and brought into partner relationships to deliver the program in remote locations | • Different views between facilitators and stakeholders as to whether remote travel allowance should have been included in budget |
| Impact<br>To what extent was there an increase in regular school attendance in the community? | **Indicator:** Changes in school attendance from baseline<br>**Target:** No target set due to lack of existing baseline data | • No changes evident in school attendance patterns since program commencement<br>• Participating schools suggest it is still too early to detect trends | Contribution Analysis Workshop<br>• Key stakeholders believed it was still too early to see firm trends due to lower than expected program participation rates and insufficient elapsed time since program commencement | • No trends evident and more time needed to identify trends in attendance rates<br>• Lack of improvement in attendance rates attributed in part to lower than expected participant numbers |
| Sustainability<br>Was there evidence of ongoing benefits beyond the program? | **Indicator:** Number and type of partnership agreements developed<br>**Target:** Not considered appropriate to numerate partnership agreements | • Few partnership agreements in place<br>• Management reports suggest this was an area that did not receive sufficient attention | Workshop and interviews<br>• Existing and potential program partners felt they should have been more involved in the program | • Few partnership agreements developed<br>• Underutilization of existing and potential program partners |

**Table 8.7** Data Synthesis and Assessment Against Evaluation Questions Using a Rubric

| Quality Criterion | Evaluation Question: Was the program of good quality? | | | | | |
|---|---|---|---|---|---|---|
| | Data Synthesis | Standards | | | | Evaluative Judgments |
| | | Excellent | Good | Adequate | Poor | |
| Evidence based | Literature review and stakeholder interviews indicate model founded on strong evidence base | √ | | | | High quality through use of solid evidence base to inform design and operations |
| Culturally appropriate | Monitoring data and stakeholder interviews indicate program did not attract sufficient target group members | | | | √ | Poor quality in relation to limited reach to culturally and linguistically diverse participants |
| Met association standards | Review report indicates program had baseline accreditation | | | √ | | Adequate quality in relation to meeting baseline standards |

| Value Criterion | Evaluation Question: Was the program of value? | | | | | |
|---|---|---|---|---|---|---|
| | Data Synthesis | Standards | | | | Evaluative Judgments |
| | | Excellent | Good | Adequate | Poor | |
| Met needs and filled a service gap | Stakeholder responses indicate model met a significant need and filled a service gap | √ | | | | High stakeholder value ascribed to meeting needs and filling a service gap |
| Positive results | Pre-post tests show evidence of increased knowledge, motivation, and intention to change behavior | | √ | | | Program valued for positive results in improved knowledge and motivation with potential for behavior change |
| Engaged effectively with stakeholders | Stakeholder forums indicate existing and potential partnerships not fully developed | | | | √ | Limited value ascribed to stakeholder engagement due to lack of developed partnerships with key agencies |

dimensions against a rubric is illustrated in Table 8.7. In addition, a column has been included at the end of the table in order to illustrate the type of evaluative judgments made following the process of data synthesis in relation to the criteria and standards.

The evaluation rubric is a valuable aid that supports consideration of a range of data in relation to questions regarding a program's quality and value. As King et al. (2013) observe, "it is the synthesis of findings where our investment in rubric development really starts to pay off" (p. 15). As illustrated in the previous evaluation rubric, the process of data synthesis has led to the formulation of a set of evaluative judgments. These evaluative judgments will subsequently lead to the determination of evaluative conclusions in relation to the evaluation questions, as discussed further in Step 4.

### Practice Example

#### Using an Evaluation Rubric

The Monitoring and Evaluation Framework for a national crime prevention program was designed to assist in identifying good practice within a broad range of individually funded projects. More than 100 projects had been funded. Evaluative activities were designed to identify which projects were successful and should be upscaled or replicated to other contexts and which projects were less effective and should be down-scaled or finalized. In order to inform these evaluative judgments, an evaluation rubric was developed. Stakeholders involved with the program determined the criteria as to what represented a successful crime prevention project and included these in a rubric. As part of the rubric, they then identified performance characteristics for each criterion at five standards, these being excellent, very good, adequate, less than adequate, and poor performance. When the monitoring and evaluation data were collected and available, a full day workshop was held. This was facilitated by the evaluator. Participants included the program funders and program partners. The purpose was to assess each individual project against the rubric. Robust debate took place as to which of the five standards were applicable to each criterion for each project. Once there was consensus, the various projects were grouped according to their rank against

*(Continued)*

> (Continued)
>
> each standard. This was followed by a process of reflection and identification of lessons as to trends in project performances and associated reasons. Projects that had been ranked as excellent or having poor performance tended to be particularly useful in highlighting lessons. Data synthesis of this kind, using the evaluation rubric and accompanying reflection, led to the identification of principles for good practice in service delivery for the program, with broader application to other related initiatives.

## Step 4: Consider Approach to Making Evaluative Judgments and Reaching Evaluative Conclusions

Answering evaluation questions involves making a range of evaluative judgments as to the extent of progress or lack of progress in relation to the performance area to which the specific evaluation question refers. The term *rendering judgment* (Scriven, 1980) can be considered to be a foundation principle of evaluation. Rendering judgment is the process where evaluators, with or without the involvement of key stakeholders, consider the available evidence (data) and then apply their values, beliefs, and expectations to the interpretation or the meaning of that data. In this manner, evaluative judgment may be regarded as a process that brings out the *value* that is encapsulated in the word *evaluation*. Scriven (2007) has argued that the word *judgment* is in fact a synonym for the term *evaluation*. The process of rendering judgment has also been described as the "essence of the evaluative function" (Patton, 2008, p. 500). Judgment is also identified as the ultimate step in what Scriven (1980) identifies as the logic of evaluation. In this schema, judgment is preceded by establishing criteria of merit and standards, measuring performance against those standards, and then synthesizing data.

While maintaining a critical and ultimate focus on reaching judgments, some evaluators find this type of sequential approach to their derivation to be too rule bound. Contrary arguments suggest that a diverse range of influences are at play, including the orientation of the evaluator and the input and views of key stakeholders (House & Howe, 1999; Hurteau & Williams, 2014). As Hurteau and Williams (2014) suggest

> the production of credible judgment is a complex process achieved through the combination of evaluator and stakeholder characteristics addressing all the elements. The contributions of professionals and their

stakeholders are intertwined as they share their values and perspectives. These are influenced by the professional's dispositions. And through their interactions or dialog, all participants clarify the problems or questions and generate and analyze information. Eventually, the professional reaches a judgment by making an argument that is judged as relatively credible by all participants because they view it as properly developed and communicated. (pp. 52–53)

As the process of making evaluative judgments draws on a combination of the evaluator's knowledge, skills, experience, and values, the evaluative decision-making process is more difficult to unpack and represent. Despite the complexities involved in the task, attempts have been made to represent the ways that professional judgments are formed by evaluators. Whether the evaluator makes the judgments alone, they are made by the evaluator in collaboration with stakeholders, or stakeholders make the judgments, are all options to be negotiated (Patton, 2008). From the perspective of the evaluator alone, Mc David et al. (2013) assert that the evaluator's values, beliefs, and expectations intersect with his or her knowledge, experience, and practical know-how to form a professional judgment. Another approach is to move beyond the single evaluator being responsible for making judgments. This entails working in partnership with program stakeholders, sharing common values, beliefs, and expectations. These factors are combined with collective knowledge and experience to form shared understandings that then lead to evaluative judgments being formed.

Data synthesis has provided an interpretation of the data arising from the integration of monitoring and evaluation data and aligned this interpretation against identified performance indicators and targets and criteria and standards to establish performance against these benchmarks. The next step is to draw inferences based on this alignment to determine what has changed or has not changed and why this was so. Evaluative judgments will thus extrapolate why anticipated changes as outlined in the program theory and the program logic have or have not taken place and whether the underlying assumptions to that change as identified in the program theory and the program logic have in fact been supported or not supported by the available data. While this judgment relates to the impact domain, additional judgments will also determine the extent to which the program was appropriately designed, effective in meeting its objectives, efficiently delivered, and sustainable in the results it generated.

For the community education case study, the discussion in Chapter 4 identified a range of assumptions. These include the two connective assumptions as to whether community education delivered would positively influence participant knowledge, motivation, and behavior and whether children attending school would go on to complete their basic education and then transition to further education, training, and employment. The first assumption may be tested more readily, while the validity of the latter would be more difficult to establish. Testing of the first assumption would likely involve examination of data collected that identify changes in participant knowledge and motivation as well as intentionality to change behavior or actual behavior change in sending children to school as a consequence of participation in the sessions. Reaching a judgment may further involve examination of data collected about those participants who did not increase their knowledge or motivation or change their behavior, or show intent to change, and the factors that mitigated against such change occurring. Identifying causal mechanisms that triggered change, or mechanisms that worked against change, would support judgments to be formed. The second assumption about school-to-work transitions is likely to require longitudinal data that could only be collected and aggregated after some elapsed time. Attempting an assessment of this assumption in the shorter term may therefore not be feasible.

Following the making of evaluative judgments, evaluative conclusions are formulated that then represent the outcome of the investigation in relation to the evaluation question and the determination of a program's quality and value. For the purpose of this text, evaluative conclusions are considered as factually oriented interpretations of the judgments that precede them.

In specifying conclusions, care should be exercised that they are easily understood, clear, and definite. While conclusions are often forward-looking, they precede the development of recommendations. Not all conclusions will necessarily lead to specific recommendations being made. Conclusions will provide considerations for program continuation and program improvement but also inform the development of lessons that can be applied to other like programs or similar situations. Conclusions may also inform more general practice in the area of program operation, such as education or health. In this sense, conclusions have a broader purpose than recommendations, which are more germane to the future of the specific program being evaluated.

The process of moving from data synthesis to judgments, and then to conclusions in relation to each evaluation question, is highlighted in the examples provided in Table 8.8. Judgments draw on data synthesis, while the process of making evaluative conclusions draws on both the preceding data synthesis and the range of evaluative judgments made.

The process of drawing conclusions, is followed by the identification of related recommendations and lessons. The relationship between evaluative conclusions, recommendations, and lessons is outlined in Table 9.2.

**Table 8.8** Evaluative Judgments and Conclusions Against Evaluation Questions

| Evaluation Questions | Data Synthesis | Evaluative Judgments | Evaluative Conclusions |
|---|---|---|---|
| **Appropriateness** To what extent did the target group participate in the program? | • Considerably less participation from culturally and linguistically diverse target group members than intended<br>• Gender balance achieved | • Program design not sufficiently tailored to meet target group's cultural needs, and this affected participation levels and impacted negatively on program quality<br>• Despite challenges, program was able to meet the needs of males who engaged with the program<br>• Assumption that families can afford to send their children to school not able to be tested | • Program was not culturally appropriate in its design, promotion, and delivery<br>• Program content and approach sufficiently met needs of males who participated |
| **Effectiveness** To what extent did participants increase their knowledge of the benefits of regular school attendance? | • Increased knowledge reported across all methods of data collection | • Program participants increased knowledge due to the program content and delivery approach being based on sound evidence<br>• Assumption that community education modules can improve participant knowledge is supported | • Evidence base used for program design and delivery approach produced intended improvements in participant knowledge<br>• Male participants responded well to approach adopted |
| **Efficiency** Was the cost of delivering the program within budget? | • Budget overruns attributed to unanticipated level of remote travel<br>• Differing views as to whether remote travel allowance should have been included in budget | • Program attempted to deliver to a wider geographic reach than was feasible within existing budget parameters<br>• Having an effective operational strategy to deliver program was an assumption that was not fulfilled and this impacted negatively on program performance | • Cost overruns due to increased travel costs to remote locations<br>• Remote service delivery options not adequately included as part of operational strategy |

**Table 8.8** (Continued)

| Evaluation Questions | Data Synthesis | Evaluative Judgments | Evaluative Conclusions |
|---|---|---|---|
| **Impact** To what extent was there an increase in regular school attendance in the community? | • No trends evident as more elapsed time needed to identify results as participant numbers increase<br>• Lack of improved trends attributed in part to lower than expected participant numbers | • Evidence of clear trends marred by lower levels of participation and possibly too little time elapsed to see results in this domain<br>• Assumption that children attending school regularly will complete their basic education was not able to be tested | • Low participation rates and short time frame limited capacity of program to identify trends since inception |
| **Sustainability** Was there evidence of ongoing benefits beyond the program? | • Few partnership agreements developed<br>• Underutilization of existing and potential program partners | • Program not able to develop an adequate level of effective partnerships, and this impacted negatively on its value<br>• Engagement with partner agencies was an assumption that was not fulfilled, and this impacted negatively on program performance | • Sustainability limited by lack of partnership development with agencies<br>• Wide geographic reach of program indicated need for greater partnership development |

In addition to evaluative conclusions that are made in relation to each evaluation question, an overall conclusion about the program as a whole can be made. This provides a succinct summary or overview as to a program's progress. Such an overall conclusion draws on and integrates conclusions to individual evaluation questions and may be included in executive summaries and other condensed formats that present the results of the monitoring and evaluation process. Following is an example of an overall conclusion related to the case study of a community education program where rates of school attendance of children are low.

> **Overall Conclusion**
>
> The program model was developed based on strong evidence. The model and its mode of delivery demonstrated capability for increasing participant knowledge about the benefits of regular school attendance. Knowledge acquisition was particularly evident for those males who attended the community education sessions. Evidence that the model would ultimately lead to behavior change in participants supporting school attendance for their children was yet to be identified.
>
> The achievement and the extent of program outcomes were constrained by three fundamental limitations in the program's design and implementation. Firstly, the program was not sufficiently tailored to meet the cultural and linguistic needs of its identified target group members. As a corollary of this limitation, the program did not gain sufficient support from the target group. Additionally, the program attempted to service a wider geographic area than was feasible within its existing budget which resulted in budget overruns. The program also did not sufficiently foster partnerships and working relationships with suitable affiliated agencies, particularly those located in remote regions with an interest in delivering community education sessions. These three factors cumulatively limited the program's achievements.
>
> Program results in increasing school attendance were thus potentially curtailed by the lower-than-intended participation rates, dispersal of program resources over a wide geographic reach, and also limited by the shorter time frames for assessing trends. The program personnel need to consider making changes to the program's design and then continue to track changes in trends for school attendance over time to demonstrate that increased knowledge will translate to attitudinal and behavior change for participating target group members.

## SUMMARY CHECKLIST

Has the Data Collection Plan

- identified data collection methods for the collection of requisite data?
- identified the main elements of required data collection tools and, in some cases, included developed tools as an attachment to the Data Collection Plan?
- identified sampling approaches required for different data collection processes?
- identified any ethical issues likely to be associated with data collection?
- considered issues of confidentiality and privacy of data?
- considered protocols for the collection of secondary data from partner agencies?

Has the Data Management Plan

- provided guidance for establishing a viable management information system to support the Monitoring and Evaluation Framework?
- provided guidance for generating required reports, including any specific actions such as cross-tabulations and statistical analyses?
- included arrangements for the review of the accuracy of data and ease of its collection?
- clarified relationships between those who collect and enter data and those who analyze and report on the data?

Has guidance been provided for data synthesis, the forming of evaluative judgments, and the development of evaluative conclusions? Specifically, has this involved:

- clarifying how monitoring data will be synthesized with the evaluation data and at what intervals this will take place?
- suggesting how judgments against each evaluation question will be formed and who will be involved in the process?
- suggesting how to develop evaluative conclusions in relation to the program and how it performed against the evaluation questions, with reference to the program theory and the program logic and their underlying assumptions?
- suggesting how evaluative conclusions will support the identification of transferable lessons and recommendations for program improvement?

## Chapter 8 Collecting, Managing, Analyzing, and Synthesizing Data

### CHAPTER REVIEW QUESTIONS

1. How would you ensure that data collected was systematically entered into a database or otherwise recorded in a timely and accurate way?
2. How would you approach the development of an associated Data Collection Plan and a Data Management Plan?
3. How would you ensure that all data collected were routinely analyzed and synthesized?
4. Who would be responsible for these roles within a program?
5. What process would you adopt to form evaluative judgments and conclusions based on the data collected, analyzed, and synthesized? Who would be involved in this process?
6. Do you foresee any challenges in reaching consensus regarding evaluative judgments and conclusions? If so, how would you manage them?

# CHAPTER 9

# Learning, Reporting, and Dissemination Strategies

# Chapter 9  Learning, Reporting, and Dissemination Strategies

*This chapter identifies learning as integral to monitoring and evaluation and therefore an important area for attention within the Monitoring and Evaluation Framework. Consideration is given as to how learning can be promoted through the associated processes of reporting and dissemination. The lessons and recommendations derived from monitoring and evaluation are a point of emphasis, with discussion of how they may be most effectively generated and structured, building on the processes of data synthesis and the identification of evaluative judgments and conclusions. Attention is also given to the related area of how to increase the usefulness of the products of the monitoring and evaluation process. Areas of use include direct application to the program and its organizational context and, from a broader perspective, to related programs and policies.*

## 1. INTRODUCTION

Advancing a learning approach within the Monitoring and Evaluation Framework is an important consideration. This involves planning for the use and dissemination of recommendations and lessons derived from the program. Learning is an important process within a program and draws on and enhances capacities for reflection, with the flexibility to change a program's focus and direction based on the recommendations identified. Recommendations and lessons are commonly incorporated in both formal and occasional reporting and other communication products. In this manner, learning has critical value in its potential transferability within organizations and to other related programs and policy contexts.

From a systemic perspective, learning has been identified as a critical to the RBM approach. Within an iterative process that connects planning and monitoring and evaluation, RBM promotes the application of evaluative conclusions, recommendations, and lessons to revisit the initial program vision and design. The intent is to improve the program and its practice. The following excerpt from the UNDP *Handbook on Planning, Monitoring, and Evaluating for Development Results* emphasizes this approach:

> Good RBM is an ongoing process. That means that there is constant feedback, learning and improving. Existing plans are regularly modified based on the lessons learned through monitoring and evaluation, and future plans are developed based on these lessons. (2009, p.11)

**Figure 9.1** Learning Approach for Program Improvement and Broader Application

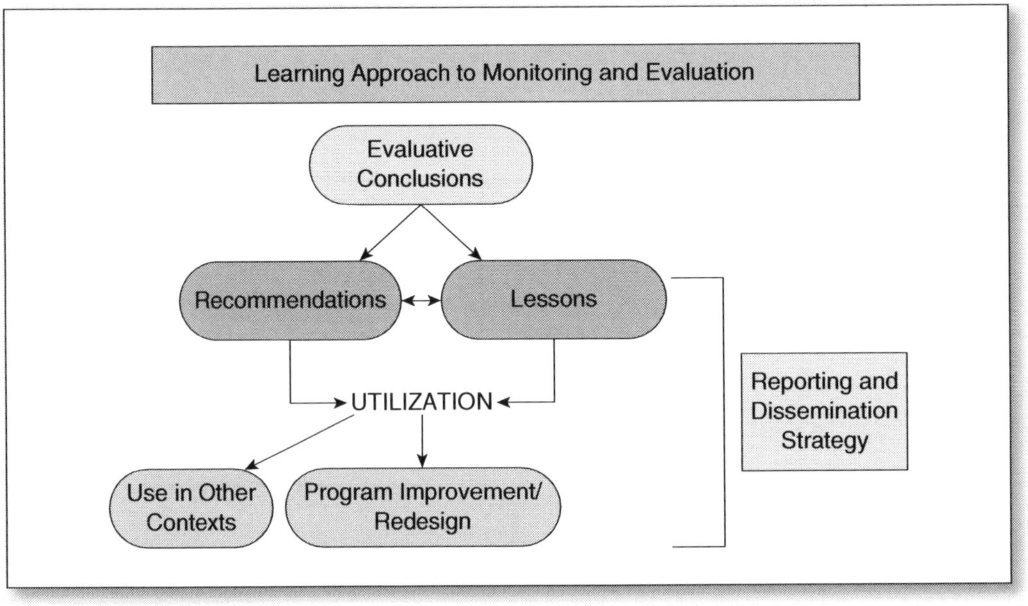

```
                Learning Approach to Monitoring and Evaluation

                              Evaluative
                              Conclusions
                             ↙         ↘
                 Recommendations  ↔  Lessons
                          ↓          ↓              Reporting and
                        → UTILIZATION ←              Dissemination
                         ↙         ↓                   Strategy
              Use in Other    Program Improvement/
                Contexts          Redesign
```

The impetus provided by a learning approach to monitoring and evaluation within a program and associated flow-on effects from the derivation of evaluative conclusions through to use are illustrated in Figure 9.1. The process of reaching evaluative conclusions was discussed in Chapter 8. This chapter considers further the development of recommendations and lessons that build on these conclusions. The figure emphasizes the critical role played by recommendations and lessons as a basis for program improvement or redesign and also for use in other contexts. This chapter also considers reporting and dissemination strategies that promote the application of the conclusions, recommendations, and lessons. The development of these is guided by the Monitoring and Evaluation Framework.

## 2. STEPS INVOLVED IN LEARNING AND REPORTING AND DISSEMINATION

Developing strategies for learning and reporting and dissemination as part of the Monitoring and Evaluation Framework involves three main steps. The first

**Table 9.1** Steps Involved in Learning, Reporting, and Dissemination

| Stage 5: Learning, Reporting and Dissemination | | |
|---|---|---|
| Steps | | |
| 1 | Consider developing or refining a learning strategy for the program that maximizes use of conclusions, recommendations, and lessons | • Consider developing or refining a learning strategy for the program that guides the learning process, identifying when and how learning is expected to occur.<br>• Ensure that the Monitoring and Evaluation Framework identifies and promotes opportunities for reflection and learning. This includes attention to:<br>  ○ linking learning to program improvement and to redesign where required,<br>  ○ identification of transferable recommendations and lessons for the benefit of other programs and contexts, and<br>  ○ increasing opportunities for the use and influence of conclusions, recommendations, and lessons. |
| 2 | Consider processes for the identification of recommendations and lessons | • Consider how to translate conclusions into recommendations and lessons that will be useful and used.<br>• Scope the need for recommendations, their nature, and number.<br>• Consider how to best engage stakeholders in identification of recommendations and lessons without compromising independence or objectivity. |
| 3 | Provide guidance on developing a reporting and dissemination strategy | • Develop a reporting and dissemination strategy that best supports potential use of evaluative conclusions, implementable recommendations, and useful lessons.<br>• Provide guidance for the production of reports and effective reporting processes.<br>• Give consideration to different types of reports and their audiences.<br>• Consider best methods for communicating messages to different audiences. |

step concerns the broader context for this work, with consideration of developing or refining a learning approach across the program. The following steps are narrower in focus. The second step concerns developing guidance as to how recommendations and lessons will be identified and disseminated. A final step considers the formulation of a specific strategy for reporting and dissemination through which the use and application of the products of monitoring and evaluation will be advanced.

## Step 1: Consider Developing or Refining a Learning Strategy That Maximizes Use of Conclusions, Recommendations, and Lessons

### Learning Strategies

An RBM approach is concerned with promoting the generation and use of learning in both the short and longer term. More immediate benefits of the application of learning may be identified in the refinements made that enhance the level of results achieved by a program, while longer term gains may be identified where programs have the capacity to use learning to improve decisions in relation to future operations. "Since there are no perfect plans, it is essential that managers, staff and stakeholders learn from the successes and failures of each program or project" (UNDP, 2009, p. 11).

More broadly, the development of a learning approach within an organization or program and associated staff may be viewed as building a core capacity (Preskill, 2008; Preskill & Russ-Eft, 2005). An ability to learn is associated with flexibility and adaptability, is a vital attribute of human resource development, and is important in building organizational expertise and intelligence. Monitoring and evaluation, and associated processes of reflection and learning, therefore have a key role in reinforcing such attributes and minimizing the possibility that mistakes are repeated.

While advancing a learning approach has multiple benefits, in practice, aims of building core capacity for learning and harnessing learning for program improvement are often compromised. Pressures of accountability on an organization or a program, and by extension on monitoring and evaluation functions, are often pronounced. They may overwhelm an intent to promote learning, particularly when accountability mandates are "introduced early and authoritatively" (Patton, 2012, p. 124). The challenge and need to maintain balance in the functions served by a Monitoring and Evaluation Framework were emphasized in Chapter 2. In this regard, both organizational and program culture and specific strategies have a key role to play.

Specific learning strategies are sometimes developed by organizations, often linked to a proactive intent to expand the focus of monitoring and evaluation beyond accountability. Such strategies typically identify needs and contexts for learning, including the type of processes required. The latter may extend from regular team meetings to discuss the results of monitoring, to dedicated events such as stakeholder meetings that reflect on formal evaluation reporting. A structured and dedicated reflective process can consider conclusions, recommendations, and lessons, whether these are of an emergent nature or the more formal products of the evaluation process. Reflection of this kind, often drawing together a range of team members including managers, is likely to prompt evidence-informed adjustments to a program's design or operations where required. For example, it may become apparent that a particular approach is not effective with a specific stakeholder group and therefore requires modification.

The Monitoring and Evaluation Framework can reinforce a learning culture at both the program and organizational levels. This can involve including an explicit expectation that the program personnel will host regular structured learning events to consider evaluative conclusions, identify lessons, and, where appropriate, consider and formulate recommendations for the program's design and future directions. Systematized inquiry and learning that occur through conscious efforts are more likely to generate useful lessons and implementable recommendations. In this context, the process of inquiry and learning becomes integrated within standard work practices. Such practice may extend from the individual across work teams and a whole program and possibly across a whole organization (Preskill & Torres, 1999).

Organizational leaders can play a critical role in building a learning culture by thinking evaluatively and supporting evaluative thinking and practice amongst staff. Reflecting this intent, Preskill (2014) emphasizes that leaders need to develop an understanding of how strategy and evaluation are linked; provide sufficient resources for evaluation; become active users of evaluative information; and consciously support the generation of learning within their organizations.

Adoption of a learning approach can pose significant challenges for organizations that operate more on a command and control model, rather than with principles of collaboration, team reflection, and problem solving. For some programs, taking corrective action based on learning generated by monitoring and evaluation may be constrained by funder requirements and resistance. This may be compounded by a program personnel's hesitance to bring issues to the notice of a funding organization. To combat such inertia, the Monitoring and Evaluation Framework can clearly signal an intent to undertake program review and refinement based on the results of its implementation. Ongoing dialogue and negotiation with funders, where required, can ease this process. This sort of adaptability stands in contrast to variations in program design that are unplanned, ad hoc, and result in compromises to a program's fidelity in implementation.

## Utilization Strategies

The manner in which evaluative conclusions are used, and the factors that impact on this use, have received significant attention in the evaluation literature (Bamberger et al., 2012; Lopez-Acevedo, Krause, & Mackay, 2012; Mayne, 2014; Patton, 2012; Stufflebeam Shinkfield, 2007; Van Dooren et al., 2010). Patton (2012) refers to the production and distribution of a utilizable report as the output but its actual use as the outcome. While the Monitoring and Evaluation Framework cannot in itself guarantee use of the conclusions, lessons, or the recommendations that are generated, it can provide guidance that may increase the chances that the information produced is actually used. Incentives may need to be developed by a program or within an organization to encourage a utilization approach, such as rewarding implementation and use of evaluation and sanctioning lack of use (Bamberger et al., 2012; Morra Imas & Rist, 2009; Wholey, 2010).

Different types of utilization can take place with most evaluators anticipating what is termed *instrumental use*, where evaluative conclusions are used to directly improve the program. However, sometimes the result is awareness raising or enlightenment, where knowledge is increased and reflective thinking is enhanced (Mayne, 2014). Whether enlightenment then translates to instrumental use will clearly vary amongst different stakeholders, with some more committed to acting on conclusions and recommendations and others more content to remain informed and reflective without taking commensurate action. Instrumental and enlightenment use are generally regarded as positive outcomes. Other less positive types of use can include symbolic use, where reports are used only in a symbolic way to justify predetermined actions, and misuse, where conclusions and recommendations are handled inappropriately or based on flawed evidence (Cousins & Shulha, 2006).

While multiple factors are likely to support the positive use of evaluative conclusions and recommendations, a range of other factors may impair their use, and by association, their potential influence (Bamberger et al., 2012; Mayne, 2014; Van Dooren et al., 2010; Wholey, 2010). These include a range of political and bureaucratic challenges affecting the use of evaluation findings, operating at the institutional and political levels; constraints in organizational cultures, structures, and leadership; and a lack of coordination in accountability frameworks.

Developing insight into how information derived from monitoring and evaluation is perceived and used by decision makers is important and can inform the design of Monitoring and Evaluation Frameworks. Van Dooren et al. (2010) identify what they term as the application of a "truth test" and "utility test" by decision makers in assessing the value of information presented to them. The former term describes decision makers' assessment as to the quality and to common sense resonance of the information, while the latter term refers to the perceived utility of the information in helping to solve immediate problems and provide new directions into the future. This schema underlines the need to ensure that conclusions and recommendations are credible and developed with good understanding of stakeholder information requirements. The success factors that may contribute to effective use of the results of evaluation and reinforce their influence are summarized in Figure 9.2 (Bamberger et al., 2012; Mayne, 2014; Van Dooren et al., 2010; World Bank, 2009).

**Figure 9.2** Factors Likely to Assist with Evaluation Use and Influence

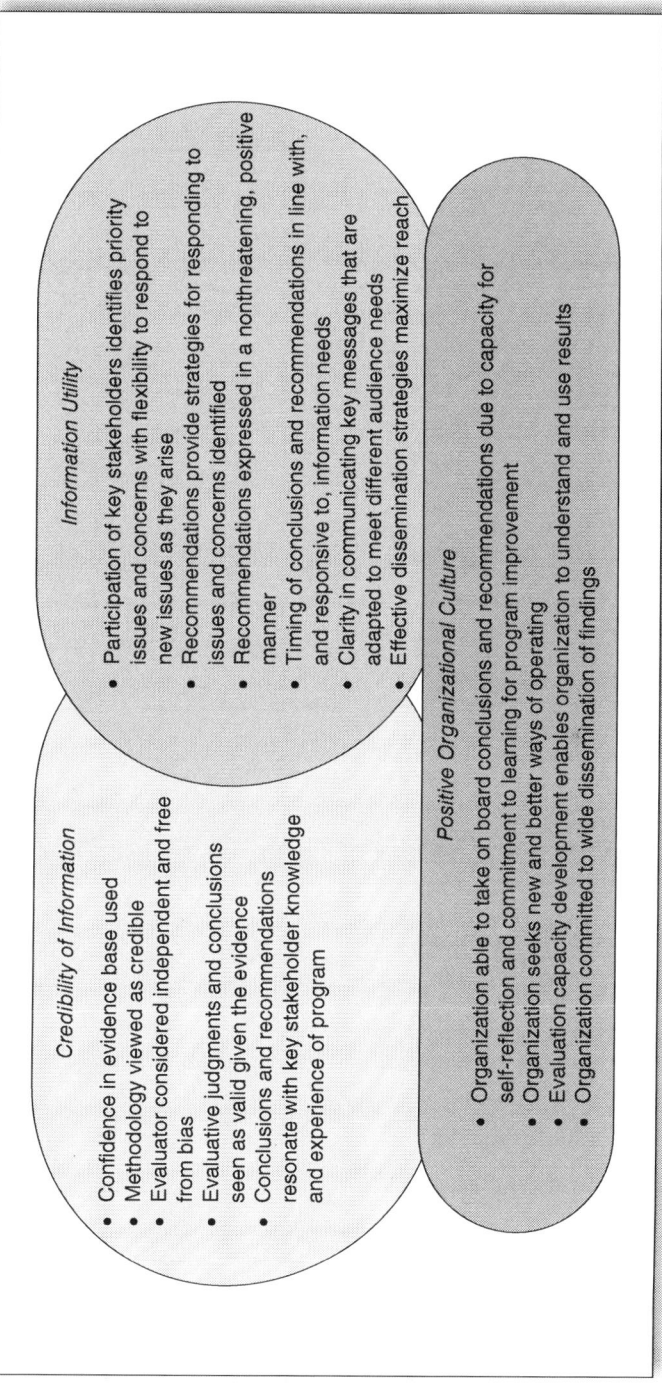

*Credibility of Information*

- Confidence in evidence base used
- Methodology viewed as credible
- Evaluator considered independent and free from bias
- Evaluative judgments and conclusions seen as valid given the evidence
- Conclusions and recommendations resonate with key stakeholder knowledge and experience of program

*Information Utility*

- Participation of key stakeholders identifies priority issues and concerns with flexibility to respond to new issues as they arise
- Recommendations provide strategies for responding to issues and concerns identified
- Recommendations expressed in a nonthreatening, positive manner
- Timing of conclusions and recommendations in line with, and responsive to, information needs
- Clarity in communicating key messages that are adapted to meet different audience needs
- Effective dissemination strategies maximize reach

*Positive Organizational Culture*

- Organization able to take on board conclusions and recommendations due to capacity for self-reflection and commitment to learning for program improvement
- Organization seeks new and better ways of operating
- Evaluation capacity development enables organization to understand and use results
- Organization committed to wide dissemination of findings

## Step 2: Consider the Identification of Recommendations and Lessons

Evaluative conclusions have been identified in this text as the outcome of the investigation in relation to each evaluation question, with an overall conclusion made for the program as a whole (Chapter 8). Lessons are derived from these conclusions and identify those principles that can be usefully applied to other like programs and related policies and strategies. In this manner, they have considerable value in augmenting program-specific, concrete evaluative conclusions and prescriptive recommendations. They add to the accumulation of knowledge pertaining to ingredients that make for successful program designs and delivery approaches.

Lessons are often referred to as *lessons learned* and can be defined as follows:

> Generalizations based on evaluation experiences with projects, programs, or policies that abstract from the specific circumstance to broader situations. Frequently, lessons highlight strengths or weaknesses in preparation, design, and implementation that affect performance, outcome, and impact. (OECD DAC, 2010, p. 26)

Lessons do not necessarily need to be identified in relation to the area covered by each evaluation question or in relation to each area of recommendation. The critical factor is that they capture the important areas of generalizable program experience. An example of a lesson is as follows:

> Effective community education programs that intend to attract participation from target group members drawn from culturally and linguistically diverse communities rely on the identification of the specific needs and requirements of that target group. The program then adjusts the educational strategy accordingly. This applies to choice of facilitator, location, timing, and type of delivery methods used. Once participating in the program, engagement with target group members will require a clear focus on participant development, learning, and well-being. Engagement also relies on trusting relationships between the facilitator and participants. For target group members from traditionally hard-to-reach groups, specialized engagement strategies will be required to maximize participation in, and engagement with, the program.

Recommendations develop conclusions into suggestions for more prescriptive steps forward. They are not always required, nor always requested, and some stakeholders are satisfied with the identification of conclusions alone so that they can develop their own recommendations based on the findings outlined.

If recommendations are to be developed, an important initial step is to clarify their purpose and use so they are realistic and implementable. Expectations regarding the number of recommendations developed and their orientation should be discussed in order to maximize their potential application to program improvement. Recommendations receive considerable scrutiny within evaluation reports. Significant contemplation time and careful attention to wording is required in their development. Otherwise, the recommendations may potentially become "a lightning rod for attack" (Patton, 2012, p. 358).

Developing recommendations in partnership with stakeholders can be a productive strategy. It provides an opportunity to test out draft recommendations and promote their relevance, applicability, and usefulness. A challenge arising in this approach, however, relates to preserving evaluator independence. Undue influence can be exerted by stakeholders in attempts to nuance recommendations in accordance with their interests. In this context, the evaluator is required to maintain a balancing act, facilitating productive stakeholder participation, while at the same time attempting to preserve sufficient evaluator independence and objectivity (Markiewicz, 2005, 2008).

Another area requiring careful diplomacy is in presenting both positive and negative recommendations. Recommendations need to respond to performance issues and identify corrections. However, where positive areas of performance, promising interventions, and innovative approaches are identified these have an important role to play in motivating personnel and forming the basis for future directions for the program.

The connections between evaluative conclusions, recommendations, and lessons are illustrated in Table 9.2. These are based on extending the evaluative judgments and conclusions, as identified in Chapter 8, into recommendations and then to lessons. Such a process can be supported through the Monitoring and Evaluation Framework and identified as forming part of program learning events conducted at key junctures in a program's life cycle. These events usually involve selected program staff and key stakeholders.

**Table 9.2** Evaluative Conclusions, Recommendations, and Lessons

| Evaluative Conclusions | Recommendations | Lessons |
|---|---|---|
| Program was not culturally appropriate in its design, promotion, and delivery. | Engage, train, and support facilitators from the respective cultural and language groups to deliver the program to these groups. | Engagement of members from specific target communities will be increased when using facilitators drawn from those target communities. |
| Program content and approach sufficiently met needs of males who participated. | Continue current content and approach for male participants. | Evidence-based program designs are important when engaging male participants in parenting programs. |
| Evidence-based content produced intended changes in improving participant knowledge. | Care should be taken to maintain content integrity given the success of the program in improving participant knowledge. | Maintaining content integrity is important to the success of program delivery across different courses and locations. |
| Cost overruns occurred due to increased travel costs to remote locations. | Agencies in remote locations that indicate an interest and are suitable to deliver the program should be contracted to do so. | When attempting to deliver a program across a wide geographic region, serious consideration should be given to forming partnerships with agencies based in remote locations. |
| Remote service delivery options were not adequately included as part of the operational strategy. | Program guidelines should be reviewed to discourage direct delivery of courses to remote regions. | Programs with limited scope and resources and working in remote locations should prioritize partnership development to assist in meeting participant needs. |
| Low participation rates and short time frames limited the capacity of the program to identify trends since its inception. | Program should conduct an analysis of school enrolment and attendance rates 12 months after implementation of the adjusted program design. | Programs attempting to identify longer term change need to carefully establish realistic time frames within which expected results will become apparent. |

> **Practice Example**
>
> ### Stakeholder Engagement in Identification of Recommendations and Lessons
>
> Engaging stakeholders in the identification of lessons and recommendations emerging from monitoring and evaluation activities can reinforce learning and the use of findings for program improvement. This orientation was apt for a program managed by a nongovernment organization aimed at improving emergency accommodation services available in rural communities. Initial scoping of a Monitoring and Evaluation Framework highlighted the need to identify whether the program's service delivery model was appropriate and effective for its context. Concerns were raised at an early stage regarding whether program resources were adequate to operate across the broad range of communities involved. Both formative and summative evaluation activities highlighted concerns with the program model. While some adjustments were made during implementation, it became increasingly apparent at the summative evaluation stage that a major program redesign was required. An extended 3-day learning workshop was therefore held. The workshop emphasized the participation of program stakeholders in order to reflect on learnings and discuss their implications. The evaluator facilitated the workshop process, which allowed stakeholders to discuss and debate recommendations and nuance them to better suit the context. This workshop process resulted in the endorsement of a useful set of recommendations focused on tailoring service delivery to a more carefully targeted and selected range of communities. Throughout the workshop, stakeholders were encouraged to actively participate in discussion and debate. This inclusive approach led to a high degree of acceptance of the new program model despite it entailing reduced levels of service delivery. Other factors contributing to the success of this process were a positive organizational culture in the nongovernment organization with committed leadership supportive of a learning approach, managers making time available for staff to participate in the workshop and associated meetings, and the production of what was seen to be a credible evaluation report upon which the learnings and recommendations were founded.

## Step 3: Provide Guidance on Developing a Reporting and Dissemination Strategy

The evaluative conclusions, recommendations, and lessons derived from monitoring and evaluation make up an important part of the accountability responsibility that a program has in relation to its progress, performance, and learning that is conveyed through formal reports and other means. The audiences for these products include both internal and external stakeholders. Reporting and dissemination represent an important avenue for reinforcing learning undertaken by a program or organization and support internal stakeholder needs and interests. External stakeholders and their needs are also critical and frequently represent a primary orientation of reporting, especially in relation to reporting to funding or governing bodies. However, other interests can be usefully served in this context, such as informing and guiding policy development. As emphasized in this section, although it is challenging to mediate and respond to different interests, a program has much to gain by first identifying and then addressing needs for reporting and information represented across both its internal and external stakeholders.

Frequently, attention to reporting and dissemination is treated as an afterthought in planning for monitoring and evaluation. Such an approach is unfortunate and ignores a vital opportunity to maximize the value and use of information and lessons derived from monitoring and evaluation. A Reporting and Dissemination Strategy developed as part of the Monitoring and Evaluation Framework includes details on audiences for the distribution of reports and other information products, key stakeholder requirements for information; the format information should be in and when the information will be required, and who is responsible for providing it (Morra Imas & Rist, 2009). A foundation for this work will be provided by the stakeholder engagement strategy, as discussed in Chapter 3, which identifies program stakeholders, their needs, and relationship to the monitoring and evaluation functions.

While formal reports are required, and play an important role in communicating with stakeholders and broader audiences, programs are increasingly diversifying the means that they use for this purpose. Such trends are reinforced in an information age where the diversity and use of electronic forms of communication are increasing exponentially. As a complement and a contrast, programs working with marginalized or disadvantaged populations are likely to want to include dissemination methods that are accessible for such groups. Therefore, this section covers a range of different means of communication but commences with a discussion of formal reporting.

## Reporting Processes

Formal reporting is an important process for telling the story of a program's achievements, limitations, challenges, and learnings. As Fitzpatrick et al. (2011, p. 464) state, "the importance of telling a story through evaluation cannot be overemphasised." A formal report will address evaluation questions, include valid and reliable performance information that highlights accomplishments against expected results and other performance, and will also demonstrate a capacity to learn and adapt (UNDP, 2011). Beyond these generic considerations, a report is likely to have a range of different audiences all with differing information needs. Reporting should thus be focussed in accordance with its core purposes and then honed and adapted to meet the information needs of intended users. Such an approach will encourage the actual use of information generated and included in a report (Patton, 2012).

Reports vary in terms of their focus and range from comprehensive reports, such as a summative evaluation report, to more focused reports related to a specific evaluative activity. An example of the latter is a report of a case study or set of case studies. A comprehensive evaluation report, which draws on both monitoring and evaluation data, would usually address all of the evaluation questions and may incorporate the evaluation domains either explicitly or implicitly to provide structure. Monitoring reports can follow a similar structure but are likely to be particularly focused on the domains of effectiveness, efficiency, and impact. The following report types are those most commonly encountered in monitoring and evaluation:

- Routine monitoring reports that track progress in implementation and actual against expected performance, identifying achievements and limitations in overall program performance
- Formative evaluation reports that establish progress to date and identify recommended areas for improvement
- Progress reports that integrate monitoring data with formative evaluation data to establish progress to date and identify areas for improvement
- Occasional reports that fulfill information needs in relation to a particular area of investigation or inquiry (e.g., workshop reports and survey reports)
- A summative evaluation report that provides a synthesis of all monitoring and evaluation data, drawing evaluative conclusions with associated recommendations and learnings identified

Additionally, a range of other types of publications may be produced that draw on or are related to the contents of the above reports. These include, for example, discussion papers, articles, and pamphlets. There is also a wide range of new media available for disseminating information in a range of different, abbreviated formats.

A broad structure for a comprehensive evaluation report is included in Table 9.3, with considerations for the preparation of each section also indicated.

**Table 9.3** Indicative Evaluation Report Structure

| Chapter Headings | Considerations |
|---|---|
| *Executive Summary* | |
| 1 **Program Overview**<br>• Context and Background to the Program<br>• Approach to Monitoring and Evaluation | • Presents the context and history of the program<br>• Identifies the purpose and approach adopted to monitoring and evaluation<br>• Outlines approach to key stakeholder engagement |
| 2 **Foundations**<br>• Program Theory<br>• Program Logic<br>• Evaluation Questions | • Program Theory outlining expected changes<br>• Program Logic outlining expected results<br>• Evaluation Questions classified under five domains |
| 3 **Methodology**<br>• Approach to Monitoring<br>• Evaluation Methodology | • Scope of the approach and methodology used<br>• Any limitations or constraints in approach or methodology used<br>• Any ethical issues that arose and how they were handled |
| 4 **Key Results**<br>• Program Context (Appropriateness)<br>• Progress Toward Objectives (Effectiveness)<br>• Program Implementation and Resourcing (Efficiency)<br>• Program Coordination and Management (Efficiency)<br>• Program Outcomes (Impact)<br>  ○ Progress against the program theory and the program logic<br>  ○ Key assumptions<br>• Sustainability<br>• Gender and other Cross Cutting Issues<br>• Overall Evaluative Conclusions | • Answers provided to the evaluation questions under each domain<br>• Presents synthesized data, assessment, and findings against each evaluation question<br>• Identifies performance against indicators and targets and criteria and standards<br>• Presents an assessment of program impact<br>• Provides an assessment of progress against the program theory and the program logic<br>• Assessment of validity of key assumptions<br>• Assessment of other areas examined, such as gender and environmental impact<br>• Presents overall evaluation conclusions |
| 5 **Recommendations** | • Focused on program continuation and/or improvement |

| | Chapter Headings | Considerations |
|---|---|---|
| 6 | Learning | • Identifies lessons that can be used to review program design and benefit future program development and similar programs and policy contexts |
| 7 | Appendices<br>• Data Collection Tools and Approaches<br>• Performance Indicators and Targets, Evaluation Rubrics, and other Analytical Frameworks<br>• Other | • Presents range of data collection tools used<br>• Identifies approaches used to sample<br>• Lists interviewees<br>• Identifies ethical approval processes (where required) and informed consent forms used<br>• Presents approaches for data synthesis and assessment, such as use of performance indicators and targets, evaluation rubrics, and other analytical frameworks |

A summative evaluation report may become a large document, and its whole contents may be of interest to only a select few. The size of such documents can act as a constraint limiting their wider use and influence. As policy makers and other key stakeholders may not actively seek knowledge to assist them in their daily decision making, knowledge must be distributed and communicated in such a way that it is likely to affect such policy decisions (Webber, 1991). A Reporting and Dissemination Strategy can prescribe the production of different types of reports to potentially maximize use. Consideration may be given to production of a multitiered report structure that includes, for example, a one-page overview for main messages, a short executive summary, and a comprehensive report. An executive summary provides a stand-alone summary of the fuller report and includes the key constructs used, such as program logic and evaluation questions; outlines the methodology and approach to data collection; summarizes the conclusions; and presents the recommendations. The use of a larger report can be further enhanced by splitting this report into a range of subreports and producing associated brochures and other publications, as well as developing a range of information sharing strategies.

A Reporting and Dissemination Strategy will foreshadow the reporting requirements and interests of funders, program partners, and key stakeholders and plan for these to be met. Customization of reports to meet different audience needs includes consideration of the function of the reports in different contexts. A report may primarily serve accountability needs or alternatively address needs for improved implementation, identification of program results, wider learning, decision making regarding the program's future, allocation of resources, or all these purposes. Van Dooren et al. (2010, p. 108) identify three related main uses for performance information, these being to "learn," to "steer and control," and to "give account." Accordingly, the production of reports may need to prioritize one purpose above the other or provide balance and address multiple purposes in any one report. Patton (2012) suggests that when a single report has multiple functions and attempts to serve multiple audiences, clear distinctions should be made between its various sections. This approach assists the reader to locate relevant sections that best meet his or her information needs.

A Reporting and Dissemination Strategy will also typically specify the range of reports and other information products required and identify when they are expected to be produced and who is responsible for producing them. It is important that, as much as possible, reports are produced at a time when their contents will be used as intended. Delineating responsibilities for producing reports is also important, especially as many people may contribute to the production process. Close management of this process may be required to ensure that the various sections of a report are effectively drawn together when required.

A Reporting and Dissemination Strategy will further identify the focus and structure of the different kinds of reports to be produced and also detail the main contents of these reports. Finally, it will scope the range of dissemination strategies to be employed. Dissemination extends beyond the production of reports to the identification of complementary means for communicating information and knowledge derived from monitoring and evaluation. This aspect is discussed further below. An example of a Reporting and Dissemination Strategy is presented in the subsequent section.

### Dissemination

The dissemination of reports and other information products is an important process that supports their potential use and influence. A range of formal and informal dissemination strategies can be adopted, which are mutually reinforcing (Patton, 2012). Formal opportunities for dissemination can include publications that are distributed in hard copy or through posting on websites. Additionally, both in-person and virtual presentation and promotional opportunities could be available. Informal opportunities for dissemination are more likely to be ad hoc and involve taking advantage of opportunities for influence as they arise. Planning for dissemination is important to maximize the chances that the reports and information products produced will reach the intended audiences for those products.

While the benefits of dissemination are apparent, it is not always undertaken. Many evaluation reports are not seen or understood by key stakeholders, with such issues often exacerbated in developing country contexts where few reports are translated into national or local languages (Bamberger et al., 2012). Additionally, dissemination is often directed to powerful stakeholders. Beneficiaries and marginalized groups who often provide the information that forms the basis of monitoring and evaluation reports are frequently neglected.

Related constraints may be placed on dissemination by political, funder, and organizational influences. These may determine whether a report or related information will be distributed and to whom it will be distributed. Often such influences may be stronger than the good intentions of an evaluation team. It is important, however, not to adopt an air of fatalism about this dimension and to actively seek out and clarify opportunities for dissemination with a funder or other governing bodies. The following material is based on an assumption that reports and other related information products will be disseminated to key stakeholders and potentially made available to broader audiences.

In developing a Reporting and Dissemination Strategy, it is important to consider how different stakeholders may respond to different media. While some stakeholders are familiar with, and expect the production of more substantial technical reports, other stakeholders may require reports that are shorter, more engaging, and easier to access. Shorter written communications that facilitate interaction with the material may assist with the process of evaluative inquiry (Preskill & Torres, 1999). As stated earlier, larger reports can be augmented with accompanying executive summaries, issue papers, summary case studies, brochures, videos, presentations, and posters. These varied communication strategies are increasingly used to disseminate key messages in a more accessible format and potentially achieve a greater level of reader impact. Additionally, in-person presentations and discussions, especially with those disadvantaged communities that may have contributed perspectives and data, can be used to verbally communicate key findings and messages. Through such means, feedback on the evaluation process and its results can be elicited and further disseminated. In some contexts, different stakeholders will have been directly involved in collecting and analyzing evaluation data, which will further reinforce their interest in evaluation results and their potential application.

Improved knowledge about effective communication techniques has enabled reports to be produced that are likely to have greater reader impact. Communication techniques include use of design principles to inform choice of graphics, typeface, color, and arrangement of material (Evergreen, 2014). While the Reporting and Dissemination Strategy is unlikely to provide specific guidance about these factors, it can suggest the level of publication quality to which a report should be produced and whether to include the services of a graphic designer as part of a report's publication. Additionally, the Reporting and Dissemination

Strategy may suggest that brochures are produced to communicate findings to broader program stakeholders and beneficiaries. Such media are likely to require high-quality publication standards. Evergreen (2014) makes the following point in support of investing in design:

> Design, ultimately, is fairly invisible. It works in the background, behind the solid research you conducted. It can undermine the quality of your study or enhance it in such a way that you get more attention as a result. (p. 164)

Additionally, Evergreen (2014) cautions that identifying the key messages that must be conveyed is a critical element to getting the design right. The quality of the presentation of a report or other publication can only go so far in attracting interest, as the content needs to be meaningful and engaging as well.

In addition to the production of written communications, there are a range of interactive means for communicating messages. Aligning the production of reports with opportunities to present and discuss findings at conferences, in workshops, and in other working sessions may also assist the communication process. Interactive opportunities of this kind could be included as part of the Reporting and Dissemination Strategy. Additionally, use of social media has become a popular means to increase the accessibly of information.

Key considerations in dissemination thus include not only the identification of audiences and their information needs but also full appreciation as to how these audiences receive, respond, react to, and use information. Ideally, dissemination should include dynamic elements that promote interaction and discussion. To get the best fit between the audiences and the methods used for dissemination, active monitoring of the impact of dissemination approaches employed is advisable.

Table 9.4 provides an example of a completed Reporting and Dissemination Strategy. The strategy is structured according to type of report or dissemination product. An alternative would be to structure the strategy on the basis of individual stakeholder groups with the information needs and potential use by each identified. An additional column could be included in the format to identify different meetings and forums that would be organized in order to discuss and consider the implications of conclusions, recommendations, and lessons associated with the reports and other publications produced.

The extent of the guidance provided for reporting and dissemination processes will vary according to the needs of each program and the scope of the Monitoring and Evaluation Framework developed. A Monitoring and Evaluation Framework developed by an internal evaluator may contain a greater level of prescriptive detail than one developed by an external evaluator. In the latter case, the operational detail may be left to the host organization to complete as a later step.

**Table 9.4** Reporting and Dissemination Strategy (example)

| Report Type | Due Date | Audiences & Their Interests | | Overall Focus | Contents | Dissemination |
|---|---|---|---|---|---|---|
| *Formal Reports* | | | | | | |
| Routine Monitoring | Each quarter | • Funder<br>• Organization<br>• Program | • Accountability<br>• Management<br>• Program improvement | • Adequacy of budget against deliverables<br>• Progress to date<br>• Improvements in performance | • Financial report<br>• Outputs delivered<br>• Performance against milestones | • Funder template to be completed<br>• Distribute to funders and within organization |
| Midterm evaluation | Mid program | • Funder<br>• Organization<br>• Program<br>• Program partners | • Management<br>• Program Improvement | • Strategies to improve performance<br>• Learning for next stage | • Reasons for success/lack of success in performance<br>• Areas for future focus | • 25-page evaluation report<br>• Print and bind<br>• Post on organization intranet<br>• Distribute to funders and partners |
| End-term evaluation | End program | • Funder<br>• Organization<br>• Program<br>• External stakeholders | • Accountability<br>• Decision making<br>• Management<br>• Learning | • Conclusions<br>• Lessons<br>• Recommendations regarding program continuation | • Overall performance<br>• Program quality and value<br>• Conclusions<br>• Lessons<br>• Recommendations | • 50-page report<br>• Desktop publish and print<br>• Distribute to key stakeholders<br>• Produce summary brochure<br>• Post full report on website |

*(Continued)*

**Table 9.4** (Continued)

| Report Type | Due Date | Audiences & Their Interests | | Overall Focus | Contents | Dissemination |
|---|---|---|---|---|---|---|
| Annual report for organization | End calendar year | • Board members<br>• Organization<br>• External stakeholders | • Management<br>• Accountability | • Overview of achievements for year<br>• Challenges | • Financial report<br>• Personnel report<br>• Performance<br>• Success stories | • Annual report format<br>• Desktop publish and professionally print<br>• Post on website |
| *Ad Hoc and Event Reports* | | | | | | |
| Case studies | Intermittent | • Funder<br>• Organization<br>• Program Partners | • Wider learning | • Strategies to improve performance | • Performance<br>• Outcomes and impact<br>• Areas for future focus | • Post on website<br>• Post on social media |
| Publications (e.g., articles, papers) | Intermittent | • External stakeholders | • Wider learning | • Sharing knowledge | • Key messages | • Journal articles<br>• Conference and workshop papers<br>• Social media |
| Summary reports | Intermittent | • External stakeholders<br>• Beneficiaries | • Wider accountability and learning | • Sharing knowledge | • Key messages<br>• Learning | • Field trip to verbally present report and discuss results with beneficiaries |

### Practice Example

### Promoting Influence Through Tailored Dissemination

A nongovernment organization providing a range of family and children's services had previously produced a range of reports on their programs but had become dissatisfied with the level of attention and use of these reports by funding organizations and government agencies. In developing a Monitoring and Evaluation Framework for a new program, the organization placed a strong emphasis on identifying and piloting news ways of disseminating lessons and maximizing influence. First, senior program personnel consulted with personnel representing funding bodies and government agencies regarding the program's connection with various current policy initiatives. They identified the type of monitoring and evaluation products that would be most useful to support the policy-making process. In response, and as subsequently reflected in the Framework, program personnel developed short reports on a 6-month basis outlining the results and emerging lessons from the program. These were then shared with funders and government agencies during regular meetings. Feedback on these reports was provided in a timely way that was useful for the program in fine tuning its focus and direction. Funder and government agency representatives were also made aware of the progress of the program in its different project areas. As the program progressed, program personnel shared the emerging results more broadly, providing a summary on the program's Web site and making presentations at several conferences. When the end-of-program report was produced, it was published in several different formats, including a shorter summary report. The summary report contained a higher concentration of graphics and photographs to make it more visually appealing to readers. Additionally, a two-page back-to-back pamphlet was produced, further summarizing the larger report. Two articles were produced for publication in selected professional journals. These added to the visibility of the program, its evaluation, and lessons learned. A workshop was held with stakeholders to explore the implications of the findings and lessons, including for upcoming policy and regulatory initiatives in the program area. Funder and government agency representatives appeared engaged and provided feedback indicating that they saw the relevance and value of the findings and lessons to their work. The emphasis on early engagement with key users and the use of a variety of dissemination methods appeared to reinforce the level of influence achieved by this program.

## SUMMARY CHECKLIST

- Has consideration been given to developing or refining a learning strategy for the program, with possible reference to its host organization?
- Is there a focus on the identification and dissemination of promising interventions and innovative approaches, as well as limitations and lessons in the Monitoring and Evaluation Framework?
- Has consideration been given to means to promote regular reflection on the lessons generated by monitoring and evaluation processes, including promoting dialogue with stakeholders for this purpose?
- Have the purposes of reports and other information products been clearly outlined (e.g., accountability, management, learning)?
- Have strategies for reporting and dissemination been clearly identified in the Monitoring and Evaluation Framework?
- Will stakeholders have an opportunity to provide feedback on the effectiveness of the reporting and dissemination strategies used?

Depending on the type and focus of reports and information products produced, to what degree are they intended to assist with the following:

  o Accountability to a range of stakeholders?
  o Operational decision making and resource allocation decisions?
  o Identifying performance issues and corrections required?
  o Identifying lessons for improved service delivery?
  o Strategic and long-term policy development and planning processes?

- Have the information needs of different stakeholders been clearly identified including funders, policy developers, decision makers, beneficiaries, and others?
- Have the types of reports or other information products that will be produced been specified including details of their audiences?
- Will reports and information products be sufficiently tailored to meet different audience needs including informing decision making and resource allocation?

# Chapter 9 Learning, Reporting, and Dissemination Strategies

## CHAPTER REVIEW QUESTIONS

1. How would you approach the development and implementation of a learning strategy for a program?

2. How can a Monitoring and Evaluation Framework promote the identification of useful and transferable lessons?

3. How would you build strategies into a Monitoring and Evaluation Framework that promote effective reporting and dissemination of the conclusions, recommendations, and lessons that are generated?

4. Who would be the main audiences for information and reports derived from monitoring and evaluation, and how might their needs differ?

5. What types of reports could be produced for the different audiences in order to meet their differing information needs?

6. Other than a written report, are there other methods that could be used to disseminate information for maximizing reach to program stakeholders?

7. How would you ensure that reports and other information products produced and disseminated have potential for influence with funders, policy developers, decision makers, and other key stakeholders?

8. What do you see as being the enablers and barriers to reports and other information products produced being used and influential?

9. How can stakeholders have the opportunity to provide feedback on the effectiveness of the reporting and dissemination strategies used?

# CHAPTER 10

# Planning for Implementation of the Monitoring and Evaluation Framework

# Chapter 10  Planning for Implementation

*Consideration is now given to planning for the implementation of the Monitoring and Evaluation Framework, taking into account the staged approach upon which it has been developed and the critical need to involve stakeholders in the process.*

*Principles of effective project management are usefully applied to guide implementation of the Framework. These include clear identification of the tasks, timelines, and responsibilities for all the steps identified in the Framework. The implementation of the Monitoring and Evaluation Framework will itself require monitoring. This will extend to review and periodic adjustment, as required, with assessment of the process of implementation and results of its use.*

## 1. INTRODUCTION TO PLANNING FOR IMPLEMENTATION

The context for the development of a Monitoring and Evaluation Framework as advanced in this text is assumed to be a program, which in turn is often located within an organization. As such, the implementation of the Monitoring and Framework is likely to be guided and governed by those arrangements already in place in the organization for internal decision making, allocation of resources, and reporting. Synergy between monitoring and evaluation and program and organizational management arrangements is to be encouraged and will generally reinforce the quality of usefulness of results achieved. Such integration is integral to the notion of Results-Based Management and promoted through this approach. As Meier (2003) highlights:

> Results-Based Management (RBM) provides the management framework and tools for strategic planning, risk management, performance monitoring and evaluation. Its primary purpose is to improve efficiency and effectiveness through organizational learning, and secondly to fulfil accountability obligations through performance reporting. Key to its success is the involvement of stakeholders. (p. 6)

Integration of monitoring and evaluation processes in this manner is ideal but cannot be automatically assumed (OECD DAC, 2006). An unfortunate tendency for monitoring and evaluation activities to operate at the margins of programs has been noted, sometimes reinforced by lack of engagement or support from leadership. Such trends underline the critical observations of Kettner et al.

(2013), who identify leadership and resourcing as key success factors for the implementation ("conversion") of a monitoring and evaluation system, "leadership and staff commitment to performance measurement, monitoring, and program evaluation is the sine qua non of a successful conversion; but commitment without resources will probably not get the job done" (p. 306).

Similarly, Van Dooren et al. (2010) observe that leadership and ownership are vital to the implementation of performance management arrangements, including monitoring and evaluation. Furthermore, they identify staff training and skills development as additional success factors, while also noting that implementation will be affected by the quality of the data produced by the system and its perceived cost-benefit. Previous sections of this text have highlighted the need for proactive strategies to build support from leadership to enhance the effective implementation of a Monitoring and Evaluation Framework.

While the preceding factors represent preconditions for success, the actual implementation of a Monitoring and Evaluation Framework requires specific and detailed attention. This need stems from the many specialized activities, such as data collection, that are carried out as part of monitoring and evaluation, which may be unlike other actions that the organization or program performs. The range of tasks involved is highlighted in Figure 10.1.

Planning for the implementation of the Monitoring and Evaluation Framework is the final stage of a six-stage process. Initial work planning is likely to have occurred to guide the development of the building blocks that formed the basis for the development of the Monitoring and Evaluation Framework. As outlined earlier, these include identification of processes for stakeholder engagement and clarification of the purpose and parameters of the Framework (Stage 1), developing key constructs and evaluation questions (Stage 2), and development of monitoring and evaluation plans (Stage 3).

The subsequent Stage 4 represents planning for data collection, management, analysis, and synthesis. The focus here is on the details of the generation and use of data from complementary monitoring and evaluation processes and the synthesis of emergent data to form evaluative conclusions. Consideration is then given in Stage 5 to approaches to learning, reporting, and the dissemination of results and lessons learned. Each of the identified stages comprises a range of constituent steps that have been discussed in detail in each of the chapters in the text.

The final stage, Stage 6, concerns the actual implementation of the Framework, for which detailed planning is undertaken. This planning is included within the completed Framework and represents a guide in relation to actions, their sequence, timing, and specific assigned responsibilities. Principles of effective project management inform the guidance provided. Such work involves a

**Figure 10.1** Work Planning for Implementation of the Monitoring and Evaluation Framework

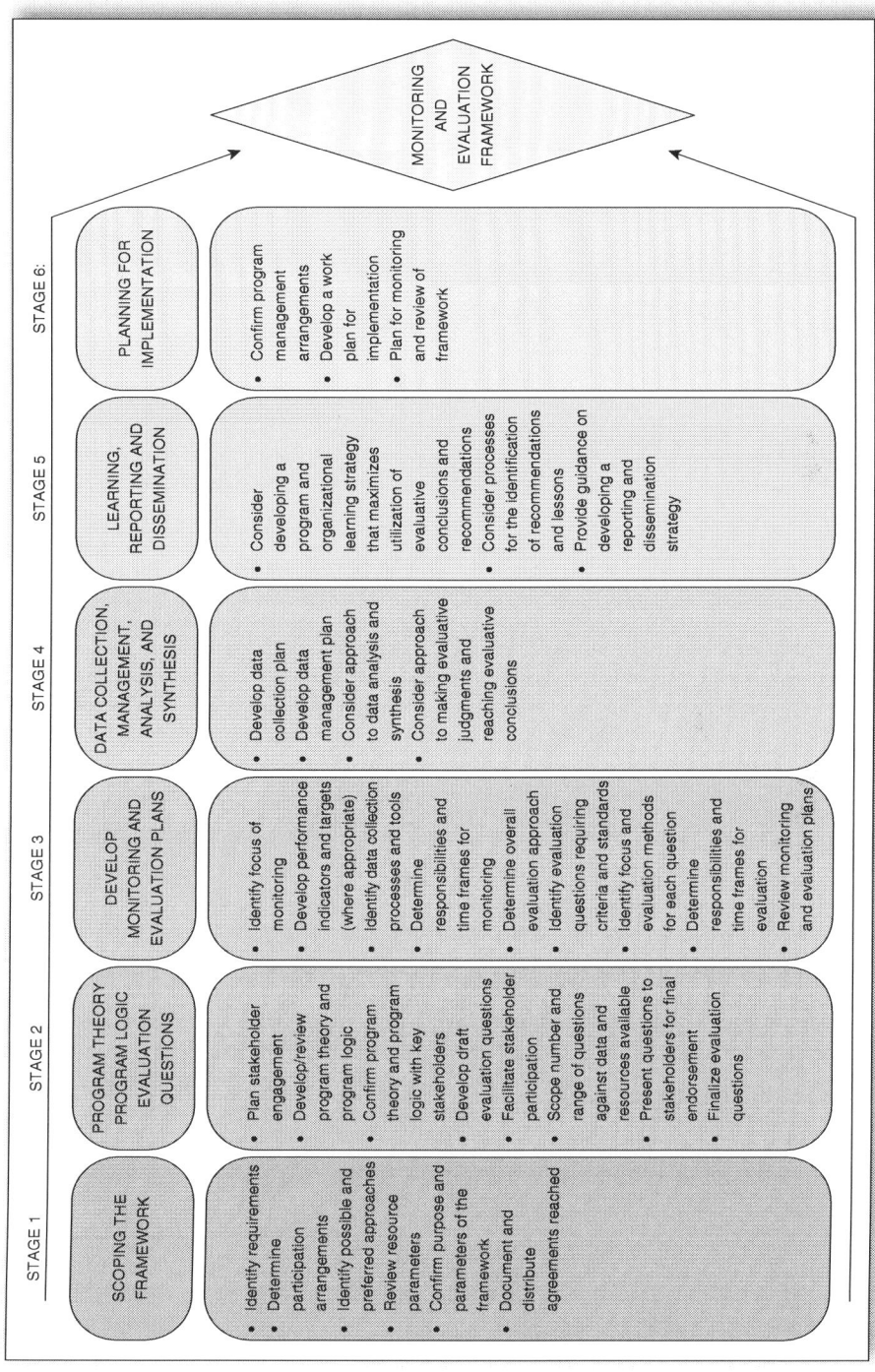

combination of forward thinking and discipline aimed at providing structure for the implementation of the Framework over time. Attention is also given here to planning for monitoring the implementation of the Framework itself and its periodic review.

## 2. KEY STEPS IN IMPLEMENTATION OF MONITORING AND EVALUATION FRAMEWORKS

The three mains steps involved in planning for implementation of the Monitoring and Evaluation Framework are identified in Table 10.1.

**Table 10.1** Steps Involved in Planning for Implementation

| *Stage 6: Planning for Implementation of the Monitoring and Evaluation Framework* | | |
|---|---|---|
| *Steps* | | |
| 1 | Confirm program management arrangements | • Provide guidance regarding program and organizational elements required for effective operation of monitoring and evaluation functions, as identified in the Monitoring and Evaluation Framework. These include the areas of management of key stakeholder relationships, personnel management, financial management, information technology, and administrative systems.<br>• Identify any specific areas of program or organizational capacity development required to implement the Framework.<br>• Provide guidance regarding any necessary adjustment or development of program guidelines and procedures to support implementation of the Monitoring and Evaluation Framework. |
| 2 | Develop a work plan for implementation | • Develop a work plan for implementation of the Monitoring and Evaluation Framework. This should identify required activities, when they are to be undertaken, and who is responsible for them. Use a Gantt chart or similar planning tool for this purpose. |
| 3 | Plan for monitoring and review of Framework | • Determine how the implementation of the Monitoring and Evaluation Framework will be monitored and reviewed. Include arrangements that will examine the relevance of the content and organization of the Framework as well as the effectiveness and efficiency of its implementation.<br>• Build arrangements for ongoing monitoring and periodic review of the Monitoring and Evaluation Framework into the work plan. Include arrangements for periodic updating of the Framework and continued focus on developing program and organizational capacity for monitoring and evaluation as required. |

## Step 1: Confirm Program Management Arrangements

Maintaining adequate support and integration of the factors required for monitoring and evaluation can present challenges for the program manager and for organizational leadership. As highlighted in Figure 10.2, monitoring and evaluation represent one of a range of interdependent program management functions. For example, the availability of effective information systems is often a precondition for data collection and analysis carried out as part of monitoring and evaluation activities. Effective personnel management is required to provide requisite capacity for monitoring and evaluation functions. Similarly, appropriate standards of budgeting and financial management represent preconditions that provide the required resources for monitoring and evaluation activities.

Integrating monitoring and evaluation functions within broader program management highlights the need for detailed planning, adequate resource allocation,

**Figure 10.2** Program Management Arrangements

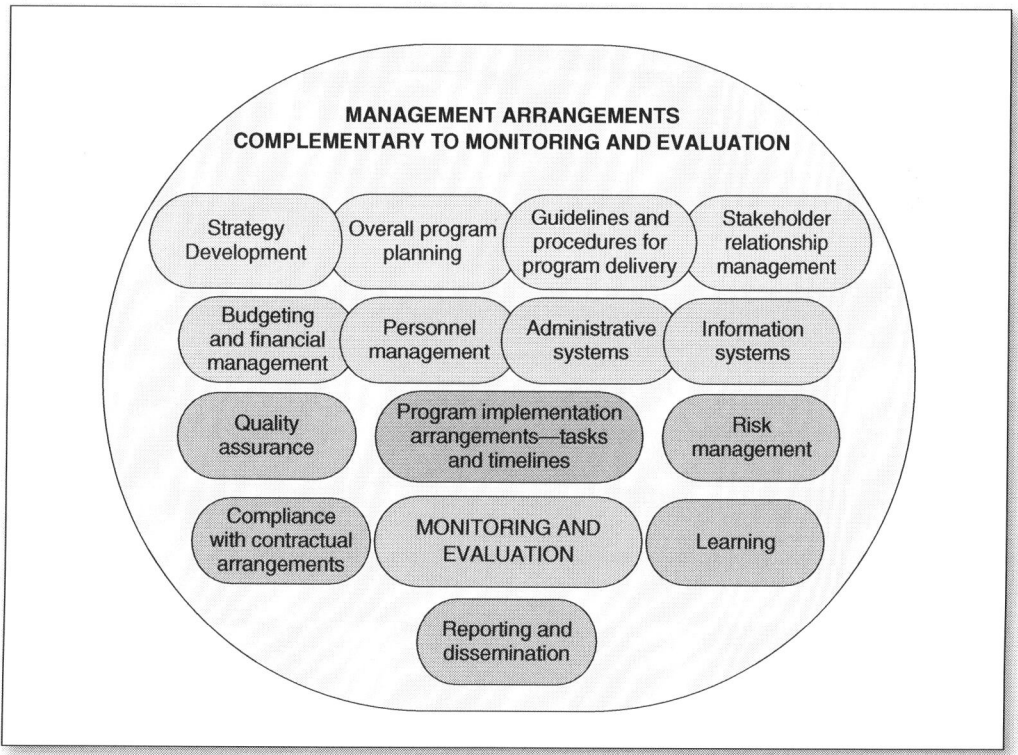

and close internal program coordination (Calley, 2011; Morra Imas & Rist, 2009). The Monitoring and Evaluation Framework can provide guidance to this process. For example, it may be that the implementation of a Monitoring and Evaluation Framework requires additional computer equipment, development of database capacities, and the recruitment and training of specialist personnel. Specific budgets may also be required, particularly for evaluation-related aspects. Such requirements can be specified within the Monitoring and Evaluation Framework.

Identifying risks associated with the Monitoring and Evaluation Framework and planning for their management is another potential aspect of integration with program management arrangements. These may be included in an existing or newly generated Risk Management Plan and possibly included as an appendix to the Monitoring and Evaluation Framework. Aspects related to the implementation of a Monitoring and Evaluation Framework may also be incorporated in a procedures or an operational manual that is maintained by the program or the host organization. Examples of areas for possible inclusion include financial management, human resource management, information management, and ethical conduct. In this manner, closer integration between the management of monitoring and evaluation and other program management functions is promoted.

### *Step 2: Develop a Work Plan for Implementation*

Work planning involves formulating detailed arrangements for the implementation of the Monitoring and Evaluation Framework. Typically this involves the identification of the different tasks to be performed and associated personnel and their specific responsibilities. These details are then incorporated in a chart or plan. An initial step in the preparation of a work plan may involve a meeting where monitoring and evaluation staff members identify what is required and feasible. Such a meeting is also likely to build their commitment and ownership of the implementation process. The absence of a work plan heightens the risk that the Monitoring and Evaluation Framework will not be successfully implemented.

In addition to narrative elements, the core of a work plan typically involves a Gantt chart (named after Henry Gantt) or a similar chart showing the project schedule. A range of computer software is available to aid the preparation of Gantt charts. With an emphasis on clear and direct visual communication, a Gantt chart identifies the various activities, when each activity is expected to start and finish, how long each activity is scheduled to last, the overlap of activities and by how much, a range of milestones, the start and finish date of the overall process, and responsible personnel. More elaborate formats may detail relationships between various tasks (dependencies), resources used for each task, and also include information on how far each task has progressed.

**Chapter 10** Planning for Implementation 249

Two charts are presented in Figures 10.3 and 10.4. The first (Figure 10.3) is a simplified example of the implementation plan for the Monitoring and Evaluation Framework for Year 1. Its focus is on establishing activities. During the first year, monitoring activities are expected to commence, as will some initial evaluation activities. Monitoring reports are to be produced each quarter, while specific evaluation activities, when combined with the monitoring reports produced, are expected to lead to the production of a formative evaluation report at the end of Year 1. Responsible teams are specified with evaluation activities being conducted by a combined internal staff and external consultant team. In the second year (Figure 10.4), monitoring activities are expected to continue with other evaluation activities also scheduled. Cumulatively, these will contribute to production of a final summative evaluation report toward the end of Year 2. A more detailed work plan can be developed both overall and for any individual component.

The timelines are illustrative only and will be dependent on the size and scale of the program and its Monitoring and Evaluation Framework. In practice, it may take less or more time to complete the various steps than is suggested in the charts. Additional time is likely to be required where a highly participatory approach to

**Figure 10.3** Work Plan for the First Year of Implementation of Framework

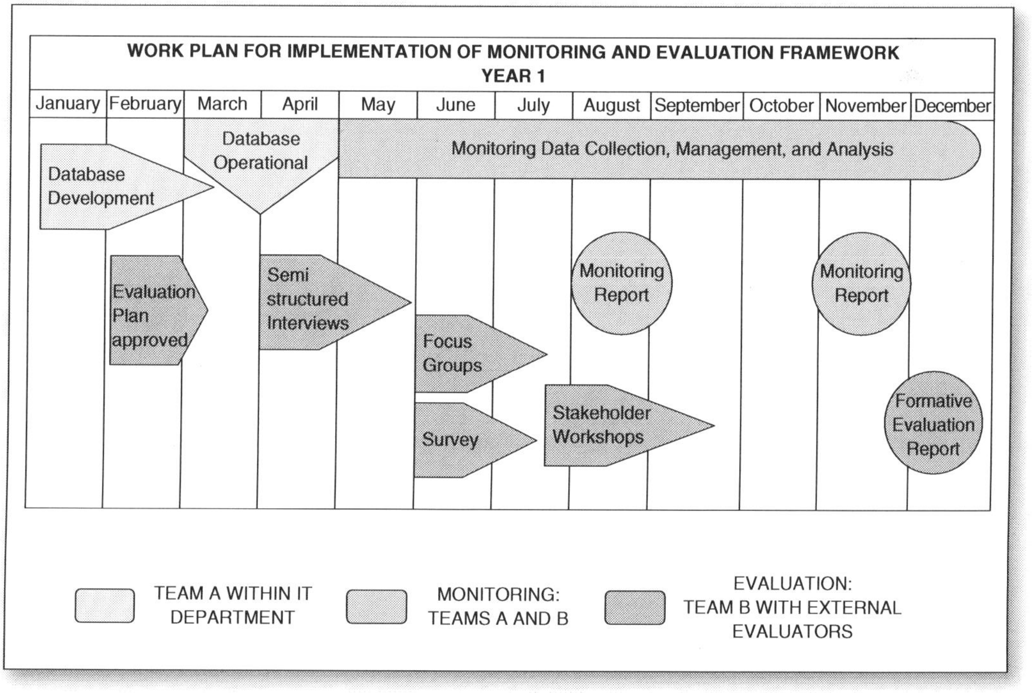

**Figure 10.4** Work Plan for the Second Year of Implementation of Framework

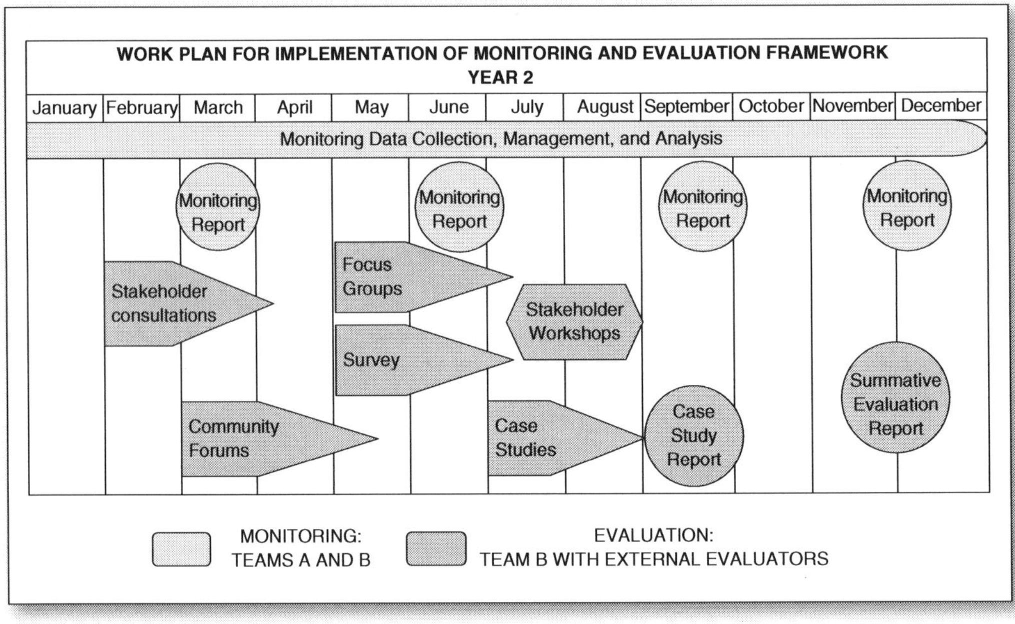

```
WORK PLAN FOR IMPLEMENTATION OF MONITORING AND EVALUATION FRAMEWORK
                                YEAR 2
January | February | March | April | May | June | July | August | September | October | November | December
        Monitoring Data Collection, Management, and Analysis

Monitoring Report (Feb/Mar)      Monitoring Report (May/Jun)      Monitoring Report (Aug/Sep)      Monitoring Report (Nov)

Stakeholder consultations        Focus Groups                     Stakeholder Workshops
                                 Survey
                                                                                                    Summative Evaluation Report
Community Forums                 Case Studies                     Case Study Report

MONITORING: TEAMS A AND B        EVALUATION: TEAM B WITH EXTERNAL EVALUATORS
```

design and implementation is adopted. In such contexts, it is not unusual for design processes to extend over a number of months with various rounds of stakeholder consultations and workshops. Monitoring processes will usually be mapped out over the entire program funding time frame, although it is highly likely that the intensity of monitoring activities will diminish toward the end of the program. The implementation of the evaluation component may vary significantly. The evaluation component could operate over most of the program cycle and involve a range of activities or possibly be concentrated around specific periods such as at the midterm and at the end of program. The summative evaluation is likely to be synchronized with the funding cycle of the program, usually coming toward the end of the funding period or at a time of review.

Flexibility is important in program management, and if obstacles or unforeseen delays are encountered, then adjustments will be required to the tasks and timeframes that are outlined in any implementation plan or chart. Where issues are experienced in relation to an agreed schedule, these should be discussed with relevant management personnel (Morra Imas & Rist, 2009). Ultimately, the value of a chart and the schedule that it contains relies on its use. Checking the progress of implementation against this chart is an important aspect of program management.

## Step 3: Plan for Monitoring and Review of Framework

As stated in the Introduction of this text, a Monitoring and Evaluation Framework is both a planning process and a written product designed to provide guidance to the conduct of monitoring and evaluation functions over the life span of a program. The viability and utility of the Framework will be tested during its early implementation. As the Framework continues to be implemented over time, a range of internal capacity issues and external challenges may be encountered. Particular approaches to monitoring and evaluation may prove to be more or less advantageous or problematic. Additionally, changes may occur in a program's focus and in expectations of its results over time. Changes of this kind will have consequences for the purpose and focus of the Monitoring and Evaluation Framework, including for the program theory and the program logic.

The fluid and changeable environment under which most programs operate underlines the need for periodic review and updating of the Monitoring and Evaluation Framework and how it is implemented. This review process is important for ensuring the sustainability of the Framework (Kusek & Rist, 2004). If not routinely reviewed, the Monitoring and Evaluation Framework runs the risk that it will no longer be seen as practical, useful, or relevant to the program or its host organization.

A periodic review process would commence with a broad assessment of the relevance, effectiveness, and efficiency of the implementation of the Framework and the results derived. Informed by this broader assessment, a range of specific areas are likely to require investigation. The latter relate to the content and organization of the Framework itself and to the organizational and program capacity to undertake monitoring and evaluation functions. Examples of these considerations are outlined in the Table 10.2.

The frequency of review of the Monitoring and Evaluation Framework will depend on the size and scale of the program, the quality of initial assessments undertaken, and capacity development activities that may have been conducted for monitoring and evaluation. Where the level of data available and the capacity for data collection and analysis are more uncertain, a review should occur soon after implementation in order to test the viability and utility of the Framework and make appropriate adjustments. Additionally, the review may focus on the extent to which a program undertaking incremental implementation of its Framework is ready to advance from one implementation step to another. When there is agreement reached as to the best timing and most appropriate intervals for a review of the Framework, these timings could be included as part of the work plan as outlined in Step 2.

**Table 10.2** Areas for Review of the Monitoring and Evaluation Framework and Its Implementation

| Overall Focus |
|---|
| - Extent to which the Monitoring and Evaluation Framework reflects an appropriate understanding of the program and its context
- Extent to which the Monitoring and Evaluation Framework provides a basis for the collection of needed and useful information for the program and its stakeholders
- Extent to which the Monitoring and Evaluation Framework has been effectively implemented
- Particular issues or constraints that may have been experienced in the implementation of the Monitoring and Evaluation Framework and which require adjustments to be made |

*Specific Areas*

| Structure of Framework | Implementation of Framework |
|---|---|
| Program theory and program logic: focus and orientation of expected results | Degree of integration of monitoring and evaluation with program management functions |
| Evaluation questions: focus and range of questions posed | Effectiveness of leadership provided in support of monitoring and evaluation functions |
| The Monitoring Plan: areas to monitor, usefulness of indicators and targets, availability of data | Adequacy of staff skills for successful implementation of the Framework and any requirements for further professional development |
| The Evaluation Plan: areas to evaluate, usefulness of selected evaluation methods, availability of data | Degree of incentives provided within the organization and program for undertaking monitoring, evaluation, and learning functions |
| Data collection, management, and analysis: feasibility and usefulness of approaches adopted | Operational effectiveness of data entry processes and database systems |
| Learning, reporting, and dissemination: feasibility and usefulness of approaches adopted | Extent required data are available and data synthesis and analysis is taking place |
| Implementation schedule and milestones: whether realistic and ability to be modified based on progress | Degree of clarity about roles and responsibilities for monitoring and evaluation, particularly coordination roles |
| Budget and staffing arrangements for monitoring and evaluation functions clearly identified | Budget and staffing arrangements for monitoring and evaluation functions clearly identified |

## SUMMARY CHECKLIST

- Do monitoring and evaluation functions appear to be well integrated within the program and host organization and their overall management?
- Have the program and/or organizational functions that are required for the Monitoring and Evaluation Framework to be implemented been identified and included as part of the Framework?
- Has an implementation plan been developed as part of the Monitoring and Evaluation Framework that identifies activities, timelines, and roles and responsibilities?
- Have these activities, timelines, roles, and responsibilities been presented in a suitable work plan or chart?
- Has a process been established for monitoring the implementation of the Framework and undertaking a periodic review as to how effectively and efficiently it is working in practice?
- Does the monitoring and review process allow for any adjustments of the Framework and associated work plan or chart, as required?
- Will program and organizational capacity for implementing the Framework continue to be monitored and reviewed and additional support provided should this be required?

## CHAPTER REVIEW QUESTIONS

1. How would you go about developing an effective and realistic implementation plan for a Monitoring and Evaluation Framework?
2. Who would you involve in the process, and why?
3. What do you see as the enablers and barriers to putting an implementation plan into operation within a program and its host organization?
4. What do you see as the key features of successful implementation of a Monitoring and Evaluation Framework?
5. How would you go about monitoring and reviewing the implementation of a Monitoring and Evaluation Framework?
6. What are the major areas that would be examined in undertaking such monitoring and review?

# CHAPTER 11

# Conclusion

This text has presented an approach to the development of Monitoring and Evaluation Frameworks that is firmly based on evaluation principles and practice and delineated into manageable stages and steps. A Monitoring and Evaluation Framework is regarded as both a planning process and a written product designed to guide the conduct of monitoring and evaluation functions over the life span of a program. After the Framework is developed, monitoring and evaluation functions are then put into operation and incorporated within the regular operations of a program. Monitoring and evaluation contribute to a program's overall value by producing conclusions, recommendations, and lessons that can be used to inform program improvement, guide decision making, and support wider learning.

Programs that are routinely adjusted based on conclusions derived from monitoring and evaluation processes have a better chance of delivering positive outcomes that will potentially improve the social, economic, environmental, or other circumstances for which the program was developed. As Monitoring and Evaluation Frameworks are more frequently developed and implemented for a range of programs across sectors and country contexts, it is anticipated that net returns for management, accountability, learning, and program improvement will become clearly evident. In this context, arguments for the benefits relative to the costs of monitoring and evaluation will be most persuasive.

The text has outlined an approach to developing a Monitoring and Evaluation Framework that is both informed by evaluation theory and is practical. Key features of this evaluation-led approach to developing a Monitoring and Evaluation Framework include the use of program theory and program logic together with the focus provided by evaluation questions categorized using the five main evaluation domains. The approach taken provides clear guidance as to how to plan for monitoring and evaluation processes in a participatory, logical, systematic, and integrated way.

# Chapter 11 Conclusion

It is anticipated that this text will provide readers with a useful and informative resource for the development of a Monitoring and Evaluation Framework and that it will be applicable to a wide range of audiences working with different socioeconomic groups in both developing and developed country contexts. The text should be particularly useful for those readers with a strong interest in positioning evaluation at the forefront of a Monitoring and Evaluation Framework.

Developing and implementing a Monitoring and Evaluation Framework requires in the first instance the acquisition of knowledge and skills required to undertake the task. Thereafter, support for the Framework's role and value are required, together with a commitment to the participatory processes involved. It is hoped that this text will contribute to the development of the required knowledge and skill areas and will also motivate and inspire readers to be confident and proactive in the use and application of Monitoring and Evaluation Frameworks. Such application has considerable power to enhance the practice of monitoring and evaluation and, by extension, build the quality of programs and their results.

SCOPE FRAMEWORK

PROGRAM THEORY & LOGIC

EVALUATION QUESTIONS

PLAN FOR DATA ANALYSIS & SYNTHESIS

PLAN FOR DATA COLLECTION & MANAGEMENT

MONITORING PLAN & EVALUATION PLAN

PLAN FOR LEARNING, REPORTING & DISSEMINATION

PLAN FOR IMPLEMENTATION

FRAMEWORK COMPLETED!

# Appendix*

# MONITORING AND EVALUATION FRAMEWORK TEMPLATE

**Proposed Table of Contents for Monitoring and Evaluation Framework**

| 1 | Purpose of Monitoring and Evaluation Framework<br><br>1.1 Key Stakeholders<br>1.2 Purpose and Focus<br>1.3 Requirements and Expectations<br>1.4 Stakeholder Capacity Building Needs |
|---|---|
| 2 | Background and Context to the Program<br><br>2.1 Program Context<br>2.2 Goal and Objectives<br>2.3 Program Design |
| 3 | Program Theory and Program Logic<br><br>3.1 Considerations<br>3.2 Participatory Approach<br>3.3 Program Theory<br>3.4 Program Logic |
| 4 | Evaluation Questions<br><br>4.1 Considerations<br>4.2 Participatory Approach<br>4.3 Finalized Questions |
| 5 | The Monitoring Plan<br><br>5.1 Approach to Monitoring<br>5.2 The Monitoring Plan |

*(Continued)*

*These documents are available for downloading at http://study.sagepub.com/dmef.

(Continued)

| | | |
|---|---|---|
| 6 | The Evaluation Plan | |
| | 6.1 Approach to Evaluation | |
| | 6.2 The Evaluation Plan | |
| | 6.3 The Evaluation Rubric | |
| 7 | Data Collection Plan | |
| | 7.1 Data Collection Plan | |
| | 7.2 Managing Potential Ethical Issues | |
| 8 | Data Management Plan | |
| | 8.1 Data Management Plan | |
| 9 | Data Synthesis, Judgments, and Conclusions | |
| | 9.1 Approach to Data Synthesis | |
| | 9.2 Forming Judgments | |
| | 9.3 Reaching Conclusions | |
| 10 | Learning Strategy, | |
| | 10.1 Organizational and Program Learning Strategy | |
| | 10.2 Identifying Recommendations and Lessons | |
| 11 | Reporting and Dissemination Plan | |
| | 11.1 Reporting and Dissemination Plan | |
| 12 | Implementation Work Plan | |
| | 12.1 Program Management Arrangements | |
| | 12.2 Work Planning | |
| | 12.3 Monitoring and Review of Framework | |
| Appendix | Monitoring and Evaluation Data Collection Tools | |

## 1. PURPOSE OF MONITORING AND EVALUATION FRAMEWORK

### 1.1 Key Stakeholders

| Stakeholder Mapping Matrix | | | | | | |
|---|---|---|---|---|---|---|
| Stakeholder Groups | Consultation Focus and Scope | Development of Key Constructs | Development of the Overall Framework | Endorsement of Final Framework | Implementation of the Framework | Audience for M&E Products |
| | | | | | | |
| | | | | | | |
| | | | | | | |

### 1.2 Purpose and Focus

### 1.3 Requirements and Expectations

### 1.4 Stakeholder Capacity-Building Needs

| Stage | Required Areas of Knowledge and Understanding |
|---|---|
| Initial Orientation | |
| Developing the Framework | |
| Implementing the Framework | |
| Managing Findings and Reporting | |

## 2. BACKGROUND AND CONTEXT TO THE PROGRAM

   2.1  Program Context

   2.2  Goal and Objectives

   2.3 Program Design

## 3. PROGRAM THEORY AND PROGRAM LOGIC

### 3.1 Considerations

### 3.2 Participatory Approach

### 3.3 Program Theory

The Program Theory is depicted in the diagram below:

## 3.4 Program Logic

**INPUTS:**

**ACTIVITIES:**

| Outputs | Short-Term Outcomes | Medium-Term Outcomes | Impacts |
|---|---|---|---|
|  |  |  |  |

**ASSUMPTIONS:**

**CONTRIBUTING POLICIES AND STRATEGIES:**

**EXTERNAL FACTORS AND CONSTRAINTS:**

## 4. EVALUATION QUESTIONS

   4.1 Considerations



   4.2 Participatory Approach



   4.3 Finalized Questions

| Domains | Evaluation Questions |
|---|---|
| **Appropriateness** | |
| **Effectiveness** | |
| **Efficiency** | |
| **Impact** | |
| **Sustainability** | |

## 5. THE MONITORING PLAN

### 5.1 Approach to Monitoring

### 5.2 The Monitoring Plan

| Evaluation Questions | Focus of Monitoring | Indicators | Targets | Monitoring Data Sources | Who Is Responsible | When |
|---|---|---|---|---|---|---|
| **Appropriateness** | | | | | | |
| **Effectiveness** | | | | | | |
| **Efficiency** | | | | | | |
| **Impact** | | | | | | |
| **Sustainability** | | | | | | |

## 6. THE EVALUATION PLAN

   6.1 Approach to Evaluation

   6.2 The Evaluation Plan

| Evaluation Questions | *Summary of Monitoring* | *Focus of Evaluation* | *Evaluation Method* | *Method Implementation* | *Who Is Responsible* | *When* |
|---|---|---|---|---|---|---|
| **Appropriateness** | | | | | | |
| **Effectiveness** | | | | | | |
| **Efficiency** | | | | | | |
| **Impact** | | | | | | |
| **Sustainability** | | | | | | |

## 6.3 The Evaluation Rubric

| Criterion | Standards | | | | Justification |
|---|---|---|---|---|---|
| | Excellent | Good | Adequate | Poor | |
| **Quality:** | | | | | |
| 1 | | | | | |
| 2 | | | | | |
| 3 | | | | | |
| 4 | | | | | |
| **Value:** | | | | | |
| 1 | | | | | |
| 2 | | | | | |
| 3 | | | | | |
| 4 | | | | | |

## 7. DATA COLLECTION PLAN

### 7.1 Data Collection Plan

| Data Collection Tools | | | | |
|---|---|---|---|---|
| | A | B | C | D |
| *Purpose* | | | | |
| *Focus* | | | | |
| *Sampling* | | | | |
| *Implementation* | | | | |
| *Potential Ethical Issues* | | | | |
| *Requiring Development* | | | | |

### 7.2 Potential Ethical Issues

| Data Collection Tools | Potential Ethical Issues |
|---|---|
| | |
| | |
| | |
| | |
| | |

## 8. DATA MANAGEMENT PLAN

| Database Requirements: | | | | |
|---|---|---|---|---|
| *Data Collected* | *Data Entry* | *Data Analysis* | *Database Reports* | *Staff Training and Orientation* |
| | | | | |
| | | | | |
| | | | | |
| | | | | |
| | | | | |

## 9. DATA SYNTHESIS, JUDGMENTS, AND CONCLUSIONS

### 9.1 Approach to Data Synthesis

| Evaluation Questions | Performance Indicators and Targets | Monitoring Data | Evaluation Data | Data Synthesis |
|---|---|---|---|---|
| **Appropriateness** | | | | |
| **Effectiveness** | | | | |
| **Efficiency** | | | | |
| **Impact** | | | | |
| **Sustainability** | | | | |

### 9.2 Making Judgments

| | Evaluation Question: | | | | | |
|---|---|---|---|---|---|---|
| | | Standards | | | | |
| Criterion | Data Synthesis | Excellent | Good | Adequate | Poor | Evaluative Judgments |
| | | | | | | |
| | | | | | | |
| | | | | | | |

## 9.3 Reaching Conclusions

| Evaluation Questions | Data Synthesis | Evaluative Judgments | Evaluative Conclusions |
|---|---|---|---|
| Appropriateness | | | |
| Effectiveness | | | |
| Efficiency | | | |
| Impact | | | |
| Sustainability | | | |

## 10. LEARNING STRATEGY

### 10.1 Organizational and Program Learning Strategy

### 10.2 Identifying Recommendations and Lessons

| Evaluative Conclusions | Recommendations | Lessons |
|---|---|---|
|  |  |  |
|  |  |  |
|  |  |  |
|  |  |  |

## 11. REPORTING AND DISSEMINATION PLAN

### 11.1 Reporting and Dissemination Plan

| Report Type | Due Date | Audience & Their Interests | Overall Focus | Contents | Dissemination |
|---|---|---|---|---|---|
| **Formal Reports** | | | | | |
| | | | | | |
| | | | | | |
| | | | | | |
| | | | | | |
| **Ad Hoc and Event Reports** | | | | | |
| | | | | | |
| | | | | | |
| | | | | | |

## 12. IMPLEMENTATION WORKPLAN

### 12.1 Program Management Arrangements

### 12.2 Work Planning

| Year | Jan | Feb | Mar | Apr | May | Jun | Jul | Aug | Sep | Oct | Nov | Dec |
|------|-----|-----|-----|-----|-----|-----|-----|-----|-----|-----|-----|-----|
|      |     |     |     |     |     |     |     |     |     |     |     |     |
|      |     |     |     |     |     |     |     |     |     |     |     |     |
|      |     |     |     |     |     |     |     |     |     |     |     |     |

### 12.3 Monitoring and Review of Framework

| Overall Focus | |
|---|---|
| *Specific Areas* | |
| Structure of the Framework | Implementation of Framework |
|   |   |
|   |   |
|   |   |
|   |   |

## Appendix

Monitoring and Evaluation Data Collection Tools

(List selected data collection tools here.)

# References

African Evaluation Association. (2006). *African evaluation guidelines*—Standards and norms. Retrieved from http://www.ader-evaluare.ro/docs/African%20Evaluation%20Association.pdf

Alkin, M. C. (2013). *Evaluation roots: A wider perspective of theorists' views and influences*. Thousand Oaks, CA: Sage.

American Evaluation Association. (2004). *Guiding principles for evaluators*. Retrieved from http://www.eval.org/p/cm/ld/fid=51

Anand, S., & Sen, A. K. (2000). Human development and economic sustainability. *World Development, 28*(12), 2029–2049.

Armytage, L. (2011). Evaluating aid: An adolescent domain of practice. *Evaluation, 17*(3), 261-276.

Asian Development Bank. (2011). *Special evaluation study on managing for development results*. Manila, the Phillipines ADB.

Asif, M. (2013). Methodological pluralism with reference to recent literature. *International Journal of Academic Research and Reflection, 1*(2), 14-25.

Astbury, B., & Leeuw, F. (2010). Unpacking black boxes: Mechanisms and theory building in evaluation. *American Journal of Evaluation, 31*(3), 363-381.

Australasian Evaluation Society. (2013). *Guidelines on ethical conduct of evaluation and code of ethics*. Melbourne, Australia: Author.

Bamberger, M. (2010, November). *Reconstructing baseline data for impact evaluation and results measurement* (Special series on the nuts and bolts of M&E systems 4). Washington, DC: World Bank.

Bamberger, M., Rugh, J., & Mabry, L. (2012). *RealWorld evaluation: Working under budget, time, data, and political constraints* (2nd ed.). Thousand Oaks, CA: Sage.

Bernard, H. R., & Ryan, G. W. (2010). *Analyzing qualitative data: Systematic approaches*. Thousand Oaks, CA: Sage.

Boll, J., & Høeberg, L. (2013). Performance management and evaluation in the Danish public employment service. *New Directions for Evaluation, 137*, 57–67.

Bryson, J., & Patton, M. (2010). Analyzing and engaging stakeholders. In J. S. Wholey, H. P. Harty, & K. E. Newcomer (Eds.), *Handbook of practical program evaluation* (3rd ed., pp. 30–54). San Francisco, CA: Jossey-Bass.

Calley, N. G. (2011). *Program development in the 21st century: An evidence-based approach to design, implementation, and evaluation*. Thousand Oaks, CA: Sage.

Canadian Evaluation Society. (1996). *Guidelines for ethical conduct*. Retrieved from http://www.evaluationcanada.ca/site.cgi?s=5&ss=4&_lang=en

Castro, M. F. (2011). Defining and using performance indicators and targets in government M&E systems. *The World Bank Prem Notes: Special series on the nuts and bolts of M&E systems*. Retrieved from http://siteresources.worldbank.org/INTPOVERTY/Resources/335642-1276521901256/ME12_v2.pdf

Centers for Disease Control and Prevention. (2006). *CDC unified process practice guides: Risk management*. Retrieved from http://www2.cdc.gov/cdcup/library/practices_guides/CDC_UP_Risk_Management_Practices_Guide.pdf

Chen, H. T. (2005). *Practical program evaluation: Assessing and improving planning, implementation, and effectiveness*. Thousand Oaks, CA: Sage.

Chen, H. T. (2013). The roots and growth of theory-driven evaluation. In M. C. Alkin (Ed.), *Evaluation roots: A wider perspective of theorists' views and influences* (pp. 113–129). Thousand Oaks, CA: Sage.

Chen, H. T. (2015). *Practical program evaluation: Theory-driven evaluation and the integrated evaluation perspective*. Thousand Oaks, CA: Sage.

Chianca, T. (2008). The OECD/DAC criteria for international development evaluations: An assessment and ideas for improvement. *Journal of MultiDisciplinary Evaluation*, 5(9), 41–51.

Chouinard, J. A. (2013). The case for participatory evaluation in an era of accountability. *American Journal of Evaluation*, 34(2), 237–253.

Clinton, J. (2014). The true impact of evaluation: Motivation for ECB. *American Journal of Evaluation*, 35(1), 120–127.

Conley-Tyler, M. (2005). A fundamental choice: Internal or external evaluation? *Evaluation Journal of Australasia*, 4(1&2), 3–11.

Cornwall, A., & Brock, K. (2005). What do buzzwords do for development policy? A critical look at 'participation', 'empowerment' and 'poverty reduction.' *Third World Quarterly*, 26(7), 1043–1060.

Coryn, C. L., Noakes, L.A., Westine, C.D., & Schroter, D.C. (2011). A systematic review of theory-driven evaluation practice form 1990 to 2009. *American Journal of Evaluation*, 32(2), 199–226.

Cousins, J. B., Donohue, J. J., & Bloom G. A. (1996). Collaborative evaluation in North America: Evaluators' self-reported opinions, practices, and consequences. *Evaluation Practice*, 17(3), 207–226.

Cousins, J. B., & Earl, L. M. (1995). *Participatory evaluation in education: Studies in evaluation use and organizational learning*. Washington, DC: Falmer Press.

Cousins, J. B., & Shulha, L. M. (2006). A comparative analysis of evaluation utilization and its cognate fields of inquiry: Current issues and trends. In I. Shaw, J. Greene, & M. Mark (Eds.), *The Sage handbook of evaluation* (pp. 266–291). Thousand Oaks, CA: Sage.

Cousins, J. B., & Whitmore, E. (1998). Framing participatory evaluation. *New Directions for Evaluation*, 80, 5–23.

Creswell, J. W. (2015). *A concise introduction to mixed methods research*. Thousand Oaks, CA: Sage.

Creswell, J. W., & Plano Clark, V. L. (2007). *Designing and conducting mixed methods research*. Thousand Oaks, CA: Sage.

Cullen, A. E., & Coryn, C. L. S. (2011). Forms and functions of participatory evaluation in international development: A review of the empirical and theoretical literature. *Journal of Multidisiplinary Evaluation*, 7(16), 32–47.

Cullen, A. E., Coryn, C. L. S., & Rugh, J. (2011). The politics and consequences of including stakeholders in international development. *American Journal of Evaluation*, 32(3), 345–361.

Dart, J. J., & Davies, R. J. (2003). A dialogical story-based evaluation tool: The most significant change technique. *American Journal of Evaluation, 24*, 137–155.

Datta, L. E. (2011). Politics and evaluation: More than methodology. *American Journal of Evaluation, 32*(2), 273–294.

Davidson, E. J. (2005). *Evaluation methodology basics: The nuts and bolts of sound evaluation.* Thousand Oaks, CA: Sage.

De Vries, M., & Nemec, J. (2013). Public sector reform: An overview of recent literature and research on NPM and alternative paths. *International Journal of Public Sector Management, 26*(1), 4–16.

Department for International Development. (2006). *Monitoring and Evaluation: A guide for DFID-contracted research programmes.* London, England/Author.

Donaldson, S.I. (2007). *Program theory-driven evaluation science: Strategies and applications.* New York, NY: Psychology Press.

Department of Planning and Community Development. (2013). *Draft local government performance reporting framework & indicators.* Melbourne, Australia: Author.

Drucker, P. F. (1954). *The practice of management.* New York, NY: Harper & Row.

Drucker, P. F. (1964). *Managing for results: Economic tasks and risk-taking decisions.* New York, NY: Harper & Row.

Dudding, B., & Nielsen, S. B. (2013). Managing for results in the U.S. not-for-profit sector: Applying complementary approaches of knowledge production at the Center for Employment Opportunities. *New Directions for Evaluation, 137*, 103–114.

Earl, S., Carden, F., & Smutylo, T. (2001). *Outcome mapping: Building learning and reflection into development programs.* Ottawa, Canada: International Development Research Centre.

Ebrahim, A. (2005). Accountability myopia: Losing sight of organizational learning. *Nonprofit and Voluntary Sector Quarterly, 34*(1), 56–87.

Evergreen, S. (2014). *Presenting data effectively: Communicating your findings for maximum impact.* Thousand Oaks, CA: Sage.

Eyben, R. (2013). *Uncovering the politics of 'evidence' and 'results': A framing paper for development practitioners.* Retrieved from http://bigpushforward.net/wp-content/uploads/2011/01/Uncovering-the-Politics-of-Evidence-and-Results-by-Rosalind-Eyben.pdf

Fetterman, D. M., & Wandersman, A. (2005). *Empowerment evaluation principles in practice.* New York, NY: Guilford Press.

Fitzpatrick, J. L., Sanders, J. R., & Worthen, B. (2011). *Program evaluation: Alternative approaches and practical guidelines* (4th ed.). Upper Saddle River, NJ: Pearson.

Fournier, D. M. (1995). Establishing evaluative conclusions: A distinction between general and working logic. *New Directions for Evaluation, 68*, 15–32.

Frechtling, J. A. (2007). *Logic modeling methods in program evaluation.* San Francisco, CA: Jossey-Bass.

Funnell, S. C., & Rogers, P. J. (2011). *Purposeful program theory: Effective use of theories of change and logic models.* San Francisco, CA: Jossey-Bass.

Greene, J. C. (1999). The inequality of performance measurements. *Evaluation, 5*(2), 160–172.

Greene, J. C. (2006). Evaluation, democracy, and social change. In I. Shaw, J. Greene, & M. Mark (Eds.), *The SAGE handbook of evaluation* (pp. 118–140). Thousand Oaks, CA: Sage.

Guijt, I. (2010). Exploding the myth of incompatibility between accountability and learning. In J. Ubels, N. Acquaye-Baddoo, & A. Fowler (Eds.), *Capacity development in practice* (pp. 277–292). London, England: Earthscan.

Hatry, H. P. (2006). *Performance measurement: Getting results* (2nd ed.). Washington, DC: Urban Institute Press.

Hatry, H. P. (2013). Sorting the relationships among performance measurement, program evaluation, and performance management. *New Directions for Evaluation, 137,* 19–32.

Hatton, M. J., & Schroeder, K. (2009). Results-based management: Friend or Foe? *Development in Practice, 17*(3), 426–432.

House, E. R., & Howe, K. R. (1999). *Values in evaluation and social research*. Thousand Oaks, CA: Sage.

House, E. R., & Howe, K. R. (2000). Deliberative democratic evaluation. *New Directions for Evaluation, 85,* 3–12.

Hummelbrunner, R. (2010). Beyond logframe: Critique, variations, and alternatives. In N. Fujita (Ed.), *Beyond logframe: Using systems concepts in evaluation* (pp. 1–34). Tokyo, Japan: FASID.

Hunter, D. E., & Nielsen, S.B. (2013). Performance management and evaluation: Exploring complementarities. *New Directions for Evaluation, 137,* 7–17.

Hurteau, M., & Williams, D. (2014). Credible judgment: Combining truth, beauty, and justice. *New Directions for Evaluation, 142,* 45–55.

International HIV/AIDS Alliance. (2001). *A facilitators' guide to participatory workshops with NGOs/CBOs responding to HIV/AIDS*. Brighton, England/ Author.

Kettner, P. M. Moroney, R. M., & Martin, L. L (2013). *Designing and managing programs: An effectiveness-based approach* (4th ed.). Thousand Oaks, CA: Sage.

King, J., McKegg, K., Oakden, J., & Wehipeihana, N. (2013). Evaluative rubrics: A method for surfacing values and improving the credibility of evaluation. *Journal of MultiDisciplinary Evaluation, 9*(21), 11–20.

King, J. A. (2005). Participatory evaluation. In S. Mathison (Ed.), *Encyclopedia of evaluation* (pp. 292–296). Thousand Oaks, CA: Sage.

Knowlton, L. W., & Phillips, C. C. (2013). *The logic model guidebook: Better strategies for great results* (2nd ed.). Thousand Oaks, CA: Sage.

Kusek, J. Z., & Rist, R. C. (2004). *Ten steps to a results-based monitoring and evaluation system*. Washington DC: World Bank.

Labin, S. (2014). Developing common measures in evaluation capacity building: An iterative science and practice process. *American Journal of Evaluation, 35*(1), 107–115.

Labin, S., Duffy, J., Meyers, D., Wandersman, A., & Lesesne, C. (2012). A research synthesis of the evaluation capacity building literature. *American Journal of Evaluation, 33*(3), 307–338.

Laudon, K. C., & Laudon, J. P. (2012). *Management information systems* (12th ed.). Upper Saddle River, NJ: Pearson Prentice Hall.

Le Menestrel, S., Walahoski, J., & Mielke, M. (2014). A partnership model for evaluation: Considering an alternate approach to the internal-external evaluation debate. *American Journal of Evaluation, 35*(1), 61–72.

Lopez-Acevedo, G., Krause, P., & Mackay, K. (Eds.). (2012). *Building better policies: The nuts and bolt of monitoring and evaluation systems*. Washington, DC: World Bank.

MacDonald, B. (1976). Evaluation and the control of education. In D. Tawney (Ed.), *Curriculum evaluation today: Trends and implications* (pp. 125–136). London, England: MacMillan Education.

Magis, K., & Shinn, C. (2009). Emergent themes of social sustainability. In J. Dillard, V. Dujon, & M. C. King (Eds.), *Understanding the social aspect of sustainability*. New York, NY: Routledge.

Markiewicz, A. (2005). 'A balancing act': Resolving multiple stakeholder interests in program evaluation. *Evaluation Journal of Australasia, 4*(1&2), 13–21.

Markiewicz, A. (2008). The political context of evaluation: What does this mean for independence and objectivity? *Evaluation Journal of Australasia, 8*(2), 35–41.

Martens, J., & Debiel, T. (2008). *The MDG project in crisis: Midpoint review and prospects for the future*. Duisburg, Germany: Institut für Entwicklung und Frieden.

Mayers, J. (2005). *Stakeholder power analysis*. London, England: International Institute for Environment and Development.

Mayne, J. (2001). Addressing attribution through contribution analysis: Using performance measures sensibly. *The Canadian Journal of Program Evaluation, 16*(1), 1–24.

Mayne, J. (2014). Issues in enhancing evaluation use. In M. Laubli Loud & J. Mayne (Eds.), *Enhancing evaluation use* (pp. 1–14). Thousand Oaks, CA: Sage.

Mayoux, L. (2005). *Between tyranny and utopia: Participatory evaluation for pro-poor development*. Retrieved from http://www.participatorymethods.org/sites/participatorymethods.org/files/between%20tyranny%20and%20utopia_%20mayoux.pdf

McDavid, J. C., Huse, I., & Hawthorn, L. (2013). *Program evaluation and performance measurement* (2nd ed.). Thousand Oaks, CA: Sage.

Meier, W. (2003). *Results-based management: Towards a common understanding among development cooperation agencies*. Retrieved from http://www.managingfordevelopmentresults.org/documents/Results-BasedManagementDiscussionPaper.pdf

Mertens, D. M. (2009). *Transformative research and evaluation*. New York, NY: Guilford Press.

Mertens, D. M., & Wilson, A. T. (2012). *Program evaluation theory and practice*. New York, NY: Guildford Press.

Morra Imas, L. G., & Rist, R. C. (2009). *The road to results: Designing and conducting effective development evaluations*. Washington, DC: World Bank.

Moynihan, D. P. (2006). Managing for results in state government: Evaluating a decade of reform. *Public Administration Review, 66*(1), 77–89.

Natsios, A. (2010). *The clash of the counter-bureaucracy and development*. Centre for Global Development. Retrieved from http://www.cgdev.org/sites/default/files/1424271_file_Natsios_Counterbureaucracy.pdf

Newcombe, R. (2003). From client to project stakeholders: A stakeholder mapping approach. *Construction Management and Economics, 21*, 841–848.

Nielsen, S. B., & Ejler, N. (2008). Improving performance? Exploring the complementarities between evaluation and performance management. *Evaluation, 14*(2), 171–192.

Nielsen, S. B., & Hunter, D. E. (2013). Challenges to and forms of complementarity between performance management and evaluation. *New Directions for Evaluation, 137*, 7–17.

OECD DAC. (1991). *Principles for evaluation of development assistance*. Paris, France: Author. Retrieved from http://www.oecd.org/dac/evaluation/50584880.pdf

OECD DAC. (2006). *Emerging good practice in managing for development results: Source book*, First Issue. Washington, DC: World Bank. Retrieved from http://www.mfdr.org/%5C/Sourcebook/1stEdition/MfDRSourcebook-Feb-16-2006.pdf

OECD DAC Network on Development Evaluation. (2010). *Evaluating development cooperation: Summary of key norms and standards* (2nd ed.). Paris, France: Author. Retrieved from http://www.oecd.org/development/evaluation/dcdndep/41612905.pdf

OECD DAC. Working Party on Aid Effectiveness. (2010). *Glossary of key terms in evaluation and results based management*. Paris, France: Author. Retrieved from http://www.oecd.org/dac/evaluation/2754804.pdf

Owen, J. M., & Rogers, P. J. (1999). *Program evaluation forms and approaches* (2nd ed.). St. Leonards, Australia: Allen and Unwin.

Patton, M. Q. (2008). *Utilization-focused evaluation* (4th ed.). Thousand Oaks, CA: Sage.

Patton, M. Q. (2011). *Developmental evaluation: Applying complexity concepts to enhance innovation and use*. New York, NY: Guilford Press.

Patton, M. Q. (2012). *Essentials of utilization-focused evaluation*. Thousand Oaks, CA: Sage.

Pawson, R., & Tilley, N. (1997). *Realistic evaluation*. Thousand Oaks, CA: Sage.

Penuel, W. R., & Means, B. (2011). Using large-scale databases in evaluation: Advances, opportunities, and challenges. *American Journal of Evaluation, 32*(1), 118–133.

Perrin, B. (1998). Effective use and misuse of performance measurement. *American Journal of Evaluation, 19*(3), 367–379.

Picciotto, R. (2013). The logic of development effectiveness: Is it time for the broader evaluation community to take notice? *Evaluation, 19*(2), 155–170.

Plottu, B., & Plottu, E. (2011). Participatory evaluation: The virtues for public governance, the constraints on implementation. *Group Decision and Negotiation, 20*(6), 805–824.

Poister, T. H. (2010). Performance measurement: Monitoring program outcomes. In J. S. Wholey, H. P. Hatry, & K. E. Newcomer (Eds.), *Handbook of practical program evaluation* (3rd ed., pp. 100-124). San Francisco, CA: Jossey-Bass.

Preskill, H. (2008). Evaluation's second act: A spotlight on learning. *American Journal of Evaluation, 29*(2), 127–138.

Preskill, H. (2014). Now for the hard stuff: Next steps in ECB research and practice. *American Journal of Evaluation, 35*(1), 116–119.

Preskill, H., & Boyle, S. (2008). A multidisciplinary model of evaluation capacity building. *American Journal of Evaluation, 29*(4), 443–449.

Preskill, H., & Catsambas, T. (2006). *Reframing evaluation through appreciative inquiry*. Thousand Oaks, CA: Sage.

Preskill, H., & Russ-Eft, D. (2005). *Building evaluation capacity: 72 activities for teaching and tracking.* Thousand Oaks, CA: Sage.

Preskill, H. S., & Torres, R. T. (1999). *Evaluative inquiry for learning in organizations.* Thousand Oaks, CA: Sage.

Pretty, J. (1995). Participatory learning for sustainable agriculture. *World Development, 23*(8), 1247–1263.

Ramalingam, B., Jones, H., Toussaint, R., & Young, J. (2008). *Exploring the science of complexity: Ideas and implications for development and humanitarian efforts* (Working Paper 285). London, England: ODI.

Rist, R.C. (2006). The 'E' in monitoring and evaluation: Using evaluative knowledge to support a results-based management system. In R. C. Rist & N. Stame (Eds.), *From studies to streams. Managing evaluative systems* (pp. 3–23). London, England: Transaction.

Rogers, P. J. (2007). Theory-based evaluation: Reflections ten years on. *New Directions for Evaluation, 114,* 63–67.

Rogers, P. J., Petrosino, A., Huebner, T. A., & Hacsi, T. A. (2000). Program theory evaluation: Practice, promise, and problems. *New Directions for Evaluation, 87,* 5–14.

Rossi, P. H., Lipsey, M. W., & Freeman, H. E. (2004). *Evaluation: A systematic approach* (7th ed.). Thousand Oaks, CA: Sage.

Schmeer, K. (1999). *Guidelines for conducting a stakeholder analysis.* Bethesda, MD: Partnerships for Health Reform.

Scriven, M. (1980). *The logic of evaluation.* Inverness, CA: EdgePress.

Scriven, M. (1981). Product evaluation. In N. L. Smith (Ed.), *New techniques for evaluation: New perspectives in evaluation.* Newbury Park, CA: Sage.

Scriven, M. (1991). *Evaluation thesaurus.* Thousand Oaks, CA: Sage.

Scriven, M. (1996). Types of evaluation and types of evaluator. *American Journal of Evaluation, 17*(2), 151–161.

Scriven, M. (2007). The logic of evaluation. In H. V. Hansen et al. (Eds.), *Dissensus and the search for common ground* [CD-ROM]. Windsor, Ontario, Canada OSSA. 1-16.

Seeds for Change. (n.d.). *Facilitation tools for meetings and workshops.* Retrieved from http://www.seedsforchange.org.uk/tools

Shandish, W., Cook, T., & Campbell, D. (2002). *Experimental and quasi-experimental designs for generalised causal inference.* Boston, MA: Houghton Mifflin.

Simons, H. (2009). *Case study research in practice.* Thousand Oaks, CA: Sage.

Slocum, N. (2003). *Participatory methods toolkit.* Brugge, Belgium: United Nations University—CRIS.

Stake, R. E., & Schwandt, T. A. (2006). On discerning quality in evaluation. In I. Shaw, J. Greene, & M. Mark (Eds.), *The SAGE handbook of evaluation* (pp. 404–438). Thousand Oaks, CA: Sage.

Stufflebeam, D. L., & Shinkfield, A. J. (2007). *Evaluation theory, models, and applications.* San Francisco, CA: Jossey-Bass.

Torres, R. T., & Preskill, H. (2001). Evaluation and organizational learning: Past, present, and future. *American Journal of Evaluation, 22*(3), 387–395.

UNESCO. (2010). *Risk management training handbook.* Paris, France: Author.

United Nations. (2008). *Review of results-based management in the Author*. Sixty-third session, Agenda items 117 & 128.

United Nations. (2012). *Report of the United Nations Conference on sustainable development, Rio de Janeiro, Brazil 20–22 June 2012*. New York, NY: Author.

United Nations. (2013). *The millennium development goals report 2013*. New York, NY: Author.

United Nations Development Group. (2011). *Results based management handbook*. Retrieved from http://www.ilo.org/public/english/bureau/program/dwcp/download/undg_rbm1011.pdf

United Nations Development Program. (2009). *Handbook on planning, monitoring, and evaluating for development results*. New York, NY: Author. Retrieved from http://web.undp.org/evaluation/handbook/documents/english/pme-handbook.pdf

United Nations Development Program. (2011). *Addendum June 2011 evaluation: Updated guidance on evaluation in the handbook on planning, monitoring, and evaluation for development results (2009)*. New York, NY: Author.

University of Wisconsin—Extension. (2003). *Enhancing program performance with logic models*. Madison, WI: Author.

Vahamaki, J., Schmidt, M., & Molander, J. (2011). *Review: Results based management in development cooperation*. Stockholm, Sweden: Riksbankens Jubileumsfond.

Van Dooren, W., Bouckaert, G., & Halligan, J. (2010). *Performance management in the public sector*. London, UK: Routledge.

Vera Institute of Justice. (2003). *Measuring progress toward safety and justice: A global guide to the design of performance indicators across the justice sector*. New York, NY: Author.

Webber, D.J. (1991). The distribution and use of policy knowledge in the policy process. *Knowledge and Policy, 4*(4), 6–35.

Weiss, C. (1983). The stakeholder approach to evaluation: Origins and promise. *New Directions for Program Evaluation, 17*, 3–14.

Whitehouse, C. (n.d.). *The ants and the cockroach: A challenge to the use of indicators*. Retrieved from http://www.mande.co.uk/docs/Indicators%20-%20The%20Ants%20and%20the%20Cockroach.pdf

Wholey, J. (2010). Use of evaluation in government: The politics of evaluation. In J. Wholey, H. Harty, & K. Newcomer (Eds.). *Handbook of practical program evaluation* (pp. 651–667). San Francisco, CA: Jossey-Bass.

Williams, B., & Hummelbrunner, R. (2011). *System concepts in action: A practitioner's toolkit*. Stanford, CA: Stanford Business Books.

W.K. Kellogg Foundation (2004). *Logic model development guide*. Battle Creek, MI: W.K. Kellogg Foundation.

World Bank. (2009). *Making smart policy: Using impact evaluation for policy making: Case studies of evaluations that influenced policy*. Retrieved from http://siteresources.worldbank.org/INTISPMA/Resources/383704-1146752240884/Doing_ie_series_14.pdf

Yarbrough, D. B., Shulha, L. M., Hopson, R. K., & Caruthers, F. A. (2011). *The program evaluation standards: A guide for evaluators and evaluation users* (3rd ed.). Thousand Oaks, CA: Sage.

Youker, B. (2013). Goal-free evaluation: A potential model for the evaluation of social work programs. *Social Work Research, 37*(4), 432–438.

# Index

Accountability, 4, 30, 31, 168
Accuracy, 42, 168
Activities, 75
Ad hoc reports, 238 (table)
Agreed evaluation questions,
   95, 96 (table)
Alkin, M. C., 161–162
American Evaluation Association,
   66, 167–168
Anti-smoking program example,
   72–73, 72 (figure), 76, 77 (figure)
Appendices, 192, 195, 274
Appreciative Inquiry, 164 (table), 167
Approaches, identifying possible/
   preferred, 60–65, 60 (figure),
   65 (table)
Appropriateness domain:
   about, 99, 101 (table), 102 (figure),
      103, 103 (figure)
   headline/subsidiary evaluation
      question examples, 105 (table)
   monitoring, focus of, 130 (table)
Armytage, L., 34
Assessment, 48–49, 103, 103 (figure)
Assumptions:
   community education case
      study, 211–212
   program logic, 75, 76, 87
   program theory, 84
Attendance records, participant,
   197 (table)
Audience for reports, 235

Bamberger, M., 9, 66, 117
Baselines, 133–134
Bouckaert, G., 142, 224,
   234, 244

Cascading, 9, 10–11, 10 (figure)
Case studies, 164 (table),
   193–194 (table), 197 (table)
   *See also* Community education
      case study
Causal inference, 174–175
Cause-and-effect evaluation
   questions, 104
Chen, H. T., 74
Chianca, T., 98
Communication techniques,
   235–236
Community education case study:
   assumptions, 211–212
   conclusion, overall, 215
   Data Collection Plan,
      192, 193–194 (table)
   Data Management Plan,
      200, 200 (table)
   data synthesis, 204, 206–207 (table)
   ethical issues in data collection,
      196, 197 (table)
   Evaluation Plan, 158–159 (table),
      173–175, 174 (table)
   evaluative judgments and
      conclusions, 211–212,
      213–214 (table)
   Monitoring Plan, 126, 127 (table),
      128, 131, 140–142 (table),
      157 (table)
   program goal, 76, 78
   program logic, 78, 79 (figure)
   program theory, 78, 78 (figure), 84
Community forums, 197 (table)
Complementarity, 15–17, 17 (table)
Comprehensive evaluation reports,
   231, 232–233 (table)

283

Concepts, foundation:
  about, 28–29, 28 (figure)
  evaluation-led monitoring and evaluation, 29, 38–40
  monitoring and evaluation, multiple purposes for, 28, 29–31
  participatory orientation, 29, 40–42
  Results-Based Management approach, 28, 31–35, 33 (figure)
  theory-based approach, 29, 35–38
Conceptual orientation, 55 (figure)
Conclusions, evaluative. *See* Evaluative conclusions
Constructivist paradigm, 64, 65 (table)
Context, 130 (table), 184–187, 260
Contribution analysis, 163 (table)
Controlled Experiment, 164 (table)
Convenience sampling, 196 (table)
Coryn, C. L., 36, 37, 41
Cost-benefit evaluation approach, 64, 164 (table)
CREAM measures/indicators, 137, 138
Credibility:
  of data, 187, 188
  of evaluation, 169
  of information, 224, 225 (figure)
Criteria, 160 (table), 169–172, 171 (table), 172 (figure), 173 (table)
Cullen, A. E., 41

Data:
  baseline, 133–134
  credibility of, 187, 188
  dependability of, 187–188
  evaluation questions and, 112 (table), 115–116
  limited, 67 (figure)
  reliability of, 67 (figure), 187–188
  use, promoting, 186
  validity of, 187, 188
Data analysis, 20, 184–187, 199, 201–202
Database reports, 199–200
Data collection:
  about, 20, 21 (figure)
  ethical issues in, 196, 197 (table)
  methods, 142–144, 145, 165–166, 166 (table), 191, 192 (figure)
  mixed-methods, 165–166
  Monitoring Plan and, 125
  organizational context for, 184–187
  primary, 143–144
  secondary, 143, 144
Data Collection Plan:
  about, 190–191, 190 (table)
  appendices, 192, 195
  community education case study, 192, 193–194 (table)
  data collection methods, 191, 192 (figure)
  ethical issues in selecting data collection tools, 196, 197 (table)
  sampling, 195, 196 (table)
  template/forms, 267
Data entry, 199
Data management, 21 (figure), 184–187, 202
Data Management Plan:
  about, 190 (table), 197–200, 198 (figure)
  community education case study, 200, 200 (table)
  data analysis, 199, 201–202
  data management system, review of, 202
  template/forms, 268
Data processes overview, 182–184, 183 (figure), 189, 190 (table)
  *See also specific data processes*
Data quality, 187–189
Data synthesis:
  about, 21 (figure), 190 (table), 203–204, 205 (figure)
  community education case study, 204, 206–207 (table)
  evaluation questions and, 204, 206–207 (table), 208 (table)
  evaluation rubrics, 208 (table), 209–210
  examples, 206–207 (table), 208 (table)
  indicators/targets and, 203
  template/forms, 269

Davidson, E. J., 104, 151, 170, 174
Decision making, 5
Dependability of data, 187–188
Descriptive evaluation questions, 104
Developmental Evaluation, 63, 164 (table)
Dissemination:
  about, 20, 21 (figure)
  interactive, 236
  in Reporting and Dissemination Strategy, 234–236, 237–238 (table), 239
  See also Reporting and Dissemination Strategy; Reports
Documentation review, 47–48
Donaldson, S. I., 35, 38, 165
Draft evaluation questions, 111 (table), 112–113
Draft program theory, 85

ECB approaches. See Evaluation capacity building approaches
Economic sustainability, 101
Effectiveness, 42, 123
Effectiveness domain:
  about, 98 (table), 99–100, 101 (table), 102 (figure), 103, 103 (figure)
  headline/subsidiary evaluation question examples, 105 (table)
  monitoring, focus of, 130 (table)
Efficiency assessment, 103, 103 (figure)
Efficiency domain:
  about, 98 (table), 100, 102 (figure), 102 (table), 103, 103 (figure)
  headline/subsidiary evaluation question examples, 106 (table)
  monitoring, focus of, 130 (table)
Ejler, N., 18
Empowerment evaluation, 163 (table)
Ethical issues in data collection, 196, 197 (table)
Evaluation:
  about, 150–151
  concepts, 39
  defined, 12, 150, 151
  empowerment, 163 (table)
  evaluation questions, role in answering, 94–95, 96 (table), 150 (figure)
  external, 176–177, 176 (table)
  formative, 123, 153–155, 154 (table)
  internal, 176–177, 176 (table)
  monitoring, complementarities between, 15–17, 17 (table)
  monitoring, differences between, 11–13, 13–14 (table)
  monitoring, overlap with, 123, 145–146
  participatory, 40–42, 163 (table)
  principles and standards, 167–169
  process, 123
  program, 9, 11
  program theory-driven, 8, 35, 38, 62, 163 (table)
  purposes, multiple, 28, 29–31
  realistic, 62, 164 (table)
  reflective, 163 (table)
  summative, 153, 154–155, 154 (table)
  transformative, 163 (table)
  use, 63, 162, 164 (table)
  utilization-focused, 40, 97, 164 (table)
  values, 39
  See also Evaluation Plan; *specific topics*
Evaluation accountability, 168
Evaluation approaches:
  about, 160 (table), 161–162, 163–164 (table), 165
  data collection methods and, 165–166, 166 (table)
  evaluation principles/standards and, 167–169
  identifying possible/preferred, 61–64
Evaluation capacity building (ECB) approaches, 57–58, 58–59 (table), 59
Evaluation domains:
  headline/subsidiary evaluation questions and, 104–105, 105–106 (table)
  OECD DAC framework, 97–99, 98 (table)
  OECD DAC framework, adaptation of, 99–102, 101–102 (table), 102 (figure)

other frameworks, 103–104,
103 (figure)
program logic and, 107–108,
108 (figure), 109–110
relationship between, 102, 102 (figure)
theory-based approach and, 37–38
*See also* Evaluation questions
Evaluation-led approach, 7–9, 29, 38–40
Evaluation Plan:
about, 20, 21 (figure)
community education case study,
158–159 (table), 173–175,
174 (table)
data collection methods, 165–166,
166 (table)
evaluation approach, 160 (table),
161–162, 163–164 (table),
165–169, 166 (table)
evaluation principles and
standards, 167–169
evaluation questions, focus of
evaluation and methods for,
160 (table), 173–175, 174 (table)
evaluation questions, identifying,
160 (table), 169–172, 171 (table),
172 (figure), 173 (table)
format, 155, 156 (table)
Monitoring Plan compared to, 125–126
qualitative methods, 165–166,
166 (table), 192 (figure)
quantitative methods, 165, 166,
166 (table), 192 (figure)
responsibilities and time frames,
161 (table), 176–177, 176 (table)
reviewing, 161 (table), 177,
178 (table), 179
steps in developing, 160–161 (table),
160–179
template/forms, 265–266
Evaluation questions:
about, 20, 21 (figure)
agreed, 95, 96 (table)
attributes of, 95–97, 97 (figure)
cause-and-effect, 104
criteria and standards, identifying,
160 (table), 169–172, 171 (table),
172 (figure), 173 (table)

data synthesis and, 204,
206–207 (table), 208 (table)
descriptive, 104
divergent versus convergent
stage for, 117
draft, 111 (table), 112–113
evaluative, 106
evaluator role in developing, 111, 117
finalizing, 112 (table), 117–118
focus of evaluation and methods for,
160 (table), 173–175, 174 (table)
headline, 104, 105–106 (table)
monitoring and evaluation role in
answering, 94–95, 96 (table),
122 (figure), 150 (figure)
normative, 104
number/range of, scoping against
available data and resources,
112 (table), 115–116
practical, 95, 96 (table)
presenting to stakeholders for final
endorsement, 112 (table),
116–117
program logic and, 107–110,
108 (figure)
program theory and, 107
stakeholder participation,
facilitating, 112 (table),
113–115, 114 (figure)
steps in developing, 110–111,
111–112 (table), 112–118
streamlining, 116
subsidiary, 104–105, 105–106 (table)
template/forms, 263
useful, 95, 96 (table)
*See also* Evaluation domains
Evaluation rubrics:
about, 170
data synthesis, 208 (table), 209–210
examples, 171 (table), 173 (table)
template/forms, 266
Evaluative conclusions:
about, 190 (table)
described, 212, 213–214 (table), 215
recommendations/lessons
and, 228 (table)
template/forms, 270

Evaluative evaluation
    questions, 106
Evaluative judgments, 190 (table),
    210–212, 213–214 (table), 269
Evaluators, 111, 117, 176–177,
    176 (table)
Event reports, 238 (table)
Evergreen, S., 236
Experimental evaluation approach,
    63–64, 164 (table)
External evaluators, 176–177,
    176 (table)
External factors, in program logic,
    75, 76, 86–87

Feasibility, 168
Fetterman, D. M., 40
Fidelity of implementation, 99–100
Field officers, 186–187
Fitzpatrick, J. L., 117, 151, 231
Flexibility, 250
Focus:
    clarifying, 48, 49
    identifying, 128 (table), 129,
        130 (table)
    of monitoring, 130 (table)
    program-level, 9
Focus groups, 197 (table)
Formal reports, 230–231,
    237–238 (table)
Formative evaluation, 123, 153–155,
    154 (table)
Formative evaluation reports, 231
Forms. *See* Template/forms
Forums, community, 197 (table)
Fournier, D. M., 170
Freeman, H. E., 78, 103, 103 (figure)
Function of Monitoring and Evaluation
    Framework, 4–5
Funnell, S. C., 84, 90, 107

Gantt charts, 248–249, 249 (figure),
    250 (figure)
Governance, 130 (table)
*Guiding Principles for Evaluators*
    (American Evaluation Association),
    66, 167–168

Halligan, J., 142, 224, 234, 244
*Handbook on Planning, Monitoring, and
    Evaluating for Development Results*
    (United Nations Development
    Programme), 219
Hatton, M. J., 34
Hawthorn, L., 211
Headline evaluation questions,
    104, 105–106 (table)
Hierarchical complementarity, 17 (table)
Honesty, 168
Hunter, D. E., 18
Hurteau, M., 210–211
Huse, I., 211

Impact assessment, 103, 103 (figure)
Impact domain:
    about, 98 (table), 100–101,
        102 (figure), 102 (table),
        103, 103 (figure)
    headline/subsidiary evaluation
        question examples, 106 (table)
    monitoring, focus of, 130 (table)
Implementation:
    about, 20, 21 (figure)
    described, 243–244, 245 (figure), 246
    evaluation capacity building and,
        59 (table)
    fidelity of, 99–100
    as monitoring area, 130 (table)
    planning for monitoring and review of
        Framework, 246 (table), 251,
        252 (table)
    program management arrangements,
        246 (table), 247–248, 247 (figure)
    steps in, 27 (table), 246–252,
        246 (table)
    work plan for, 246 (table), 248–250,
        249 (figure), 250 (figure), 273
Independence, 169
Indicative evaluation reports,
    231, 232–233 (table)
Indicators:
    about, 129 (table), 131
    application of, 136 (table), 137
    baselines and, 133–134
    common, 131–132

CREAM, 138
   data synthesis and, 203
   debates on use of, 134–135
   examples, 139–140, 140–141 (table)
   judicious use of, 135–136, 136 (table)
   other attributes, 137
   selection criteria, 136–137
   selection of, 132–133
   SMART/SMARTER, 137–138
   types and features, 138–139 (table)
   *See also* Targets
Inference, causal, 174–175
Information, credibility of, 224, 225 (figure)
Informational complementarity, 17 (table)
Information orientation, 55 (figure)
Information technology (IT), 184
Information utility, 224, 225 (figure)
Inputs, 75
Inquiry, systematic, 167
Instrumental use, 224
Integrative complementarity, 17 (table)
Integrity, 168
Interactive dissemination, 236
Internal evaluators, 176–177, 176 (table)
Interviews, 193–194 (table), 197 (table)
IT. *See* Information technology

Joint Committee on Standards for Educational Evaluation, 168
Judgments, evaluative, 190 (table), 210–212, 213–214 (table), 269

Kettner, P. M., 30, 243–244
Key Evaluation Checklist, 104
King, J., 209
King, J. A., 41
Knowlton, L. W., 74
Kusek, J. Z., 46, 48–49

Learning:
   about, 21 (figure)
   as Monitoring and Evaluation Framework purpose, 4, 30–31
   in Results-Based Management, 219, 222
   strategies, 221 (table), 222–223, 271

Learning approach, 219–220, 220 (figure), 222
Learning evaluation approach, 62–63, 164 (table)
Lessons, 221 (table), 226, 228 (table), 229, 271
   *See also* Recommendations
Lipsey, M. W., 78, 103, 103 (figure)

Mabry, L., 9, 66, 117
Management:
   monitoring, focus of, 130 (table)
   as Monitoring and Evaluation Framework function, 4
   performance, 18, 19 (figure), 32, 124–125, 125 (figure)
   program, 246 (table), 247–248, 247 (figure)
   stakeholder, 56–57
   *See also* Results-Based Management
Management information system (MIS), 184
Martin, L. L., 30, 243–244
Mayoux, L., 42
McDavid, J. C., 211
McKegg, K., 209
Meier, W., 243
Merit, 152
Mertens, D. M., 162, 201–202
Methodological complementarity, 17 (table)
Methodological paradigms, 64–65, 65 (table)
Methods evaluation theories, 162
MIS. *See* Management information system
Mixed-methods data collection, 165–166
Mixed-methods paradigm, 64, 65 (table)
Monitoring:
   defined, 12
   effectiveness of, 123
   evaluation, complementarities between, 15–17, 17 (table)
   evaluation, differences between, 11–13, 13–14 (table)
   evaluation, overlap with, 123, 145–146

evaluation questions, role in answering, 94–95, 96 (table), 122 (figure)
future of, 145–146
levels of, 123–124, 124 (figure)
purposes, multiple, 28, 29–31
role of, 121–123, 122 (figure)
*See also* Monitoring Plan; *specific topics*
Monitoring and Evaluation Framework:
about, 1–2
cascading, 9, 10–11, 10 (figure)
content areas, 19–20
evaluation-led approach to, 7–9
function and purpose of, 4–5
investing in, 2–3
program-level focus of, 9
program planning and, 3
stages overview, 20, 21 (figure), 22–27 (table)
*See also specific topics*
Monitoring and Evaluation Planning Workshop, 114
Monitoring and review of Framework:
implementation, 246 (table), 251, 252 (table)
template/forms, 273
Monitoring Plan:
about, 20, 21 (figure)
community education case study, 126, 127 (table), 128, 131, 140–142 (table), 157 (table)
data collection processes/tools, 142–144, 145
Evaluation Plan compared to, 125–126
focus, identifying, 128 (table), 129, 130 (table)
format, 126, 126 (figure), 156 (table)
indicators and targets, developing, 129 (table), 131–142
responsibilities and time frames, 144
reviewing, 161 (table), 177, 178 (table), 179
steps in developing, 128–129 (table), 128–144
template/forms, 264

Moroney, R. M., 30, 243–244
Morra Imas, L. G., 104
Most Significant Change technique, 115, 135, 163 (table)

Needs assessment, 103, 103 (figure)
Nielsen, S. B., 18
Noakes, L. A., 36, 37
Nonprobability sampling, 195, 196 (table)
Normative evaluation questions, 104

Oakden, J., 209
Objectivity, 169, 188
Occasional reports, 231
Operational orientation, 55 (figure)
Organisation for Economic Co-operation and Development, Development Assistance Committee (OECD DAC), 97–102, 98 (table), 101–102 (table), 102 (figure), 226
Organizational complementarity, 17 (table)
Organizational culture, positive, 225 (figure)
Outcome mapping, 163 (table)
Outcomes, 75
Outputs, 75

Participation arrangements:
evaluation capacity building (ECB) approaches, 57–58, 58–59 (table), 59
stakeholder management, 56–57
stakeholder mapping and selection, 50–55, 52 (table), 53 (table), 55 (figure)
Participation evaluation approach, 61, 163 (table)
Participatory evaluation, 40–42, 163 (table)
Participatory orientation, 29, 40–42
Patton, M. Q., 40, 51, 94, 97, 152, 223–224, 234
Performance indicators. *See* Indicators

Performance management, 18, 19 (figure), 32, 124–125, 125 (figure)
Perrin, B., 136
Phillips, C. C., 74
Picciotto, R., 98
Pipeline logic model, 74–75, 85
Political influences, 67 (figure), 142
Positivist paradigm, 64, 65 (table)
Practical evaluation questions, 95, 96 (table)
Practice Examples:
　cascading, 10–11
　data collection, building capacity for, 186–187
　data gaps in monitoring, 145
　dissemination, promoting influence through tailored, 239
　evaluation capacity building, 59
　evaluation methodologies, building capacity for use of, 167
　evaluation questions, streamlining, 116
　evaluation rubric, 209–210
　formative and summative evaluations, 154–155
　indicators, 132–133
　program logic consultation, 82–83
　program logic to generate evaluation questions, 109–110
　program logic workshops, 88–89
　program planning, 3
　purpose and focus, reaching agreement on, 49
　purposes, multiple, 5
　routine monitoring and periodic evaluation, 14–15
　stakeholder engagement in identification of recommendations/lessons, 229
　stakeholder management, 56–57
　stakeholder mapping and selection, 54
Pre-post surveys, 193–194 (table), 197 (table)
Preskill, H., 223
Primary data collection, 143–144
Probability sampling, 195, 196 (table)

Process, 42
Process evaluation, 123
Program evaluation, 9, 11
Program Evaluation Standards, 168
Program improvement, 4
Program-level focus, 9
Program logic:
　about, 19–20, 21 (figure), 71
　community education case study, 78, 79 (figure)
　defined, 36
　described, 74–76, 77 (figure)
　developing, 81 (table), 85–89, 86 (figure)
　evaluation domains and, 107–108, 108 (figure), 109–110
　evaluation questions and, 107–110, 108 (figure)
　mapping software, 75, 85
　program theory, interconnection with, 86 (figure)
　program theory versus, 74
　reservations about, 37
　school-based anti-smoking program example, 76, 77 (figure)
　stakeholder engagement strategy, planning, 80 (table), 81–82
　stakeholders, confirming with, 81 (table), 89–90
　template/forms, 262
　workshops, 88–89
　See also Program theory
Program management arrangements, 246 (table), 247–248, 247 (figure)
Program monitoring. See Monitoring
Program planning, 3
Program process assessment, 103, 103 (figure)
Programs versus projects, 9
Program theory:
　about, 19–20, 21 (figure), 71, 163 (table)
　community education case study, 78, 78 (figure), 84
　defined, 36
　described, 72–73, 72 (figure)
　developing, 80–81 (table), 83–85
　evaluation questions and, 107
　mechanisms in, 73

program logic, interconnection
    with, 86 (figure)
program logic versus, 74
reservations about, 36–37
school-based anti-smoking program
    example, 72–73, 72 (figure)
stakeholder engagement strategy,
    planning, 80 (table), 81–82
stakeholders, confirming with,
    81 (table), 89–90
template/forms, 261
    *See also* Program logic
Program theory assessment,
    103, 103 (figure)
Program theory-driven evaluation,
    8, 35, 38, 62, 163 (table)
Progress reports, 231
Projects, 9
Propriety, 168
Purpose, 4–5, 48, 49, 66, 68, 259
Purposive sampling, 195, 196 (table)

Quality, 152, 170–171, 171 (table)
Quasi-experimental approach, 64

RBM. *See* Results-Based Management
Readiness assessment, 48–49
Realist evaluation, 62, 164 (table)
Real World Evaluation, 66
Recommendations, 221 (table),
    227, 228 (table), 229, 271
    *See also* Lessons
Reflective evaluation, 163 (table)
Relevance, 42, 98 (table), 99
Reliability of data, 67 (figure),
    187–188
Rendering judgment, 210
Reporting and Dissemination Strategy:
    about, 20, 221 (table), 230
    dissemination, 234–236,
        237–238 (table), 239
    example, 236, 237–238 (table)
    reporting processes,
        231, 232–233 (table),
        233–234, 237–238 (table)
    template/forms, 272
    *See also* Dissemination; Reports

Reports:
    about, 20, 21 (figure)
    ad hoc, 238 (table)
    audience for, 235
    comprehensive evaluation,
        231, 232–233 (table)
    database, 199–200
    event, 238 (table)
    formal, 230–231, 237–238 (table)
    formative evaluation, 231
    occasional, 231
    progress, 231
    routine monitoring, 231
    summative evaluation, 231, 233
    *See also* Dissemination; Reporting and
        Dissemination Strategy
Requirements, identifying, 47–49
Resources, 65–66, 67 (figure),
    112 (table), 115–116
Results, 4, 30, 130 (table)
Results-Based Management (RBM):
    about, 7, 28
    adopting, 34–35
    critiques of, 32–34
    defined, 32
    as foundation concept, 28, 31–35,
        33 (figure)
    learning in, 219, 222
    life cycle approach, 32, 33 (figure)
    management approaches, similar, 32
    monitoring and evaluation processes,
        integration of, 243
    performance management and, 32, 124
Rights, 42
Risks, 87, 248
Rist, R. C., 46, 48–49, 104, 145
Rogers, P. J., 37, 84, 90, 107
Rossi, P. H., 78, 103, 103 (figure)
Routine monitoring reports, 231
Rubrics. *See* Evaluation rubrics
Rugh, J., 9, 41, 66, 117

Sampling, 195, 196 (table)
Sanders, J. R., 117, 151, 231
School-based anti-smoking program
    example, 72–73, 72 (figure),
    76, 77 (figure)

Schroeder, K., 34
Schroter, D. C., 36, 37
Schwandt, T. A., 152
Scoping the Monitoring and Evaluation Framework:
  about, 21 (figure), 44–46
  approaches, identifying possible/preferred, 60–65, 60 (figure), 65 (table)
  evaluation capacity building approaches, 57–58, 58–59 (table), 59
  participation arrangements, 50–59
  purpose and parameters of Framework, confirming, 66, 68
  requirements, identifying, 47–49
  resource parameters, reviewing, 65–66, 67 (figure)
  stakeholder management, 56–57
  stakeholder mapping and selection, 50–55, 52 (table), 53 (table), 55 (figure)
  steps overview, 22 (table), 46–47 (table)
Scriven, M., 12, 36, 104, 151, 153, 170, 210
Secondary data collection, 143, 144
Self-selection sampling, 196 (table)
Semistructured stakeholder interviews, 193–194 (table), 197 (table)
Sequential complementarity, 17 (table)
Shinkfield, A. J., 36, 201
Simple random sampling, 196 (table)
SMART/SMARTER measures/indicators, 87–88, 137–138
Snowball sampling, 196 (table)
Social justice evaluation approach, 62, 163 (table)
Social Return on Investment, 64, 164 (table)
Social sustainability, 101
Staff capacity, 185, 186–187
Stake, R. E., 152
Stakeholder evaluation approach, 61–62, 163 (table)
Stakeholders:
  capacity-building needs, 259
  engaging, 55 (figure), 56–57, 80 (table), 81–82, 229
  evaluation questions, presenting, 112 (table), 116–117
  interviews, 193–194 (table), 197 (table)
  managing, 56–57
  mapping and selection, 50–55, 52 (table), 53 (table), 55 (figure)
  participation of, 55, 55 (figure), 112 (table), 113–115, 114 (figure)
  program theory/program logic, confirming with, 89–90
  strategies for dealing with, 67 (figure)
  template/forms, 259
  types and roles, 51, 52 (table)
Standards, 160 (table), 169–172, 171 (table), 172 (figure), 173 (table)
Stratified random sampling, 196 (table)
Stufflebeam, D. L., 36, 201
Subsidiary evaluation questions, 104–105, 105–106 (table)
Summative evaluation, 153, 154–155, 154 (table)
Summative evaluation reports, 231, 233
Surveys, pre-post, 193–194 (table), 197 (table)
Sustainability domain:
  about, 98 (table), 101, 102 (figure), 102 (table)
  headline/subsidiary evaluation question examples, 106 (table)
  monitoring, focus of, 130 (table)
Systematic inquiry, 167
Systems evaluation approach, 63, 164 (table)

Table of contents, 257–258
Targets:
  about, 129 (table), 131
  application of, 135, 136 (table)

baselines and, 133–134
data synthesis and, 203
setting, 141–142, 142 (table)
*See also* Indicators
Template/forms:
　appendix, 274
　background and context of program, 260
　Data Collection Plan, 267
　Data Management Plan, 268
　data synthesis, judgments, and conclusions, 269–270
　Evaluation Plan, 265–266
　evaluation questions, 263
　evaluation rubric, 266
　implementation workplan, 273
　learning strategy, 271
　monitoring and review of Framework, 273
　Monitoring Plan, 264
　program logic, 262
　program theory, 261
　purpose of Monitoring and Evaluation Framework, 259
　recommendations and lessons, 271
　reporting and dissemination plan, 272
　stakeholder capacity-building needs, 259
　stakeholders, key, 259
　table of contents, 257–258
Theory-based approach:
　about, 29
　adopting, 37–38
　evaluation questions and, 37–38
　as foundation concept, 29, 35–38
　reservations about, 36–37
　steps in, 35
　strengths of, 37–38
　understanding of, 35–36
Transformative evaluation, 163 (table)

United Nations Development Programme (UNDP), 219
University of Wisconsin–Extension, 74–75
Upward accountability, 30, 31
Use evaluation, 63, 162, 164 (table)
Useful evaluation questions, 95, 96 (table)
Utility, 168
"Utility test," 224, 225 (figure)
Utilization-focused evaluation, 40, 97, 164 (table)
Utilization strategies, 223–224, 225 (figure)

Validity of data, 187, 188
Value, 152, 171–172, 172 (figure), 173 (table)
Valuing evaluation theories, 162
Van Dooren, W., 142, 224, 234, 244

Wandersman, A., 40
Wehipeihana, N., 209
Westine, C. D., 36, 37
Williams, D., 210–211
Wilson, A. T., 162, 201–202
Winnowing, 115
W.K. Kellogg Foundation, 74–75
Work plan for implementation, 246 (table), 248–250, 249 (figure), 250 (figure), 273
Workshops, 88–89, 114
Worth, 152
Worthen, B., 117, 151, 231

Printed in Great Britain
by Amazon